Linking EU and National Gove

Linking EU and National Governance

Edited by
Beate Kohler-Koch

OXFORD
UNIVERSITY PRESS

Great Clarendon Street, Oxford OX2 6DP

Oxford University Press is a department of the University of Oxford.
It furthers the University's objective of excellence in research, scholarship,
and education by publishing worldwide in

Oxford New York

Auckland Bangkok Buenos Aires Cape Town Chennai
Dar es Salaam Delhi Hong Kong Istanbul Karachi Kolkata
Kuala Lumpur Madrid Melbourne Mexico City Mumbai Nairobi
São Paulo Shanghai Taipei Tokyo Toronto

Oxford is a registered trade mark of Oxford University Press
in the UK and in certain other countries

Published in the United States
by Oxford University Press Inc., New York

© the several contributors 2003

The moral rights of the author have been asserted

Database right Oxford University Press (maker)

First published 2003

All rights reserved. No part of this publication may be reproduced,
stored in a retrieval system, or transmitted, in any form or by any means,
without the prior permission in writing of Oxford University Press,
or as expressly permitted by law, or under terms agreed with the appropriate
reprographics rights organization. Enquiries concerning reproduction
outside the scope of the above should be sent to the Rights Department,
Oxford University Press, at the address above

You must not circulate this book in any other binding or cover
and you must impose this same condition on any acquirer

British Library Cataloguing in Publication Data

Data available

Library of Congress Cataloging in Publication Data

Data available

ISBN 0-19-925225-4 (hbk.)
ISBN 0-19-925226-2 (pbk.)

1 3 5 7 9 10 8 6 4 2

Typeset by Newgen Imaging Systems (P) Ltd., Chennai, India
Printed in Great Britain
on acid-free paper by
Biddles Ltd., Guildford and King's Lynn

Contents

List of Figures	vii
List of Tables	viii
List of Abbreviations	ix
List of Contributors	xi
Preface	xiii

1. Contrasting Images of European Governance   1
   Helen Wallace

2. Interdependent European Governance   10
   Beate Kohler-Koch

3. Links between National and Supra-national Institutions: A Legal View of a New Communicative Universe   24
   Armin von Bogdandy

4. National Systems' Adaptation to the EU System: Trends, Offers, and Constraints   53
   Andreas Maurer, Jürgen Mittag, and Wolfgang Wessels

5. Compounded Representation in EU Multi-Level Governance   82
   Arthur Benz

6. The Making of a European Public Space: The Case of Justice and Home Affairs   111
   Klaus Eder and Hans-Jörg Trenz

7. Policy-Making in Fragmented Systems: How to Explain Success   135
   Hubert Heinelt, Tanja Kopp-Malek, Jochen Lang, and Bernd Reissert

8. Policy Implementation in a Multi-Level System: The Dynamics of Domestic Response   154
   Jochen Lang

9. Structuring the State—The Case of European Employment Policy   175
   Frank Deppe, Michael Felder, and Stefan Tidow

10. Horizontal Enforcement in the EU: The BSE Case and
    the Case of State Aid Control   201
    Jürgen Neyer and Dieter Wolf

Index   225

List of Figures

4.1	European legislation in force, 1983–1998	57
4.2	Decision-making modes in the Council of Ministers, 1952–2001	61
4.3	Evolution of decision-making procedures 1957–2001	61
4.4	Legal output of the Council and the Commission, 1952–1998	62
4.5	Legal output of policy fields in comparison—agriculture, trade, and customs policy against economic and social legislation	63
4.6	Typology of member states' 'adaptation' modes	66
4.7	Models of horizontal coordination and vertical hierarchy	69
5.1	Basic problems in the compounded representative system of the EU	90
8.1	Coupling of structural funds and national policies	158
8.2	Domestic responses to change of the structural funds regulations	160

List of Tables

5.1	The Agenda 2000 process	93
5.2	Effects of inter-institutional linkages on the quality of representative democracy	104
6.1	Types of European public spheres	119
8.1	The pattern of policy change	171
10.1	Infringement procedures in the EU, 1995–1999	204
10.2	Annual total amount of state aids in the EU	213

List of Abbreviations

AAmpol	Aktive Arbeitsmarktpolitik (active labour market policy)
ADAPT	European Social Fund Community initiative 'adaptation of the workforce to the industrial change'
AFSJ	area of freedom, security, and justice
AFSSA	Agence Française de Sécurité Sanitaire des Aliments
BSE	bovine spongiform encephalitis
BT-Drs	Bundestagsdrucksache (parliamentary document)
BVerfGE	Sammlung der Entscheidungen des Bundesverfassungsgerichts (collection of the German Constitutional Court's decisions)
CAP	common agricultural policy
CELEX	Communitatis Europae Lex
CEN	Comité Européen de Normalisation (European Committee for Standardization)
CENELEC	Comité Européen de Normalisation Electrotechnique (European Committee for Electronical Standardization)
CFSP	common foreign and security policy
CoR	Committee of the Regions
COREPER	Comité des Représentants Permanents (Committee of Permanent Representatives)
COSAC	Conférence des Organes Spécialisées dans les Affaires Communautaires et européennes des Parlements de l'Union européenne (Conference of the Community and European Affairs Committees of Parliaments of the EU)
D	Deutschland (Germany)
DCL	Directory of Community Legislation in Force
DFG	Deutsche Forschungsgemeinschaft (German research council)
DG	Directorate-General
DM	Deutsche Mark
EC	European Community
ECHS	Export Certified Herds Scheme
ECJ	European Court of Justice
ECSC	European Coal and Steel Community

ECR	European Court Report
ECU	European currency unit
EEC	European Economic Community
EMS	European Monetary System
EMU	Economic and Monetary Union
EP	European Parliament
ERDF	European Regional Development Fund
ESC	Economic and Social Committee
ESF	European Social Fund
EU	European Union
FF	French Franc
GDP	gross domestic product
IGC	Intergovernmental Conference
INGO	international non-governmental organization
IR	Ireland
JHA	justice and home affairs
MEP	member of the European Parliament
NAP	national action plan
NATO	North Atlantic Treaty Organization
NGO	non-governmental organization
OJ	Official Journal of the European Communities
OJ C/L	Official Journal, C series/L series
PR	public relations
QMV	qualified majority voting
S	Sweden
SEA	Single European Act
SSC	Scientific Steering Committee
TEC	Treaty establishing the European Community
TEU	Treaty on European Union
UK	United Kingdom
USA	United States of America
WTO	World Trade Organization

List of Contributors

Benz, Arthur
Professor of Political Science
Institute of Political Science
FernUniversität Hagen
Germany

Deppe, Frank
Professor of Political Science
Institute of Political Science
Philipps-Universität Marburg
Germany

Eder, Klaus
Professor of Sociology
Institute of Social Sciences
Humboldt Universität zu Berlin
Germany

Felder, Michael
Lecturer in Political Science
Faculty of Political Science
Gerhard-Mercator-Universität
Duisburg
Germany

Heinelt, Hubert
Professor of Political Science
Institute of Political Science
Technische Universität Darmstadt
Germany

Kohler-Koch, Beate
Professor of Political Science and
International Relations
Faculty of Social Sciences
Universität Mannheim
Germany
Jean-Monnet Chair for European
Integration

Kopp-Malek, Tanja
Lecturer in Political Science
Faculty of Sociology
Universität Bielefeld
Germany

Lang, Jochen
Federal Ministry of
Transport, Building
and Housing
Germany

Maurer, Andreas
Research analyst
German Institute for International
and Security Affairs
Stiftung Wissenschaft und Politik
(SWP)
Germany

Mittag, Jürgen
Lecturer in Political Science
Research Institute for Political
Science and European Affairs
Universität zu Köln
Germany

Neyer, Jürgen
Heisenberg Fellow of the Deutsche
Forschungsgemeinschaft
Department of Political and Social
Sciences
Freie Universität Berlin
Germany

Reissert, Bernd
Professor of Political Science
Department of Economics

Fachhochschule für Technik und
Wirtschaft Berlin
Germany

Tidow, Stefan
Civil Servant in the
Minister's Office Federal
Environment Ministry.
Germany

Trenz, Hans-Jörg
Lecturer in Sociology
Institute of Social Science
Humboldt-Universität zu Berlin
Germany

Wallace, Helen
Director of the Robert Schuman
Centre for Advanced Studies
European University Institute
Italy

Wessels, Wolfgang
Professor of European Politics and
Integration
Research Institute for Political
Science and European Affairs
Universität zu Köln
Germany
Jean-Monnet Chair for European
Integration

Wolf, Dieter
Managing Director of the
Collaborative Research Centre 597
Universität Bremen
Germany

Bogdandy, Armin von
Director at the Max Planck
Institute for Comparative Public
and International Law
Germany

Preface

'European Governance' ranks high on the present political and research agenda. The political discourse initiated by the White Paper on Governance and propelled by the European Convention highlights the particular salience of the topic. Academic research, on its part, has drawn attention to the fundamental challenges of organising responsive and responsible governance beyond the nation state. While joining in the broad discussion on 'European Governance', this book chooses a special focus. It takes a close look at the interdependence and interaction of the European and national political systems and investigates to what extend a system of penetrated governance has emerged. The individual contributions give evidence of the many faces of interconnectedness and explore the ambivalence of institutional and policy transformation resulting from Europeanization.

All contributions originate from the research programme 'Governance in the European Union' initiated under the auspices of the German Research Council (Deutsche Forschungsgemeinschaft, DFG). This programme has stimulated a vivid academic debate on the nature and challenges of European governance both within the confines of the EU arena and the wider system of member states. It has produced a broad range of theory-oriented empirical research by scholars from different disciplines which – as Helen Wallace notes – reflect in spite of their European orientation a characteristic German view.

I would like to give my thanks to the authors for their readiness to consider the findings of their projects in the light of the particular focus of this book, namely of the intermingling levels and spheres of governance within a highly dynamic system of multi-level policy-making. I am also very grateful to the German research council for its generous support facilitating an intense research co-operation for a period of meanwhile nearly 8 years. Last but not least, I would like to express my special thanks to Nikola Jung who supported the production of this volume during its several stages and contributed significantly to its successful completion.

Mannheim, June 2003
Beate Kohler-Koch

1

Contrasting Images of European Governance

Helen Wallace

'Governance' has become the catchword in both academic and practitioner discussions of how the European Union (EU) currently operates, as well as in the competition of propositions to improve the operating performance of the EU. In the absence of a European government, governance, a fuzzier concept, has emerged as an apparently more malleable term for addressing the way in which the EU operates. Well before it became so fashionable as a term of art among practitioners, the academic community had embraced 'governance' as a usefully broad frame for analysing the diffuse range of political processes through which policies emerge and politics is practised in and around the EU.

One reason for the adoption of governance is as an antidote to traditional studies of government, a term which implies a tidier and more ordered hierarchy of authority and more concentrated focus of politics than we find in many contemporary societies. Another reason is that the political process of the EU is incomplete, polity not state, and indeed built from a consortium of states each of which has a government of its own. A third reason is that a focus on governance creates space for an extended analysis of EU politics and policy without taking a position on what the end result of the process of European political integration might be, allowing us to analyse what happens at the meso-level of EU politics (Pollack, Jachtenfuchs, and Wessels 2001).

Governance is, however, by virtue of its fuzziness, also a contested term. As Rhodes (1996) has pointed out, there is a range of different usages of the term, some more precise than others. But there may be more to this range than careful analytical distinctions. Social scientists are, to some extent, the product of both the intellectual and the social traditions in which they deploy their professional skills. Hence, we can observe some differences in and contrasts between the commentaries that come from different parts of Europe, just as we can observe differences among politicians from different political traditions and contexts. Several years ago, the research councils in Germany and the UK each made a decision, independently of each other but almost simultaneously, to invest in ambitious programmes of academic research on European integration, both following incidentally a prior decision in Norway to fund the ARENA programme.[1] The proposal submitted to the Deutsche Forschungsgemeinschaft (DFG) explicitly titled its programme 'European Governance', with the focus squarely on the processes operating in and around the EU. The British Economic and Social Research Council (ESRC) took a self-consciously different approach by adopting a 'pan-European' frame of reference, deliberately looking at developments across the continent, including other European organizations as well as the EU, and encouraging a good deal of cross-country comparison.[2] Within the German programme the EU was thus the central preoccupation, whereas within the British programme the EU was only one of several concerns. Both programmes sought to involve a range of social sciences, but both programmes in practice acquired a bias towards political science, a reflection not of design, but perhaps rather of the character of the academic market in the two countries. A further distinction is relevant. The German programme has a deliberately tight focus as a requirement of its funding, with a strong emphasis on 'basic' research and rigorous methodology, and with no remit to emphasize 'applied' studies. In contrast the British programme, while also aiming at scholarly insights, has as a condition of funding the need to generate outputs that could be relevant to practitioners, or 'users' in ESRC terminology.

This volume draws together many of the findings from the first wave of those projects within the DFG programme which link EU and national levels of governance. It draws on a rich vein of new research. The comments that follow are intended to highlight where the main differences seem to lie between the works emerging from these two programmes. As we shall see, they seem, indeed, to present contrasting images of European governance.

---

[1] ARENA is a multi-disciplinary programme for Advanced Research on the Europeanization of the Nation-State operating under the Norwegian research council. Its primary objective is to establish high quality research in Norway on the dynamics of European integration and on how a more active European level affects the policies, identities, and institutions of the nation state.

[2] For further details of the One Europe or Several? Programme see www.one-europe.ac.uk.

1.1 EU-Europe versus the EU and Europe

An initial and striking contrast is between the notion of the EU as the lynchpin of Europe and an alternate view of the EU as only one of several manifestations of European integration. Running through the German analyses is the assumption that the EU is the central frame for examining transnational and multilateral Europe. Thus the EU is the primary given factor around which European governance operates. Little reference is made in the collection of studies to other European fora, and not much attention is paid to the wider global context. In this sense the German studies treat the EU as somewhat self-contained and self-defined. This makes the task of analysis rather tidy. The member states are circumscribed by the EU, their politics increasingly framed and penetrated by the EU, with its extending policy repertoire and expansive institutional arrangements. Areas of argument or evidence of stresses and strains are addressed within the boundaries of the EU integration process, rather than as some kind of friction between the EU and possibly countervailing versions of interdependence.

British scholarship tends to come at this subject from different starting points. Thus, while generally not denying the considerable importance of the EU, British scholars are more ready to acknowledge the actual or potential contributions of other European organizations to the management of European policy predicaments or European cross-country political processes. Hence, to assign a policy role to the EU or to locate a political debate within the EU institutional setting is a choice, but only one possible choice. Underlying this notion of choice between frameworks is an assumption that whether or not to assign a policy power to the EU—or to an alternative framework—requires a cost–benefit analysis of what might follow, as well as of options for managing the shared policy area in terms of what form of governance might be appropriate.

To take an obvious illustration the evolving debate on European security and defence exemplifies this contrast. It is a slightly unfair case to cite in relation to the rest of this volume, since this particular collection of DFG projects has little to say about issues of European security and defence, apart from the very interesting research by Eder and Trenz on *inter alia* internal security issues. Other projects in the DFG programme will, in due course, have more to add here. The ESRC programme in contrast has several projects that deal with European external security, in which the North Atlantic Treaty Organization (NATO) framework plays an obvious part, a framework which to British eyes is indeed a European framework in terms of its essential purposes. Why the contrast? It is hard not to see the difference of frame as rooted in different national experiences. To pursue the NATO point a little further, NATO has provided an external guarantee of German—or at least West German—democratic integrity, while at the same time being a forum in which German positions and preferences became fixed rather than bargained. It has, thus, seemed less interesting as an arena or model of European governance in terms of its ramifications inside German politics than the EU, where in marked contrast Germany plays a central part and where changes in German preferences, priorities, or behaviour have large systemic consequences.

Looked at from a British perspective, NATO has been a framework which has persistently offered an alternative arena for achieving core British objectives as regards European defence and security. But it has also provided an alternative method of managing transgovernmental cooperation. Thus, the more 'intergovernmental' methodology of NATO can appear an efficient and effective strategy for the realization of major national goals via multilateral cooperation, rather than a 'second best'. In addition, of course, NATO is a forum in which British voices have been persistently loud and running with the grain of the predominant consensus, whereas within the EU British voices have been more confused and inconsistent.

Here, then, is an important difference in situation between the two countries which seems to have had a shaping impact on the intellectual climate in which European integration is discussed. Whether or not this difference continues to mark the debate in the two countries in the light of recent developments remains to be seen. Scholars are always challenged by the fact that they generally run behind rather than ahead of events. Over the past decade, following the end of the cold war and the unification of Germany, the geopolitical context of West European integration has radically altered. This may have produced a convergence of orientations between Germany and Britain. On the one hand the experience in former Yugoslavia induced a fundamental reconsideration of the British approach to European defence and a readiness, even enthusiasm, to make the EU an operational frame for pushing forward enhanced European cooperation (Howorth 2001), a choice which marks a willingness to entertain a different institutional methodology. On the other hand, the 'normalization' of German European policy since unification may have enabled Germany to become a country 'like any other' within NATO, as well as within the EU (Hyde-Price and Jeffery 2001). At least at the level of governmental policy, subsequently endorsed by the Bundestag,

German reactions to the events of 11 September 2001 seemed to confirm this trend. The key point here is not whether or not the DFG programme should have included projects dealing with defence and security issues, but rather how far the EU-defined frame of reference encapsulates the discussion of different models of governance, while the ESRC programme deliberately encourages (for better or worse) a more eclectic approach.

1.2 How comfortable a fit with national politics and national policies?

It has become a commonplace in studies of Europeanization that national experiences of Europeanization vary a good deal from one European country to another and that much depends on how comfortable a fit there is between the domestic and the European arenas as regards politics and policies. Germany and Britain are arguably at opposing ends of the range in terms of the 'goodness of fit' between the country and the European arenas, in so far as the European arena is EU-defined. Thus typically German scholars tend to a more linear view of the shading of the national— or sub-national—into the European arena of governance. Also typically German scholars, like German practitioners, tend to be comfortable with the notion of the European arena of governance to which German political and institutional methods and practices can be expected to migrate. Indeed, one detects a kind of nervousness in German commentary that the future EU may be less receptive to imports from German practice. British scholarship is more often sensitive to the tensions between European governance and a kind of competing national arena, marked by significant tensions and contrasts of methods, habits, and practices.

Here, too, differences in the contexts of both national politics and national experiences of the EU seem to make an important difference. There is a convenient parallelism between the development of the modern German polity and the embedding of the European Community (EC)/EU experiment in integration. These two phenomena evolved along the same timeline over the past fifty years with a kind of benign complementarity that has encouraged a 'good fit' between these two processes. Contemporary German governance is, of course, clearly framed by the corollary of West European integration, with the enhanced advantage that the EC/EU has also been much shaped by continuous experience of active contributions to the operating procedures and routines of German institutional and political practice and norms (Hyde-Price and

Jeffery 2001). Indeed, to the outside observer the assumption of synergy or complementarity is striking, even though within the German commentary this feature of the EU is much more implicit than explicit. Since modern Germany has become a rather successful polity, moreover, the export of German practices and norms to the European arena looks like common sense and the projection of good practice, even best practice, particularly given German experience in enabling a diffuse and polycentric federation to function. Here, it should be stressed that most of the German projects are comparative (usually comparing Germany with France and the UK), although generally taking German experience as the defining point of reference, perhaps especially in the pulling together of the legal and political dimensions of integration which is such a strong characteristic of German scholarship.

The UK case is very different. Here, we have an old polity, with different traditions and experience, as well as significantly different operating norms and practices, struggling to come to terms with European integration, managed through an institutional framework which bears rather few imprints of British political methodologies. Thus British scholarship is, perhaps, more sensitive to the issues of what makes for a good fit between national and European governance, and is more explicit about the tensions, and perhaps more alert to the disjunctions. The ESRC programme carries rather little of this as regards the UK specifically, since the programme was deliberately cast to encourage cross-country comparison rather than to focus on British experiences of European integration. Where the difference in British commentary shows through in particular is in the way issues relating to enlargement are discussed, a strong and deliberate emphasis of the ESRC programme. Here, British-based scholars tend to approach the question of what kind of fit to expect between candidate countries and the EU *acquis* in a rather open-minded way, often suggesting that the process of adaptation should be two-way, rather than the simple export of EU templates to the newly arriving member states. Another point should be added here. The relevant research community of the ESRC programme, and indeed of the wider research community based in Britain, is much more pluri-national in composition than the counterpart German research community—thus, scholars of more than twenty nationalities (all based in British research institutions) are included in the ESRC programme and its projects. This factor builds a more heterogeneous range of perspectives into the programme; this seems to encourage both a critical approach to British practice and conventional wisdoms, and to generate a strong empathy for concerns and practice in other European countries, including the EU candidate states.

1.3 Designer Europeanization versus organic Europeanization

It is typical of studies of European governance, wherever rooted, to be concerned with the informal as well as the formal processes of politics, with the informal behaviour of institutions as well as the formal rules and procedures. In both the German and the British programmes, as in the wider research community, it is clear that the new institutionalist literature has had an enormous impact on ways of thinking about European governance. Here, we all owe a debt to scholars such as Johan Olsen who has made so rich a contribution to contemporary European scholarship. Incidentally, it is striking how far the Norwegian ARENA programme, under the tutelage of Olsen, has encouraged the spread of cosmopolitan approaches to the understanding of European governance; and it is striking just how far the ARENA programme has worked to escape the confines of national scholarship and local context. Nonetheless, there is something of a contrast to be drawn between a reflex among German scholars to sympathize with 'designer Europeanization', while British scholars veer more often towards 'organic Europeanization'.

What does this contrast mean in practice? Perhaps two features stand out. One is that more of German scholarship engages more readily than British scholarship with the normative dimension to European governance. In the British context we are all acutely aware that to be normative risks being trapped in the contest between Europhiles and Eurosceptics, not a productive route for dispassionate analysis. Our German colleagues can regard the normative as more normal. Several of the projects reported in this volume engage with normative issues, and productively so. Within the British scholarly community the normative dimension enters more through the vector of social constructivism, an increasingly popular approach among students of integration. Since this is also an increasingly popular approach among German scholars, we may be beginning to see here the emergence of a kind of sympathetic coalition between the constructivists from the two countries vis-à-vis other schools of analysis.

The other contrast which stands out is the way in which the German discussion (at least in the projects reported in this volume) seems to be more bound by the established routines of European integration, and with suggesting design changes that might be made to enhance their performance. The British-based discussion seems to be more open to organic developments and innovations in European governance—and indeed the subtitle of the ESRC programme is 'the dynamics of change across contemporary Europe', deliberately encouraging a more speculative approach. Thus, the

British programme has produced a range of commentary on newly emerging policy regimes, in particular, including the 'open method of coordination', aspects of justice and home affairs, and the emerging European regime for foreign, security and defence policies. These are reported in a special issue of the *Journal of Common Market Studies* published in November 2001. The introduction to this special issue (Wallace 2001) deliberately stresses the importance of both evolutionary and experimental forms of regime-building as strong features of the current phase of European policy and political integration. In particular contributors to the issue stress the open-ended character of many current developments in the EU and the alternative methodologies being adopted in contrast to the inherited 'Community method'.

Here again, there are, perhaps, different historical comparisons in the mental frames of the two research communities. British scholars examining European integration carry in their minds images of a pre-integration Britain, as well as of post-integration Britain, just as, incidentally, British scholars—and politicians—carry images of pre- and post-welfare state Britain. British scholars are perhaps more disposed than their German colleagues to play with the notion of alternative patterns of transnational integration in different periods or for different purposes. It would, of course, be quite unfair to claim that German scholarship generally—let alone all the projects reported in this volume—are locked into notions of designer Europeanization. Nonetheless, German analysis bears many imprints of the self-conscious and deliberate efforts to mould European institutions to respond to the array of transnational policy challenges facing the EU, in contrast to generally more agnostic British scholarship.

1.4 In conclusion

This volume contains an impressive array of new research from a vigorous and productive German research programme, with much more to come as other projects yield their findings. It deserves to be read with care by scholars from elsewhere and from different research traditions. The projects reported merit attention both for their individual findings and for the way in which they refract the political and social background from which they emerge and to which they respond. It is also welcome that so deliberate an effort has been made to bring this new German research to the attention of the wider research community by publication in English, since transnational publication provides an excellent channel for better-informed debate over what is after all a shared research agenda. Mainstream British and American scholarship may benefit from cosmopolitan recruitment, but it suffers from its monoglot weakness of overdependence on English language sources. The same accusation cannot be levelled at the German research community, which draws on more multilingual sources and commentary, and which is also currently much involved in forms of internationalization, as German universities increasingly operate in English and recruit students, researchers, and faculty from further afield. But then more intellectual competition might be a benefit all round.

References

Howorth, Jolyon (2001). 'European Defence and the Changing Politics of the European Union: Hanging Together or Hanging Separately?', *Journal of Common Market Studies*, 39/4: 765–81.

Hyde-Price, Adrian G. V. and Jeffery, Charlie (2001). 'Germany in the European Union', *Journal of Common Market Studies*, 39/4: 689–718.

Pollack, Mark A., Jachtenfuchs, Markus, and Wessels, Wolfgang (2001). 'Theorizing European Integration and Governance', *Journal of Common Market Studies*, 39/2: 197–264.

Rhodes, R. A. W. (1996). 'The New Governance: Governing without Government', *Political Studies*, 44/5: 652–67.

Wallace, Helen (2001). 'The Changing Politics of the EU: An Overview', *Journal of Common Market Studies*, 39/4: 581–94.

2

Interdependent European Governance

Beate Kohler-Koch

2.1 Divergent views on governance

'European governance' ranks high on the present research agenda on Europe[1] and has attracted considerable attention in public debate.[2] It has opened a wide variety of issues, ranging from explorations into the nature of the European multi-level polity and the democratic quality of the European Union (EU)[3] to the analyses of the processes and politics in specific issue areas and, more recently, to the investigations into the Europeanization of national political systems. It is not astonishing that, because of this expanding interest, there is little agreement on the meaning of 'European governance'.[4] Despite varying definitions, a rather

---

[1] There are already at least three book series on European governance: (1) 'Themes in European governance', Cambridge: Cambridge University Press, series editors: Andreas Follesdal and Johan P. Olsen, (2) 'Governance in Europe', Lanham, Maryland: Rowman & Littlefield, series editor: Gary Marks, (3) 'Regieren in der EU', Baden-Baden: Nomos, series editor: Beate Kohler-Koch.

[2] In public debate, it was above all promoted by the European Commission publishing the White Paper on European governance (Commission 2001), which—with the active support of the Commission in form of hearings and conferences, a special newsletter and an interactive electronic discussion platform—has been debated widely (see, among others, Joerges, Mény, and Weiler 2001).

[3] For the sake of convenience, the term 'EU' will be used whenever I refer to the general phenomena of the former EC and the present three pillars of the EU. Only when referring to the particularities of the first pillar, will I be more precise and use 'EC'.

[4] Altogether, governance has a rather opaque meaning. It has been introduced in International Relations to exemplify the particularities of governing without governments (Rosenau and Czempiel 1992). In comparative politics, it has the connotation of catching deep-going changes in the way governments exert political power and enter into close relations with societal actors. Some have used the term to describe 'a *new* process of governing' (Rhodes 1997: 15) in a polity still dominated by the policy-making of a government. Those who link governance to the operation of governments do it on analytical and normative grounds. They believe that governments still play a leading role in political steering and

narrow understanding of governance prevails. As most studies concentrate on the process of policy-making and implementation, the interest is focused on mainly three aspects: on the ways and means of accommodating diverse interests, on setting targets for public action and on the production of public goods. This policy perspective misses out on two important dimensions. First, it fails to grasp the intimate relationship between policy-making and politics in terms of the continuous struggle for political power and legitimacy. Second, it takes the constitutional conditions of policy-making for granted. This limited view is supported by the predominant rational choice approach, which conceptualizes governance as organizing exchange under given constraints.

This book takes a different approach. The focus is not on policy-making but on governance in a broader sense. While it takes a neo-institutional approach, it includes the shaping and changing of the constraints on political action as being part of governance: 'governance involves affecting the frameworks within which citizens and officials act and politics occurs, and which shape the identities and institutions of civil society' (March and Olsen 1995: 6). According to this position, governance concerns both the organization of collective decisions in a given institutional setting among actors with pre-established preferences and resources, and the shaping of constraints relevant for political action, in particular, by building and restructuring institutions. Political institutions are favoured objects of governance because they offer orientation for behaviour. In recent decades, the EU has been subject to continued efforts of institutional change. Most noticeable have been the Treaty revisions negotiated in successive Intergovernmental Conferences. Less noticeable, but not less important than these kinds of intentional 'constitutional politics' are the unintended effects of day-to-day routines linking closely the different levels of governance in the EU system.

insist that governing as portrayed in the normative theory of democracy should be the benchmark for any new form of governance (Pierre and Peters 2000: 12). Though the EU has, at best, some state-like qualities, Armstrong and Bulmer chose an analogous approach. Their emphasis is upon 'how different institutional *configurations* [...] can impact upon governance capacity' (Armstrong and Bulmer 1998: 55). Quite a different perspective prevails among authors who put emphasis on state–society relations. Some define the term in a way to include any deliberate attempt of political steering involving public and private actors (Héritier 2001: 185) or use it to cover also the corresponding activities by societal actors (Mayntz 1998: 7–8). Still others apply it just to '*horizontal forms of interaction*' between independent but interdependent actors who '*regularly arrive at mutually satisfactory and binding decisions by negotiating with each other and cooperating in the implementation of these decisions*' (Schmitter 2002: 53). For a short overview of the recent history of governance theorizing, see Kooiman 2002.

In order to explore the implication of interdependence, this book also takes a more embracing view than usual. Whereas most studies either analyse how the EU itself is governed or examine the impact of the EU on member state policy-making, the contributions to this volume investigate the interrelationship between EU and national governance. They give evidence of the high degree of interconnectedness between the different levels of governance and the constraints and costs associated with it. The way in which decision-making powers are exerted at one level has repercussions at other levels. These do not just change the constraints economic and social actors face, but they also alter the conditions of governing. Quite obviously, the EU and member states together constitute a system of institutionalized interdependence in governance. Therefore, it is worthwhile not just to keep record of the degree of interconnectedness, but also to examine the sensitivity and vulnerability of the individual systems involved in the complex texture of multi-level governance.[5] While European integration, thus, puts considerable pressure on the systems affected, interconnectedness also provides opportunities for mutual learning and stimulates adaptive capacities to manage a changing environment.

2.2 Linking EU and national governance

The individual chapters of this volume give evidence that interconnectedness has many faces. Linking EU and national governance has an impact on the organization of both the policy-formulation and the policy-implementation process, and it contributes to the restructuring of power between the legislative and the executive as much as it touches upon the public–private divide in governance. Furthermore, the contributions highlight that interconnectedness is brought about by different mechanisms. It comes, first of all, with the organization of decision-making at both levels and with sub-national legal integration and strategies of national compliance. In addition, the proliferation of EU programmes has contributed to an ever-closer linkage between the administrations involved in policy implementation. Policy networks tie governance across different levels of authority and shift public–private relations. The new modes of political steering like the open method of coordination, which have been

---

[5] With this terminology I refer to the concept of international interdependence as it was introduced by Keohane and Nye in 1977 (Keohane and Nye 1989).

introduced in recent years, have accelerated this kind of interaction. Soft mechanisms, such as benchmarking and monitoring, connect systems of governance as effectively as binding agreements, not least because they trigger social contagion effects across borders that are difficult to control.

Joint decision-making is the main source for connecting systems of governance. With the expansion of the functional scope of the EU, an ever-growing number of national actors has become involved in European negotiations and is now part of a governance process which is quite distinct from that at home. The chapter by Maurer, Mittag, and Wessels (Chapter 4, this volume) gives account of 'a remarkable and persistent shift of attention, of individual and institutional resources' from the national to the EU level. The extent and intensity of participation of politicians and civil servants in preparing, formulating, implementing, and evaluating EU policies are impressive. This results in a growing demand for national coordination, which is accentuated by the segmentation of negotiating arenas and the fragmentation of EU policies. Furthermore, the authors point to the effects of a progressing institutional differentiation in the EU system which comes along with the introduction of new bodies and novel procedures of European governance. It goes without saying that this process of institutional growth and increasing complexity is a challenge to the functioning of established structures and processes at the national and sub-national level.

Another strong link between national and sub-national governance is established by the common legal framework. From a lawyer's point of view it is not so much the formulation of supra-national law as its application and enforcement that penetrates national systems of governance. In his contribution, von Bogdandy (Chapter 3, this volume) brings to light how even inconspicuous legal provisions have the effect of bringing national administrations and the Commission closely together and thereby generate an interpenetration of the national legislative processes. For instance, within the realm of technical standards and regulations member states are required to inform the Commission and other member states of any relevant legislative proposal. Subsequently, the notification obligation with its broad material scope of application has, according to von Bogdandy, led to the establishment of 'an autonomous administrative communication and information network'. This networking effect is of high importance as it has 'given impetus to a change in the European legislative culture' by creating a European communicative universe in its own right.

2.3 Sensitive interdependence in European governance

It is quite obvious that interconnectedness is associated with costs and constraints. All member states struggle with the challenge of adjusting their internal governance structures in order to compensate for the loss of control which both the executive and the legislative have incurred. Since the early 1990s, governments have increased their efforts to introduce effective mechanisms for internal administrative coordination. By streamlining the flow of information and communication at home, they want to ensure the formulation of coherent national strategies and to put political weight behind stated positions. It is noteworthy that all member states introduced new mechanisms but that the requirements of adaptation have neither led to fundamental modifications of national institutions nor to uniform patterns of reform (Maurer, Mittag, and Wessels, this volume). Apart from the path-dependency of institutional change, which makes differentiated national settings visible, variations have to be attributed to the autonomy of national actors who have a certain latitude to choose the kind of adjustment they think to fit best. The optimal solution may, however, not be at hand because political actors are restricted with regard to their choices by domestic interest constellations and by party competition. In consequence, even highly influential actors such as national governments, time and again, fail to establish efficient procedures for the successful coordination and presentation of national positions at the EU level (von Bogdandy, this volume).

Change in national patterns of governance is mainly the indirect effect of being entrenched in the EU system of joint policy-making. Member states have been very cautious to transfer any competence to the Community which would empower the latter to impose changes in national governance. Nevertheless, such changes come through the backdoor, for instance, by stimulating the voluntary adaptation of 'best practice' in governance or as strings attached to subsidy programmes like the structural funds. In the case of subsidy programmes, member states can only benefit when they are willing to accept 'laid down' procedures and when they open the policy-making process to relevant actors as defined by the Community. As Lang (Chapter 8, this volume) shows, the European Community's (EC's) structural funds policy is a telling example of how the simultaneous implementation of European and national programmes bring about frictions, influence formal and informal governing patterns, and sometimes change the role of public and private actors. It is a well-researched policy field for exploring institutional spillover. In many cases, the same implementation agencies are in charge of administering both the European and the national programmes and, consequently, they seek to harmonize procedures and instruments for the sake of efficiency. The theoretical argument is that organizations have a limited set of standard operating procedures and will reduce complexity in order not to hamper their performance.

The empirical evaluation of the adjustment strategies reveal that, quite obviously, EC demands did not fit easily with established governance patterns. It is worthwhile reflecting that in, his comparative study, Lang found only one case out of twelve which could be classified as 'absorption'. In other words, it was the exception that the regulatory requirements of the EC actually met the domestic structural policy regulations and could be transposed without further institutional changes. In all other cases, a change in governance became necessary. National and sub-national political actors faced hard choices, and the strategies which they opted for may be taken as an indicator of how they rated the costs of adaptation.

When member states could not respond to the EC regulatory demands within the given institutional framework, they chose 'isolated implementation' as a short-term option. That is to say, within the same policy field they developed a parallel governance system, which operates alongside established national governance structures. From a medium-term perspective, the costs of operating two different sets of policy administration were reduced either by transforming isolated implementation into 'symbolic' adaptation or by 'material' change. Lang talks of symbolic change when EC requirements are met in a formal way, but policy decisions are arrived at via informal proceedings which conform to national traditions. This indicates long drawn-out resistance and may be taken as a valid indicator for intolerable costs of changing national patterns of governance. On many occasions, domestic actors did not comply with European principles and norms of governance despite their involvement in EC networks.

Despite such resistance, in about half the cases examined material change took place, at least in the long run. However, this change can hardly be attributed to learning effects within the policy field. Lang points out that material change in sector specific governance was only arrived at after a concurrent change in the overall domestic governance context. The overall context was not contaminated by the Europeanized sector but responded to other, external developments, that is, changes in the overall setting of national governance. These findings confirm that governance structures of individual policy fields are deeply embedded in national contexts and that a demand for compliance is likely to spread interdependence sensitivity across sectors which explains the opposition to material change. National and sub-national public actors attribute a higher value to optimizing national institutional arrangements than to comply with EU governance regulations. Therefore, they resist even strong pressures to introduce EC designed governance mechanisms and rather react in accordance with domestic requirements.

2.4 Soft and hard cases of interdependence vulnerability

In the case outlined earlier, it is noteworthy that domestic political actors enjoy a considerable degree of autonomy, even when new governance mechanisms are imposed by law. The case illustrates how difficult it is to validate vulnerability stemming from interdependence in governance. Vulnerability can be defined as a member state's liability to suffer protracted costs despite efforts of adjustment over a period of time (Keohane and Nye 1989: 13). This concept has been criticized for being vague and, indeed, when vulnerability rests on the relative availability and costliness of the alternatives that various actors face (Keohane and Nye 1989: 13), time makes quite a difference. The capacity to adjust varies depending on the time horizon; what has been identified as vulnerability in a short-term perspective may look different in the long run. Sometimes, adjusting to new modes of governance may fail in the short run but with diminishing costs, due to external developments, it may be executed quite easily later on.

Equally ambivalent is the assessment of national patterns of adjustment across member states. It has been argued, quite convincingly, that the EU system of network governance is closer to and, therefore, absorbed more easily by neo-corporatist systems such as Germany than by hierarchically organized state-centred polities such as France (Kohler-Koch 1999: 20–6; Schmidt 1999: 156–7, 2001). Nevertheless, it is difficult to find cases where the necessity to adapt to a changed environment has jeopardized the ability of member states to govern effectively. Furthermore, a valid assessment has to take into account the quality of outcome. When EU governance patterns could be absorbed with minor difficulties due to system similarities, a member state was exempted from the requirement of deep cutting reforms. Other member states, confronted with the necessity to invest in costly adjustments, finally decided in favour of thorough reforms. When successful, they did not only make efficient sector governance more sustainable, but also furthered the readiness and the capacities for adjustment. At the end, the experience of vulnerability was the key to the development of adaptability.

In an analysis which is focused on efficiency and effectiveness, it is difficult to assess whether or not linking EU and national governance may provoke vulnerability. From a normative perspective, it is far easier to spot deficiencies. It is, first of all, the ensuing democratic deficit that comes to mind. There is a broad consensus that a substantive derogation of parliamentary control would threaten the democratic identity of the EU member states.[6] Theoretical reflections and empirical research have provided more than enough evidence that European integration has tipped the balance of power between parliament and government in favour of the executive. The lack of parliamentary control both at the national and at the EU level is widely deplored and the standard remedy is to further enhance parliamentary powers.

Quite a different perspective is offered by Benz (Chapter 5, this volume) who argues that the democratization of the EU is also a problem of linking national and European institutions of democracy. His contribution highlights the sensitivity and vulnerability particularly of national parliamentary democracies. In the early years of European integration, national parliaments made little efforts to penetrate the world of executive negotiations in EC policy-making. This complacency has changed with the widening scope of EU competence and the increasing public awareness of the European democratic deficit. In different ways and to varying degrees national parliaments have adjusted their institutional structures in order to get a better grasp of European political developments and to control their own governments more efficiently. They have obliged the executive to better inform them on the EU agenda and the state of negotiations in EU affairs, they have extended their powers to have a say in EU decision-making and they have established their own informal channels to gain independent access to information from Brussels directly.

Improving parliamentary control and exerting it according to the logic of representative democracy is, however, not just a matter of paying more attention and of institutional adjustment. National parliaments face a 'negotiation-accountability dilemma' (Benz, this volume). Party competition in national parliaments puts the executive under pressure to give

---

[6] See the ruling of the German Constitutional Court 1994.

priority to partial interests and thus instigates competitive bargaining in the Council. The stricter parliamentary surveillance within the member states the more difficult it is to reach a negotiated compromise in the Council. Parliaments have learned to deal with this dilemma and, irrespective of constitutional rights, in daily practice they renounce the role of an external veto player. 'They realize that propositions forcing the government into distributive bargaining may bring about outcomes that are problematic even from the national point of view' (Benz, this volume). Therefore, instead of issuing binding decisions, parliaments—and this means the majority party group(s)—use informal ways to influence the national negotiation position. This tendency to arrive at mutual agreements outside the formal institutions also applies to the relationship between the European Parliament (EP) and the Council. Benz makes out a 'de-institutionalization' of decision-making: It is not the parliament but individual members who have access and exert influence on the executive, and positions are not negotiated in public but behind closed doors. The lack of transparency injures public accountability. The paradoxical result of upgrading parliamentary powers in EU decision-making may be a deterioration of the democratic quality of representative structures: '[...] political practice resembles the pre-democratic pattern of representative government' (Benz, this volume). There is no easy remedy, because the accountability deficit results from the combination of incompatible logics of legitimate governance. Linking EU and national governance in the multi-level system of the EU is a precarious attempt at reconciling the competitive logic of majoritarian democracies, prevalent in member states, with the consociational logic of the European negotiation system.

Another equally important and ambiguous case is presented by Deppe, Felder, and Tidow (Chapter 9, this volume). They argue that linking EU and national governance modifies statehood not only by the transfer of competence from the national to the supra-national level, but also by shifting the balance between the realm of the political and the economic in member state systems. Even soft ways of governing like the open method of coordination in employment policy have such a far-reaching effect. By propagating shared objectives, setting targets, and defining benchmarks, the handling of national employment policies is put under external pressure. Though not legally imposed, the announcement of a particular regime which carries all connotations of representing 'best practice' weakens the argumentative position of those who disagree, be they in government or be they opposing forces outside government. Opening the domestic debate on employment governance to intergovernmental coordination is by no means a neutral exercise. The framing of objectives and strategies is conditioned by the properties of the EC. With the given decision-making structures and a predominantly neo-liberal philosophy laid down in the Treaty, the EC has a propensity to privilege market integration to political steering and to give precedence to the criteria of economic rationality. Therefore, Deppe and his co-authors conclude that linking EU and national governance draws a new demarcation line between the spheres of the public and the private and in this way furthers what they call 'the uneven Europeanization of statehood': While the material regime of employment governance is developed in the institutional context of the EC, the political mediation of competing interests remains tied to the member state.

In international affairs, the asymmetric vulnerability in an interdependent relation has been identified as a source of power for one side or the other. Whenever a country has the capacity to inflict costs of adaptation on others, it has a superior standing. Asymmetric interdependence also occurs in the EU, since changes in governance are less costly to some actors than to others and since the capacity to resist change is distributed unevenly. This asymmetry can explain why some countries are more eager to advance integration which, as a general rule, implies an even closer interdependence between EU and national governance. In addition, the congruence of EU governance with governing structures in individual member states does not happen by chance. Irrespective of whether the design is the negotiated outcome of intergovernmental conferences or exported in an informal way, member states are quite aware of benefits and costs involved in alternative institutional arrangements and will push their own preferred model. We still lack systematic comparative research to know the conditions and the system properties which allow some member states to export their governance patterns to the EU and to burden other members with the costs of adjustment. But compared to international relations, neither the institutional structures nor the prevailing regime of cooperation of the EU support the use of such power to gain a significant competitive advantage over others.

Nevertheless, the effect of power differentials should not be underrated. When member governments face harsh criticism at home and fight to ward off unwanted effects of EU regulations, those which carry weight discard binding obligations and, although with some hesitation, disrupt consented governing arrangements. Neyer and Wolf (Chapter 10, this volume) present exemplary cases of non-compliance that occurred when member states were willing and able to challenge the unity of European law. More interesting than the violation itself is the strategy of both Community institutions and other member states to avoid lasting damage. Even though the Commission and the European Court of Justice (ECJ) could have exerted hierarchical power and could have sanctioned the deviant behaviour, the EU opted for 'horizontal enforcement'. Member governments and the Commission created an institutional framework for continuous discourse in order to approximate the competing conceptions. Squaring the circle to maintain the principles, norms, and procedures of European governance and to pay tribute to the needs of the distressed member state was arrived at by linking EU and national governance even closer. The defiant member state becomes a target of observation and criticism at the European and the national level. It gets incorporated into a dense network of European-level consociation and it is subjected to the monitoring and the political pressures of national actors, which have been empowered by the Community. This non-hierarchical, non-coercive strategy illustrates best that the EU has reached a high degree of penetrated governance.

2.5 The virtues of sensitivity and vulnerability of the EU system

Sensitivity and vulnerability are not only characteristics of national political systems, but they apply to the EU political system as well. Thus, at the European level, we can also observe processes of learning and adjustment to challenges in the environment that aim at improving structures and procedures of decision-making both with respect to efficiency and with respect to public legitimacy. The case of the EU structural funds reforms provides an illustrative example for successful organizational learning especially at the European level, even though, according to Heinelt et al. (Chapter 7, this volume), this is true in a quite different way from what is assumed by mainstream interpretations.

According to conventional wisdom, adaptation has been smooth thanks to the satisfactory functioning of policy networks and the emergence of encompassing policy communities. In regional policy, and in particular in the structural funds policy, the dispersion of jurisdiction across different levels and the splitting up of decision-making into multiple arenas is most pronounced. In consequence, an increasing number of relevant actors have to be coordinated and '[. . .] negotiated solutions incur exponentially rising and eventually prohibitive transaction costs' (Scharpf 1997: 70). The development of policy networks has been conducive to lowering the coordination costs of multi-level governance. Empirical research has underscored the importance of such networks and many authors attribute the successful performance of the EU structural funds policy to the formation of cross-cutting networks, which bring together public and private actors from the national, the sub-national, and the EU level. These networks are considered to be ideal breeding grounds for learning processes and the emergence of policy communities, which share interpretations of problematic situations, agree on common objectives and consent on problem-solving strategies. The stories told sound reassuring: Networks facilitate the spread of guiding principles and norms of governance and assist the exchange of experience of best practices. Furthermore, they provide for 'organized feedback loops' between policy implementation and policy formulation and in this way improve the capacity for reform. Although Heinelt et al. discard the supposition of closely knit network structures and present empirical evidence of vertical and horizontal fragmentation, they stress the favourable opportunities for mutual learning in networks. Whenever the differentiation of issue competence and their allocation to different arenas of decision-making is combined with a coherence mechanism which functions according to the logic of loosely coupled systems, a change in governance may, nonetheless, come about by organizational learning and may spread across levels and arenas. It is just the coexistence of autonomy and coordination and the involvement of all relevant actors in these overarching networks that allow for flexible adaptation.

Finally, Eder and Trenz (Chapter 6, this volume) provide an interesting example of EU capacities for adjustment activated in response to demands arising from public spheres in the EU. Thus, they address another quite unusual normative perspective of European governance. They draw attention to the interplay between patterns of governance and public attention. Whereas the academic debate concentrates on the democratic deficiencies of the supra-national organization of multi-level governance, a critical public quite obviously takes it as a normative model to measure the appropriateness of other modes of EU policy-making. In a comparative perspective, cooperation in the field of justice and home affairs is a stumbling block because the prevailing informal intergovernmentalism does not even live up to the modest requirements of transparency, responsiveness, and accountability established in the realm of the Community method.

Both form and content of EU security governance provoked resistance Beyond the reach of public control, governments settled on agreements which threatened to encroach on civil liberties. Against this background, permissive consensus was wearing down by critical monitoring which forced political actors to present themselves to an observing public. Eder and Trenz describe the effect as a 'turn from institutional "self-reference" to "outside-reference" '; or as the turn from secrecy to publicity and transparency' (Eder and Trenz, this volume). When political actors start to observe and interpret how they resonate in public, they will feel obliged to take action to make their objectives understood and accepted. In this way, the public voicing of protest and the responding activities of decision-making aimed at gathering public support started a virtuous circle resulting in the expansion of a European public space. 'Public resonance structures' developed beyond the control of executive gatekeepers and undermined national predominance in the definition of the public space. By furthering a transnational political discourse, they gave weight to generalized values of legitimate governance. Democratic accountability was strengthened to the extent that governments engaged in intergovernmental negotiations felt monitored by an attentive public. Eder and Trenz argue that European political actors 'become increasingly reflexive on the contingencies of their interaction with the public' and that they learn that political action can only be justified 'on the basis of arguments and the performance of public debates. [. . .] What counts is that European institutions take on the normative premises of the public sphere as a framework for collective will formation' (Eder and Trenz, this volume).

Further empirical research is needed to provide more valid evidence on issues such as the state of transnational public spheres in Europe and the consequence of cultural and interest heterogeneity on its formation: To what extent will the EU discourse in one policy area become integrated in the respective national arenas and under what conditions will it expand beyond sector confines? On what issues is it plausible to assume that preferences can be aggregated across borders as easily as within a nation? Apart from the functional dynamics which propel the emergence of a European public space, the normative implications have to be considered. Though transnational resonance structures may enhance the transparency of EU decision-making and improve political responsiveness, they are no substitute for democratic accountability. Those who put emphasis on responsible government based on democratic representation may discount these improvements by pointing to the negative impacts on national democracies. A final assessment may be long in coming, as it is just the multifaceted interconnectedness of EU and national governance that produces the complexity and ambiguity of European integration and also provides for its ongoing dynamism.

References

Armstrong, Kenneth A. and Bulmer, Simon J. (1998). *The Governance of the Single European Market*. Manchester: Manchester University Press.

Commission (2001). *White Paper on European Governance*. COM (2001) 428 final. Brussels. http://europa.eu.int/eur-lex/en/com/cnc/2001/com2001_0428en01.pdf.

Héritier, Adrienne (2001). 'The White Paper on European Governance: A Response to Shifting Weights in Interinstitutional Decision-Making', in Christian Joerges, Yves Mény, and Joseph H. H. Weiler (eds.), *Mountain or Molehill? A Critical Appraisal of the Commission White Paper on Governance*. Cambridge, Mass.: Harvard Law School, 73-7.

Joerges, Christian, Mény, Yves, and Weiler, Joseph H. H. (eds.) (2001). *Mountain or Molehill? A Critical Appraisal of the Commission White Paper on Governance*. Cambridge, Mass.: Harvard Law School.

Keohane, Robert O. and Nye, Joseph S. (1989). *Power and Interdependence* (2nd edn). New York: Harper Collins.

Kohler-Koch, Beate (1999). 'The Evolution and Transformation of European Governance', in Beate Kohler-Koch and Rainer Eising (eds.), *The Transformation of Governance in the European Union*. London: Routledge, 14-35.

Kooiman, Jan (2002). 'Governance: A Social-Political Perspective', in Jürgen Grote and Bernhard Gbikpi (eds.), *Participatory Governance. Political and Societal Implications*. Opladen: Leske + Budrich, 121-39.

March, James G. and Olsen, Johan P. (1995). *Democratic Governance*. New York: The Free Press.

Mayntz, Renate (1998). *New Challenges to Governance Theory* (Jean Monnet Chair Papers, 50). Florence: European University Institute.

Pierre, Jon and Peters, B. Guy (2000). *Governance, Politics and the State*. Houndsmills: Macmillan.

Rhodes, Rod A. W. (1997). *Understanding Governance. Policy Networks, Reflexivity and Accountability*. Buckingham, Philadelphia: Open University Press.

Rosenau, James N. and Czempiel, Ernst-Otto (1992). *Governance without Government: Order and Change in World Politics*. Cambridge: Cambridge University Press.

Scharpf, Fritz W. (1997). Games Real Actors Play Actor-Centred Institutionalism in Policy Research. Boulder, Col.: Westview Press.

Schmidt, Vivian A. (1999). 'National Patterns of Governance under Siege: The Impact of European Integration', in Beate Kohler-Koch and Rainer Eising (eds.), *The Transformation of Governance in the European Union*. London: Routledge, 155-72.

—— (2001). 'Europeanization and the Mechanics of Economic Policy Adjustment', *European Integration online Papers*, 5/6.

Schmitter, Philippe C. (2002). 'Participation in Governance Arrangements: Is there any Reason to Expect it will Achieve "Sustainable and Innovative Politics in a Multilevel Context"?', in Jürgen Grote and Bernhard Gbikpi (eds.), *Participatory Governance. Political and Societal Implications*. Opladen: Leske + Budrich, 51-69.

3

Links between National and Supra-national Institutions: A Legal View of a New Communicative Universe

Armin von Bogdandy

Since the European Union (EU) is a Union of law, links between supra-national and national governance occur within a legal framework. This contribution will focus on these links within the field of EU legislation, that is, the procedures and the enactment of abstract and general rules usually termed as 'secondary law'. Legislation provides a good example to study the links between the supra-national and the national authorities, since it is a process which—in the Union far more than in the German federal system—hardly occurs without the participation of the constituent members. This holds true not only for 'grand' legislation, which involves the participation of the Commission, the Council, and usually the Parliament, but also for the legislative process delegated to the Commission within the framework of the so-called comitology (DellaCananea 1990: 655; Falke and Winter 1996: 541 *ff.*; Joerges and Falke 2000). Given this focus on the legislative framework, this contribution will not investigate the links concerning the application and enforcement of the supra-national law. Nevertheless, it should be mentioned that the legal framework in those fields is far more developed than is the legal framework with respect to legislative procedures (Scheuing 1994: 289 *ff.*; Hufen 1999: 99 *ff.*; Pitschas 1999: 123 *ff.*). The difference is not surprising, since it is rather analogous to the national situation. Legislation and rule-making, in general, are usually governed only by the constitution and

---

Thanks to Reimer von Borries, Ulrich Everling, and Karsten Sach for helpful discussions, to Andreas Maurer for helpful critique, and to my assistants Felix Arndt and Philipp Dann for collaboration. The English translation is the work of Mr Eric Pickett. The subject of this article is developed in greater detail in von Bogdandy (2000c).

internal procedural rules while their application and enforcement are subject to detailed legislation.

The argument of this chapter proceeds in three steps. First, it develops and explores three points on an abstract and fundamental level: the concerns that those links generate, a conceptual framework, and the pertinent European constitutional law. The second part focuses on the Commission and draws, in particular, on the rules which link it to the national governments. The third part focuses attention on the national level: it investigates the procedures concerning the German participation in the Council.

3.1 General remarks

3.1.1 Why bother?

It is generally acknowledged that the Union is characterized by both a particularly rich exchange of information and a well-developed communication network (Schreckenberger 1997: 389, 394). The numerous concerns that the links between the supra-national and national authorities generate can best be understood from the national perspective. These links, in effect, place considerable pressure on the German administrative bodies and particularly the federal ministries. They can even be seen as a challenge to the traditional understanding of national statehood (Héritier et al. 1994: 19 ff., 60 ff., 386 ff.). In this paper, only a few of the many problematic aspects can be mentioned. One of them is that the unity of the state is lost due to these relationships. Accordingly, in many instances there is no unifying line throughout the national positions in Brussels. As problematic as the postulate of the unity of the state might be (Dreier 1991: 211 ff.), it nevertheless is a fundamental principle when it comes to the representation of the state in foreign relations (Grewe 1988: § 77 paragraph 83; Häberle 1995: 298, 309). Moreover, one can also observe a tendency in which the administration is beginning to lose its ties to the state. In view of the reciprocal relationship between the administration and the state, the importance of this process can hardly be overstated (de Tocqueville 1978: 35 ff., 190 ff.; Friesenhahn 1958: 9, 12). The empirical evidence shows that a communication network has developed out of the innumerable administrative communications within the Union which is now transcending the boundaries of each member state. If one considers—for example, in line with a systems theory approach—a social system as the sum of the specific communicative acts (Luhmann 1995: 50 ff.), then one administrative system emerges which receives its input both from communicative acts of the European and the national actors (von Bogdandy 1999: 12 *ff.*, 32 *ff.*, 2000). The concept of the 'stateless market' as a consequence of integration has been successfully introduced (Joerges 1991: 225 *ff.*; Kapteyn 1996). Is this market regulated by a stateless administration?

This development touches on central postulates of contemporary constitutionalism. The democratic principle, in particular, appears to be at risk by the consequences of this administrative communication and information network. Information and communication processes are not neutral social operations. The type of information communicated and the 'reality' which this information (re)constructs fundamentally affect the decision-making process (Berger and Luckmann 1977: 49 *ff.*). The existence of an autonomous administrative communication and information network does not necessarily provide a reason to fear the emergence of an authoritarian bureaucracy, since the professional ethics of most of those involved should be above that. Yet it provides sufficient ground to be concerned that a one-sided perception of reality may become predominant in the decision-making process. Moreover, in view of the scope and importance of the law promulgated on the European level, a certain redundancy of the traditional national parliamentary mechanisms for setting policy occurs. This may have significant consequences for social and political integration at the national level.[1]

In addition, many practical considerations make the relationships within the Union appear to be particularly challenging for the member states. Owing to its polycentric structure, the Union, as a governance authority, is far more reliant on discourse than the national political systems. The information and communication aspects of the relevant procedures thereby gain correlatively greater importance. Hierarchy operates far less as a selection mechanism and is largely absent from the European processes when it comes to determining whether a piece of information is relevant (Hoffmann-Riem 2000: 317, 370 *ff.*). Consequently, in many European proceedings, the national actors must successfully negotiate in order to realize their interests. This assumes a mastery of information about interests and technical data (Mény, Muller, and Quermonne 1996: 5 *ff.*).

3.1.2 *The conceptual approach*

Despite the undisputed salience of the information and communication network of the Union, the conceptualization of this complex system of exchange between national and supra-national actors has always been

---

[1] This is the fundamental insight in BVerfGE 89: 155, 186.

controversial. Therefore, this enquiry attempts to project the processes by which information is transported and communications are organized onto a specific conception of the Union. This conception, developed elsewhere with reference to the constitutional development in the Maastricht and Amsterdam Treaties, is summarized by the concept of the supranational federation (von Bogdandy 1999: 61 ff.). Its concretization in light of information and communication relations is particularly promising. Eberhard Schmidt-Aßmann thinks that the most promising reconstruction of the contemporary administrative law would be based on a theory of administrative communication (Pitschas 1993: 219 ff.; Schmidt-Aßmann 1998: 236 ff.). The legal scholar and later sociologist Niklas Luhmann even sees the core of social processes in communicative operations (Luhmann 1995: 50 ff.). Accordingly, the reality of each social unit lies in the communicative acts which constitute it. Joseph H. Weiler describes the Union as a whole as a new form of 'transnational discourse' (Weiler 1991: 2403, 2483). Against this background, the information and communication relations are not just secondary in nature in that they represent elements which have to be fitted into the rigid framework of the institutions; rather, they themselves build the framework, they are the institutions. One may expect that the legal foundation of these communicative acts sheds important light on the form of the sovereign authority.

This thesis concerning information and communication relations suggests the hypothesis that a certain order specific to the Union is discernable. Despite the fragmentation of actors, procedures, and areas of action, the Union is evolving as a single organization and polity (Kohler-Koch 1999). The internal vertical and horizontal flows of information and communication processes in the Union show a specific quality and density, distinguishing it from other transnational relations. It is also characteristic that there is a lack of the statal decision-making mechanism, namely hierarchy, which gives the communication structures their peculiar stamp. The significantly greater heterogeneity and the reciprocal mistrust which accompanies it require specifically legal responses. Another substantial aspect of this order is the dependence of the Union on the promulgation of 'good laws' in the sense of providing efficient regulation (Ipsen 1972: 1049; Majone 1998: 5, 28). Lacking 'natural' legitimacy, the Union is especially dependent on constructing an efficient information network (Scharpf 1999: 30). This has consequences for the necessary quality of the information flow to the Union organs and its successful processing.

A theory only makes sense in relation to other theories (Craig 1999: 1, 3 ff.; Kaufmann 1997: 224 ff.). With regard to the information and communication relations, the difference to the rather technocratic conception of order (Hans Peter Ipsen's *Zweckverband* (1972), Giandomenico Majone's regulatory state (1998)) lies in the emphasis on the political quality of relations. As opposed to the nation–state conceptions (Kirchhof 1992; Moravcsik 1993), the conception proposed here emphasizes that the national governments do not dominate the information and communication relations and that a unique quality of dialogue characterizes the communicative relations between the member states. The core rebuttal of the federal state conceptions (Louis 1997; Mancini 1998; along these lines also Pernice 1999) is that the current communication structures cannot be understood as being at the heart of a parliamentary system with the Council as (only) a secondary chamber. In contrast to the conception of the Union as nothing more than a communication and interaction network of loosely structured, only partially overlapping circles (Ladeur 1997: 33 *ff.*), the supra-national federalism conception emphasizes the organization's unity, dimensions concerning territory and citizenship and thus its role as a polity.

3.1.3 Federal loyalty as overarching constitutional principle

If the Union is considered to be a single polity, the first question that emerges is whether the diverse links between the supra-national and the national level are held together by an overarching constitutional principle. The search for such a principle is suggested by a comparative look at federal constitutions such as the constitution of the Federal Republic of Germany, where the principle of federal loyalty (*Bundestreue*) plays precisely this role (Bauer 1992: 8 *ff.*). The meaning of federal loyalty is at the centre of the issue with which this contribution is concerned, namely, with the creation of obligations to inform, consult, and collaborate (Bauer 1992: 346 *ff.*).

While the EU is not a federal state, according to the theory applied here, it is considered to be a federal polity (von Bogdandy 2000*a*). Above all, statehood is characterized by coercive means and a redistributional function. These are two elements which the principle of federal loyalty does not address. Yet as the Union is a federal polity, one would expect it to have a principle analogous to federal loyalty. In fact, the European Court of Justice (ECJ) has developed a principle of loyal cooperation, which obliges the Union's organs as well as the national authorities (Due 1991: 15 *ff.*, 35; Zuleeg 1997: Article 5 paragraph 1).[2] The relevant decisions are

---

[2] Case 230/81, Luxemburg/Parliament, ECR 1983: 255, 287; Case 2/88, Zwartfeld, ECR 1990, I-3365: 3372.

based largely on Article 10 TEC (formerly Article 5 TEC) and, thus, are initially valid only for the Union's activities under the EC Treaty. However, since the Amsterdam Treaty has come into force, there are good reasons to extend this obligation—at least in principle—to all activities of the Union (Everling 1998: 185, 192, 194).

The principle of federal loyalty entails a common responsibility of all participating authorities for the realization of law within the Union's jurisdiction (Schmidt-Aßmann 1998: 30). Nevertheless, the limits of the functional capacity of such a principle are evident. The principle of federal loyalty alone cannot construct an effective federal state (Schlink 1982: 145 ff.), the principle of loyal cooperation alone does not provide the basis for an effective supra-national polity (Meier 1989: 237, 245 ff.). Only in very few cases, such an abstract principle as loyal cooperation can be expected to have a direct regulatory function; far more detailed and precise rules and procedures of the information and communication processes are required for day-to-day business. This is especially true for the EU, which can rely neither on a basic trust nor on an intuitive reciprocal acquaintance on the part of the various authorities, but faces a good measure of ignorance and mistrust (Louis 1997: 5, 7; Moreau Defarges 1998: 152, 160).

3.2 The Commission's links as a power base

A major player in the process of policy-making at the European level is the Commission. The Commission has neither a police force nor an army, little money and hardly a party base. So does it have political power at all? Certainly, there are its competencies according to the treaties and secondary law, which have provided the Commission with some measure of power. This aspect has been investigated by the institutionalist approach (Wessels 1996; Jachtenfuchs 1997, 1999; Scharpf 1997). There is another, so far little noticed basis of power of the Commission in the process of legislation, and this is knowledge. There is no institution in Europe that is legally equipped to have as much knowledge as the Commission. This knowledge concerns facts, interests, and preferences in most fields regarding the Union's competencies.[3]

In order to grasp this aspect, the analysis will start with the competence of legislative initiative in the Union, which lies with the Commission. This competence is usually an exclusive one as the member states enjoy

---

[3] This view is rejected by Moravcsik (1999).

a concurrent initiative competence only in a few areas (Article 67 paragraph 1 TEC, Article 34 TEU; compare also Article 48 TEU). Areas in which the Commission lacks the competence of legislative initiative do not allow for legislative activity as is the case, for example, in foreign relations (Article 22 paragraph 1 TEU). This refers to an important point to bear in mind: the experiences made in the second and third pillars after the Maastricht Treaty came into force have shown that the member states and the Council's secretariat are hardly in the position of being able to make useful legislative proposals (Timmermans 1996: 133, 145). This very fact explains why the Amsterdam Treaty expanded the Commission's initiative competence. Obviously the effective synthesis of the relevant information and positions requires a specialized and autonomous body endowed with extensive competencies. In short, it requires the Commission.

Yet even if an autonomous organ for gathering and synthesizing information appears to be scarcely dispensable for successful transnational legislation, this says nothing about the procedures for the actual gathering of information and its processing as well as about the role of the member states in this process. The spectrum of possible alternatives ranges from a highly autonomous administrative procurement and processing of information over diverse forms of cooperation with other sovereign and private actors to models of mere supervision of negotiations conducted by interested societal groups (von Bogdandy 1995: 102 *ff.*). In the following, some empirical data will be presented, then the current legal framework will be described and, finally, some problems will be examined.

3.2.1 *The Commission's practice: Some empirical data*

As a relatively small and spatially localized entity, the Commission has hardly all the information and knowledge about empirical conditions and interests which would be necessary for producing convincing legislation for such a heterogeneous area as the Union.[4] In comparison to the state ministries, the Commission is a small organization; moreover, the fact that it is understaffed is beyond question. The Commission and the French ministries were typified when Yves Mény, one of the most knowledgeable individuals of both institutions, stated that the Commission, in contrast to the French ministries, does not claim to possess a 'monopoly of legitimate expertise' (Mény, Muller, and Quermonne 1996: 14).

---

[4] Mazey and Richardson (1996: 41) term the Commission a 'bourse' or 'market place' of ideas and innovations.

According to Yves Mény, it is unimaginable that the Commission would rely solely on its internal expertise for a legislative initiative. Instead, the legitimacy and acceptance of its initiatives are rather dependent on the involvement of the relevant public and private actors. The Commission depends more than a national ministry on external information.

The Commission uses many methods for gathering information. The flow of information is particularly intense when the Commission's projects are known. To this end, the Commission has developed an exemplary information policy, the principles of which are contained in the Communication of the Commission on Openness in the Community (European Commission 1993b). Pursuant to Annex I point II 2 of the communication, an annual working programme of the planned legislative proposal activities is to be published,[5] announcing the projects and the individual steps. However, it is not seldom the case that this programme is undermined by the Council's presidency. Despite its legal independence concerning the proposition of legislation, the Commission can scarcely ignore the presidency, since it has control over the Council's agenda.

The development of new or especially important political fields is often conducted by using green and white papers, which represent an important instrument of information policy.[6] Regarding these papers, the Communication of the Commission on Openness in the Community formulates relevant principles, too. In a green paper the Commission explores the nature of the topic, describes the problem and the possible principles for future regulation. At the same time, the Commission requests commentary, which in part—following the American example[7]—is organized as an Internet discussion forum. The Council generally presents its position and critique in the form of conclusions of the presidency, so that the national administrations are already involved in the Commission's projects at this stage. These conclusions are the formal determinations of a political position; they are usually passed unanimously. White papers contain a higher degree of policy development in that they foresee concrete legal acts.[8] The best known is the White Paper on the Single Market.

The green and white papers do not prescribe any specific means concerning the flow of information to the Commission. It appears that, with

---

[5] http://europa.eu.int/comm/off/work/1999/index_de.htm.
[6] http://europa.eu.int/comm/off/green/index_de.htm.
[7] See, for example, www.ftc.gov/bcp.
[8] http://europa.eu.int/comm/off/white/index_de.htm.

regard to the harmonization of laws, the Commission sometimes autonomously finds the necessary information by constructing its proposal out of the various national regulations which are to be harmonized (Interview von Borries). In the normal case, by contrast, the Commission relies on external expertise. National civil servants, lobbyists for interest groups (industry or non-governmental organizations, NGOs), or corporations are involved in the preparatory phase. Their involvement is crucial for the information gathering process, the exploration of different alternatives and the formation of a first consensus as well as for the facilitation of later transformation and implementation (Mentler 1996: 102 ff.).

Consequently, the responsible Commission functionaries often conduct extensive consultations during the drafting stage. The Commission has access to the national civil servants and experts most importantly through the many EU working groups. These working groups are usually formed within the comitology framework—with the goal of accompanying the Commission's own implementation acts—by acts of the Council (and, perhaps, the Parliament) (Glatthaar 1992: 179 ff.; Falke and Winter 1996: 541 ff.; Wessels 1996: 171 ff.). Nevertheless, there are also projects in which the Commission relies on private interest groups for information and does not involve the civil servants of the member states (Diekmann 1998: 259). Considering the importance of information in the early phases of a project, the true meaning of the flow of information becomes ever more evident.

3.2.2 The patchy legal framework

There is no general act which regulates the Commission's gathering of information. The Treaty itself does not foresee such a general act;[9] only a right to access to documents has been laid down in Articles 207 paragraph 3 and 255 TEC (Curtin and Meijers 1995: 391 ff.). Nevertheless, the ECJ has developed a number of procedural rules for the EU organs based on primary law (Hartley 1998: 411 ff.; Priebe 1999: 71 ff.). So far, at best, only the preliminary outlines of a limitation on discretion with respect to the gathering of information in the legislative process are ascertainable.[10] Accordingly, the rules of procedure of the Commission do not answer this question. A more detailed regulation can be found in the code of conduct

---

[9] Case T-194/94, *Carvel & Guardian Newspapers* v. *Council*, ECR 1995, II-2765.

[10] Case C-41/93, *French Republic* v. *Commission*, ECR 1994, I-1829: paragraph 35 ff.; Case C-263/95, *Germany* v. *Commission*, paragraph 27.

regarding representatives of interest groups, but this regulation is not legally binding (European Commission 1993a; Kohler-Koch 1996: 196 ff; Schaber 1997; Diekmann 1998: 209).

However, the EC has some interesting regulations pertaining to specific rule-making procedures. Of particular importance are the procedural rules of the anti-dumping regulation. The relevant regulation contains explicit legal requirements with regard to the gathering and processing of information. Largely in accordance with the public international law requirements of the WTO,[11] Article 5 paragraph 10 Council Regulation (EC) No 3283/94[12] stipulates that the beginning of the procedural process and the facts of the case shall be publicized in the Official Journal. Article 5 paragraph 11 provides that exporters, importers, and pertinent interest groups have to be informed. Article 6 paragraph 5 states not only that the interests affected have a right to be heard, but even foresees an adversarial process for establishing the facts of the case. The rights of the parties concerned are complemented with the right to access to documents according to Article 6 paragraph 7 (Nettesheim 1994: 226 ff.). Nevertheless, according to informed observers, these procedural provisions are insufficient to establish 'fairness' in the proceedings: the Commission's practice is usually described as being one-sided in the favour of European producers (Bierwagen 1990: 143 ff.; von Bogdandy and Nettesheim 1993: 465 ff.). In sum, there is a lack of general legal norms which secure equal access to information and which aim at ensuring that the Commission convincingly processes the information. Thus, for example, the criteria by which the partners are chosen are little known (Mény, Muller, and Quermonne 1996: 14; Diekmann 1998: 212).

The broad discretion the Commission has puts it into a powerful position. This position is justified because it allows the Commission to maintain control in the initiative phase, in particular with respect to the member states. Nevertheless, if democracy is understood either in terms of the sceptical–liberal tradition as an effective control of the rulers or in terms of the radical–democratic tradition as the opportunity to (effectively) participate, the rather opaque and potentially one-sided processes of gathering and processing information endanger democratic principles. Due to selective access, these communication and information flows threaten to develop into an autonomous governance–administrative

---

[11] Agreement on Implementation of Article VI of the General Agreement on Tariffs and Trade 1994 (OJ 1994/L 336/119).

[12] Council Regulation (EC) 3283/94 concerning protection against import dumping from non-European Community members states (OJ L 349/1).

'technoculture', leading to a one-sided perception of reality. This deficient system may, however, be compared to that of the political system of the nation-state. Then, the information exchange in the EU can actually be seen as more open than the corresponding processes in most member states, and the Commission's information gathering seems of better quality than, for instance, that of the German ministries (Mény, Muller, and Quermonne 1996: 15; Interview Sach). Yet how should the deficiencies be remedied?[13]

A further point regards the impact of the European system on the national administrative systems through the partial suspension of hierarchical structures (Interview Sach). According to the traditional understanding, the Commission's request for assistance from a national official must be processed through the ministry's internal hierarchy. However, in practice, the invitations to the Commission's meetings are usually sent by the Commission's officials to the relevant national civil servants directly by email, thereby circumventing the internal hierarchy.

3.2.3 Member states' reporting obligations

The Commission's power in legislative procedures is grounded in its right to initiate legislation and its superior knowledge. In certain areas this is built on a highly efficient regime of the member states' secondary legal obligations to inform the Commission. At the centre of a legal and administrative microcosm of the relevant legislative obligations concerning information lies Directive 98/34/EC, which provides for information procedures in the field of technical standards and regulations.[14] Its main objective is to establish preventive control and to coordinate member state legislation under the Commission's leadership. By means of transparency and the exchange of information already at the legislative proposal stage, new obstacles to the single market should be avoided (Anselmann 1986: 937). Technical standards and regulations which would have to be repealed by the Union's harmonization should not be enacted in the first place (European Commission 1998: 10–12). To realize this idea, the member states are required to inform the Commission and other member states already during the drafting stage, that is, when the projected national legislation is still a bill. This is the so-called notification obligation. The member state is prevented from adopting its draft technical

---

[13] For the debate see von Bogdandy (2000b: § 31 2c) and de Búrca (1999: 74 ff.).
[14] Directive from 22 June 1998 (OJ L 204/37). Originally Directive 83/189/EEC (OJ L 109/8).

regulation during a certain period (standstill clause) and the parties informed are given the opportunity to react to the proposed regulation. This directive has created a new culture of integrated legislation.

3.2.3.1 Procedures and actors

The information procedures require that notification by the member states is to be given during all phases of the regulatory process. The notification requirement affects, first, all plans concerning future regulation. The Commission is thereby informed in advance. On a second level, the concrete draft is subject to the notification requirement. The Commission forwards this information to the other member states. The notification includes the title of the draft, the product which is its object, the main content of the regulation envisaged as well as the reasons for the draft and information about its legal and technical environment (Fronia 1996a: 105; European Commission 1998: 36). The Commission and the other member states are thus informed of the relevant aspects of the proposed regulation, hence their opportunities to evaluate it are significantly increased. The member states are required to give notification at the drafting stage, so that significant changes can be made. The notification is completed when the definite text of the technical regulation is communicated to the Commission pursuant to Article 8 paragraph 3.

A further aspect of the information procedures concerns the standstill clause and possible reactions. The first notification automatically invokes a three-month standstill obligation, during which the informing member state may not enact the regulation. During this time, the Commission and the other member states scrutinize the compatibility of the draft with their own regulations and with the single market requirements. There are three possible reactions to the draft (European Commission 1998: 41-2):

1. The Commission and the other member states can refrain from commenting on the draft. Then the draft can be enacted after the three-month period.
2. The Commission and the other member states can respond with a comment or detailed opinion. There is no obligation to take a comment into consideration, even if there is usually a reaction in practice. The Commission and the member states respond with a detailed opinion if they consider the draft as an interference with the single market, Article 9 paragraph 2 of the directive. An opinion is intended to alter the measure envisaged in order to eliminate the possible restrictions on trade that may result from it. In this case, the standstill obligation is

extended for an additional three months. The state concerned is required to respond to the opinion, though not to amend its draft in line with it. The sole legal consequence is that, after submitting a detailed opinion, the first phase of the breach of treaty procedure according to Article 226 TEC (formerly Article 169 TEC) has been fulfilled.[15]

3. And finally the Commission (though not the member states) has the power of suspending the national legislation, that is, of completely blocking it and assuming responsibility for the regulation itself. This happens if the Commission takes the view that an EU regulation is more appropriate than a national one (Article 9 paragraphs 3 and 4).[16] In this case, the Union must adopt its legislation within a specific period of time, usually twelve months after notification. During this time, the member state concerned has to stay inactive.[17]

As an administrative microcosm, the information procedures involve a variety of actors. The Commission's central position becomes apparent from the description of the procedures. The Directorate-General III (Industry), in particular department III/B/1 for technical regulations and department III/B/2 for standards, organizes and serves the proceedings. It is responsible for informing the member states and the broader public. Within the framework of their competencies, the two European standardization organizations CEN and CENELEC are responsible for the proceedings' technical functioning. They analyse, process, and store the data that are sent to them by the member states.

National agencies which enact technical standards within the meaning of the directive are also obliged by the notification requirement. In addition to the Commission, there is a standing committee, which is inserted between the diverse actors. This committee is composed of representatives of the member states and is chaired by a representative from the Commission (Article 5). It has initiative and clarification functions with

---

[15] According to the Commission's report on the practice of the procedure (for 1992–4), the member states made extensive use of the opportunity to make a comment or detailed opinion. Approximately 50 per cent of the notifications lead to a comment by other member states and nearly 20 per cent to an opinion (KOM (96) 286: 26). The Commission uses its opportunity with similar intensity.

[16] Motivation no. 16 of Directive 98/34/EC explicitly bases this extended standstill obligation on Article 10 TEC (formerly Article 5).

[17] The importance of this obligation is, in practice, small. Between 1992 and 1994 only about 5 per cent of the cases were subject to Union standardization, in 1996 the Commission was motivated by only 1 per cent of the member state notifications to make its own proposal (for more details see OJ 1997/C 311/2).

regard to the proceedings. The information network reaches even further. The importance of the involvement of private economic interests in the information proceedings has consistently increased with their revision.[18] With the directive's first amendment in 1988, the possibility of directly obtaining information was introduced for private interests.

3.2.3.2 Scope of application and implementation

The importance of the information proceedings for the entire legislative process becomes even more obvious if the directive's broad material scope of application is considered.[19] Today, it includes all product-related regulations. More precisely, it includes all regulations concerning the features of manufactured or agricultural products, their production, usage, recycling, or disposal as well as all those regulations which forbid production, import, market introduction, or usage of a product. About half of the relevant legislation of the individual states falls within the scope of the information process. With regard to the remaining half, the legislation is in any event concerned less with autonomous national regulation than with the translation of Community legislation (Fronia 1996a: 107). The whole product-related technical legislation is thus subject to Union regulation in one form or another.

The information process as a mechanism for promoting coordination of legislation does not remain limited to technical standards regulations, but has rather been extended to other areas of law. Thus the information process has achieved a scope of application far beyond that foreseen in Directive 98/34/EC. The most extensive expansion recently occurred when Directive 98/48/EC of 20 July 1998 was adopted so that the application of the information procedures was extended to the information society services.[20] With this expansion, the entire development of a new and evolving legal field is left to the cooperative form of the information process.

---

[18] In more detail Motivation nos. 7 and 24 of Directive 98/34/EC. The European Parliament (EP) has introduced just this point into the legislative process for new codification (Ausschuss 'Normen und technische Vorschriften', Vademecum zur Richtlinie 98/48, Dok. S-42/98-DE (endg): 42). The manual even contains a plea by the Commission to private persons to participate in the proceedings (European Commission 1998: 58).

[19] Since 1983, this has been significantly extended several times. For the development see Fronia (1996a: 101 ff.), European Commission (1998: 14 ff.).

[20] The information society services concerned comprise the services rendered against payment, electronically and at the individual request of a service recipient, excluding radio and television broadcasting services which are covered by Directive 89/552/EEC. http://europa.eu.int/scadplus/leg/en/lvb/l21003.htm.

The obligations of the member states would have little effect and the Commission would be correspondingly weak if they were not directly applicable. The breakthrough came with the ECJ decision in case C-194/94, CIA Security, of 30 April 1996[21] (Slot 1996: 1035; Fronia 1996b: 383; Capelli 1997: 713 *ff.*; Everling 1998: 449). In this decision, after a long fight by the Commission, the Court affirmed direct applicability and thus opened the way for private suits to achieve compliance with the notification obligation. The Court stressed the meaning of direct applicability by elaborating on the material importance of the whole process for the single market. National courts (and agencies) are thereby prohibited from applying non-notified national technical rules. The importance of this decision for the practice of the notification process is considered to be enormous (Slot 1996: 1043; Fronia 1996b: 383; Everling 1998: 452) because the willingness of the member states to cooperate in the information process has significantly increased and the Commission's position vis-à-vis the member states has been strengthened (Slot 1996: 1047; Fronia 1996b: 384). In fact, the rate of participation has increased considerably. In 1996, when the CIA decision was announced, the number of notifications rose by more than a quarter in comparison to the previous year, from almost 400 to 523 notifications.[22] In 1997, the number nearly doubled again, with 900 (!) drafts being notified.

3.2.3.3 A new legislative culture

The importance and effect of the information process can be encapsulated in three points. The importance of this process for the protection of the single market, the economic core of the European project, is obvious. Joachim Fronia speaks of an 'unavoidable precautionary instrument for the single market's efficient functioning' (Fronia 1996a: 101). With regard to the Union's administrative communication, this clarifies significant aspects of the central position of the Commission within the European communication system. It is the leading coordinator of the process. Inside of the Commission, the lines of information and action come together. Consequently, the Commission gets an excellent overview of all legislative activities of the member states and is thus able to intervene efficiently in the member states' legislative activities. The Commission is not only well informed about the current legislative projects, but also about future activities. Just as much as the Commission can set the pace

---

[21] Case C-194/94, *CIA Security International* v. *Signalson*, ECR 1996, I-2201.
[22] OJ 1997/C 311/2.

and direction of legislation through its position in the Union's legislative process, it can utilize the information process to affect the member states' legislative processes. As the central nerve of the legislatively relevant administrative communication, it has de facto become the control and coordinating centre of all legislation relevant to the single market.[23]

Finally, the information processes have given impetus to a change in the European legislative culture, affecting both the Union and the member states. Above all, it has led to the establishment of an intensive cooperation and interpenetration of the national processes, which is characteristic of European legislation. The member states' extensive use of their possibilities to react to draft technical rules, which show a culture of a common production of technical standards and regulations demonstrates this change. The pertinent national political processes are opened up to massive foreign influences. All levels of legislative activity are affected, that is, not only the semi-governmental standardization organizations, but also all legislation of the parliament and the executive. By extending the process to the area of information services, the consultation and coordination obligations have further increased in political and economic importance.[24]

3.3 The links between the German government and the Council

The communicative universe at the European level not only comprises information and communication processes around the Commission as central actor but also processes of coordination and cooperation with the Council as another centre of prime importance for the linkage of EU and national governance. It is generally acknowledged that the Union is characterized by both a particularly rich exchange of information and a well-developed communication network (Schreckenberger 1997: 389, 394). The following part will investigate the legal framework of the communicative universe around the Council at both the supra-national and national level, taking Germany as an example. The analysis will focus on an issue pertaining to the German administration which is identified as being particularly crucial to reform: the development of a European policy in the German federal ministries and in the chancellery with a view to the German participation in the Council and its working groups. Above all,

---

[23] The procedure is, therefore, seen in the Commission as the 'ideal instrument of regulatory policy' (Fronia 1996a: 109).   [24] Vademecum zur Richtlinie 98/48: 42.

the problems can be seen to lie in the information and communication areas: the inadequate flow of information between the German ministries, the confusion caused by diverse German positions, the often unclear policy objectives, and the lack of political weight behind stated positions. Although various governments have shown themselves to be successful in carrying through their long-term European perspectives and constitutional policies, their operative policies within the framework of the European institutions are considered to have little success owing to insufficient organization (Birgelen 1998: 103 ff.; Bulmer, Jeffery, and Paterson 1998: 12, 14 ff.; Janning and Meyer 1998: 267, 272 ff.; Kohler-Koch 1998: 285 ff.). In this part, I will first describe the communicative space in which the German positions are to be explored. In a second step, the national procedures for linking the European and national levels are examined. Finally, possible reforms to these procedures will be discussed.

3.3.1 *The supra-national level*

The German position has to be explored with respect to the Council, the most powerful organ of the Union, and its working groups.[25] The Union's polycentric and fragmented structure becomes evident here. The Council and its working groups are composed of pluralities, meet in different compositions and thus do not have the central mechanism of unity building at their disposal: a hierarchy (Reflexionsgruppe 1996: paragraph 106; Wuermeling 1996: 167, 168 ff.). The decision-making on the ministerial level is prepared by the many conferences on the lower levels, which meet in the Committee of Permanent Representatives (COREPER) and the Council's working groups (Röhl 1994: 409; Mentler 1996; Hayes-Renshaw and Wallace 1997). The central group for the processing of information in preparation of the actual decision is the COREPER. The power and influence of the ministers is rather limited in large part due to the fact that the ministers' 'speaking notes' are prepared by their civil servants. The COREPER meets on average twice a week (Wessels 1996: 173). According to Articles 19 and 20 of the Council's Rules of Procedure, it establishes the Council's working groups, while the number and tasks of the latter are determined by the agenda of the current Council presidency (Council of the European Union 2001/2002). Already in 1990, there were a total of about 40 working group meetings per week. In view

---

[25] The importance that the Council is given here is not to be understood in the sense of intergovernmentalism.

of the enormous increase of tasks created by the Maastricht and Amsterdam Treaties and the extension of relations with the Eastern neighbours, it can be expected that this number has increased even more.

In many respects, the Council and its working groups rather seem to be a multifaceted process of 16 different politico-administrative systems engaged in continuous consensus building than a standing institution. The importance of this observation results from the fact that it allows for a comparison between the Council and those state organs that have a similar position of power in the national system. Only the national parliament or government come into consideration (VerLoren van Themaat 1996: 249, 251 ff., 258 ff.). Both the government and the national parliament (the latter because of its party political structure) constitute far more firmly established and hierarchical institutions. Of particular importance is the ruling majority which—as the opposition—is characterized by a more or less clear-cut hierarchy of individuals. By and large, a party political structure as well as a personification of political power are lacking on the European level. One may object that even in the state systems a strict hierarchy no longer predominates (Vesting 1990: 211 ff., 1992: 4 ff.; Steinberg 1998: 396 ff.). Nevertheless, a qualitative difference remains, as the state systems display a tendency to focus the political power on the government's leadership precisely because of the intra-state consequences of integration. Ironically, it is participation in the Union's fragmented and polycentric system that facilitates the centralization of political power in the national government (Moravcsik 1997: 211 ff.).

The fact that many institutions participate in arduous proceedings leads in many cases to a complex situation. Against this background, it is important to bear in mind that the actors involved come from different (national) contexts and represent quite different interests. In short, a great number of different elements must work together. The difficulty in dealing with this complexity is that the traditional instrument by which complexity is managed, namely hierarchy, is, in practically all important aspects, excluded as a solution or strategy in the Union, precisely because of its fundamentally polycentric organization.[26] It is neither imaginable that one member state performs a hierarchical role,[27] nor that a political party can seize a hierarchical position within the Union's political

---

[26] A strengthening of hierarchy is to be found only in the Commission through the strengthening of the position of the Commission's president (Article 219 paragraph 1 TEC).

[27] As in the German Reich under Prusssia's hegemony, see Hallstein (1979: 503, 505). Neither does the 'German-French' tandem exercise a hegemonic function (de Schoutheete 1992: 106, 108 ff.).

system.[28] Consequently, the Union's mechanisms for dealing with complexity are only rarely one-sidedly hierarchical. Rather, they are contractual or cooperative in the sense that they tend toward consensus building between different politico-administrative systems (Scharpf 1997: 520 ff.). This shows that the Union as a governing authority is constitutionally more inclined to dialogue than the traditional state. Successfully presenting factual information and interests of the Federal Republic in the Union's process of political consensus building is correspondingly important.

The negotiations in the Council, the COREPER, and in the Council's working groups cannot be understood as being only a strategic bargaining of hardened positions, although the effective political support of the home government is an important negotiating resource. Nor can the results be understood as simply representing an average of the diverse Council members' current power. In the processes of consensus building one also finds elements of a collective search for a convincing solution (Joerges and Neyer 1997: 609 ff.).[29] This results from the fact that there is a competition between legal orders and models and that the competing suppliers of various regulatory models must convince the potential buyers.[30] Even Fritz Scharpf now assumes a 'truth finding potential' that does not, in this form, exist at the member state level (Scharpf 1997: 143). Successful negotiation, however, predicates that trust must be established between the colleagues and that the respective positions of the actors must be presented according to the logic of the European communicative universe (Interview Sach). Against this background, the internal German procedures regarding the formulation of the German position will be examined.

3.3.2 *The German procedure*

This section will examine how the German positions are formulated and whether the procedures satisfy the conditions for a successful policy in the European communicative arena. The following considerations will exclude those aspects that are already the object of more detailed studies, namely the cooperation of the German government with the federal parliament

---

[28] Here, one thinks of a chairman or general secretary of a European party who would effectively control the party members in the various organs of the Union.

[29] In political science terms, this means that Germany's position and behaviour cannot be understood in terms of the so-called realist theory, according to which the state is a monolithic actor acting solely on the basis of strategic considerations (Bulmer, Jeffery, and Paterson 1998: 92 ff.).

[30] See in detail Héritier et al. (1994: 194 ff.) on regulatory competition in the Union.

(*Bundestag*) and the federal representation of the German *Länder* (*Bundesrat*) (Pernice 1998: Article 23 paragraph 104 *ff.*). Instead, this contribution will concentrate on the process within the federal government, which has not been studied much so far.

The internal preparation and the presentation of the German positions in the Council, the COREPER, and the Council's working groups are conducted according to the general principles of how the German government works. The crucial norm is Article 65 of the Basic Law (*Grundgesetz*) which lays down three principles: the autonomy of the individual ministers to guide their ministries (*Ressortprinzip*), the chancellor's competence to issue policy guidelines (*Richtlinienkompetenz des Kanzlers*), and the principle of joint cabinet decision-making (*Kabinettsprinzip*). They are concretized in two sets of internal rules: the rules of procedure of the government and the common rules of procedure of the federal ministries.[31] According to the principle of ministerial autonomy, the substantive work rests with specialized functionaries of the individual ministries; expertise is the leading criterion for competence. The ministries' European units, by contrast, have (only) a coordinating and service function (Interview Borries). The principle of this division of labour was decided by the German government during the early period of integration when it chose not to centralize the European political tasks in a single ministry for European affairs (Kühn 1994: 10 *ff.*). If a project affects more than one unit, a decision by the heads of the units concerned has to be taken. If they fail to reach a consensus, the issue is 'sent up the ladder', eventually reaching the committee of state secretaries for European affairs. The cabinet scarcely plays a role (Kühn 1994: 7).

The fact that the cabinet hardly deals with these issues is considered to be the first deficiency. The EU decision-making system requires the government to exercise highly developed and concentrated orientation and steering skills if it is to successfully present its preferences in the European space (Bulmer, Jeffery, and Paterson 1998: 16, 55; Janning and Meyer 1998: 275). In the national legislative process the government can realize its policies even at a relatively late stage due to its many constitutional and political resources of power. However, in the non-hierarchical European

---

[31] The chancellor's competence to issue policy guidelines has only been used once within the context of operative policy, namely in June 1999 by chancellor Schröder in connection with the determination of the German position on the disposal of old cars. Chancellor Kohl, in contrast, employed this competence for the strategic development of the Union (for more detail see Bulmer, Jeffery, and Paterson 1998: 26 *ff.*). For earlier usage of the competence see Kühn (1994: 3 *ff.*). For the government's procedure see von Bogdandy (2000b: § 311).

political process, it can only be achieved at a high price, if it is possible at all. The 'Banana-case' is an excellent example of a European policy where the German government acted far too late (Selmer 1998: 39 *ff.*).

Furthermore, treating the development of national legislative projects and the development of the German position on European projects as being procedurally the same does not do justice to a number of differences between them. With the Commission's initiative, a project has already been called into existence. Moreover, the German government and its ministries are not the masters of their time; it is the Council presidency that sets the agenda. The sequence of developments in the Council's working groups can be very rapid.[32] A further important difference lies in the addressees of the position which is to be presented. It has to be distinguished between addressees stemming from the national political system (like the *Bundestag* or the *Bundesrat*) and addressees at the European level (i.e. Commission and Council), since the recipients are different with regard to their tasks, preferences, and policy styles. The strategy and tactics employed in negotiating should be chosen according to the person contacted, that is, whether a member of the *Bundestag* or a Spanish official has to be convinced in the process. Yet a control of 'EU suitability', even if it is only concerning the comprehensibility of the German position, seldom occurs. In addition, the high internal consensus requirements deprive the German positions of any flexibility.

The determination of the German position follows different paths. With respect to the Council's working groups, the internally responsible person, which is generally the person responsible for the respective policy within the German ministries, is usually sent to their meetings in Brussels. It is the exception that only personnel from the German permanent representation are involved in the meetings. The government usually does not issue instructions. Rather, it is the civil servants themselves, who represent the policy line of their unit, who may have been coordinated with other units (Mentler 1996: 48 *ff.*). The individual ministries have a large degree of latitude to pursue individual aims, which do not necessarily reflect the aims of the federal government. The result of this proceeding is a strong compartmentalization of European policy-making in Germany (Bulmer, Jeffery, and Paterson 1998: 28). In some cases it is not even clear who the head of the German working group is, thereby leading to internal conflicts that are played out on the European level. One can hardly

---

[32] A noticeable consequence is that the circles affected are less involved in the preparation of the German position than they would be in a comparable national regulatory process.

speak meaningfully of the external unity of a state at this stage. Consequently, the result is that the German influence on policy formulation in Brussels tends to be limited, since the government is failing to develop a clear policy line and to muster strong political backing (Bulmer, Jeffery, and Paterson 1998: 29 ff., 99 ff.).

The preparation for the German position in the COREPER, which directly affects the Council's decision-making, follows a different line. Here, the agenda for COREPER meetings is given to the coordinating unit, which was previously located in the federal ministry for economy and since 1998 has been located in the federal ministry for finance.[33] The coordinating unit requests proposals for the relevant instructions from the civil servants who are internally responsible for the topics. The European units of the ministries concerned sent their proposals to the coordinating unit of the finance ministry, which basically functions as a mailbox. A meeting under the rotating chairmanship of the finance ministry and foreign ministry is held every Tuesday. During these conferences, the agenda of the following COREPER meeting is discussed. The expert civil servants prepare speaking notes that contain the German position including proposals for amendments. These speaking notes can be short statements or detailed instructions for the modification of certain rules. All instructions to the COREPER are signed by the head of the finance ministry's department E and are sent by email or fax to the German permanent representation. However, it still appears questionable whether this procedure does indeed succeed in giving sufficient coherence to the government-administrative European policy. The German decision-making processes for the formulation of European policies can be understood in the same way as the rest of the German political decision-making processes: namely as a process to overcome institutional pluralism (Bulmer, Jeffery, and Paterson 1998: 93). Against this background, the importance of information exchange and consensus building in the Commission described in the second part becomes even more evident.

3.3.3 *Consequences and deficiencies*

The clumsiness of the German procedures for formulating a position can be measured against a legal yardstick of the Union, namely the obligation of loyal cooperation contained in Article 10 TEC (Everling 1993: 936, 946).

---

[33] The foreign ministry first created its own European department in 1993 (Kühn 1994: 5; Bulmer, Jeffery, and Paterson 1998: 28).

It requires a minimum degree of efficiency in the national preparation for participation in the Union's procedures and thus represents a legal requirement on the internal processes. However, these requirements are extremely vague, as the discussion of Article 23 II–VI Basic Law has demonstrated. The German procedures do not appear to create difficulties of such magnitude that they would violate the Union principle.

In the relevant literature that in part compares the German situation with the British procedures, which are seen as being especially operationally (not strategically!) efficient, the following reform proposals for making Germany's European policies operationally more effective are particularly prominent (Bulmer, Jeffery, and Paterson 1998: 102; Diekmann 1998: 260 *ff.*; Hermes 1998: Article 65 paragraph 7; Janning and Meyer 1998: 272 *ff.*). These reform proposals can in large measure be realized through the government's organizational competence (Böckenförde 1964; Hermes 1998: Article 64 paragraphs 8 *ff.*, Article 65 paragraphs 46 *ff.*). The most important proposal is that the German government and in particular the chancellery should use its potentially hegemonic position within the institutionally pluralistic German political system (von Bogdandy 2000*b*: § 1 and passim). More specifically, this would entail activating the cabinet on European issues. Also under consideration is the creation of a new, authoritative minister for European affairs within the chancellery who would be responsible for coordinating the tasks of the other ministers and the COREPER (Janning and Meyer 1998: 278).

The question arises whether the aim of becoming more effective is worth striving for. From the national perspective, this goal is clearly desirable, since the federal government is politically responsible to its citizens and, thus, is held accountable with regard to the degree to which it succeeds in advancing their interests in the European arena. At the same time, however, the German government officials are also tied to the Union's aims in two ways (Article 2 TEU, Articles 2 and 3 TEC): directly when they are part of the Union's institutions and indirectly in all other circumstances through Article 10 TEC. These norms obligate them to protect the interests of all citizens of the Union, not just those of their own country. Moreover, should a conflict arise, the principle of the supremacy of European law is applicable.[34] Nevertheless, the effective presentation of German interests and positions remains a legitimate concern also under European law. This is all the more true as the Union depends on effective

---

[34] Case 6/64, *Costa* v. *ENEL*, ECR 1964: 1251.

national interest representation. The European common weal can only be realized through a synthesis of the plurality of interests and positions that exists within the Union. A bad presentation of specific interests from one part of the Union therefore damages the aggregation process which should lead to the convincing formulation of the European 'common good'.

References

Anselmann, Norbert (1986). 'Die Rolle der europäischen Normung bei der Schaffung des europäischen Binnenmarktes', *Recht der internationalen Wirtschaft—Außenwirtschaftsdienst des Betriebs-Beraters*, 32/12: 936–41.

Bauer, Hartmut (1992). *Die Bundestreue*. Tübingen: Mohr.

Berger, Peter and Luckmann, Thomas (1977). *Die gesellschaftliche Konstruktion der Wirklichkeit* (5th edn). Frankfurt a. M.: Fischer.

Bierwagen, Rainer (1990). *GATT Article VI and the Protectionist Bias in Antidumping Laws*. Deventer and Boston: Kluwer.

Birgelen, Georg (1998). 'Europapolitische Meinungsbildung in Deutschland', in Werner Weidenfeld (ed.), *Deutsche Europapolitik*. Bonn: Europa-Union, 103–27.

Böckenförde, Ernst-Wolfgang (1964). *Die Organisationsgewalt im Bereich der Regierung*. Berlin: Duncker & Humblot.

Bulmer, Simon, Jeffery, Charlie, and Paterson, Willam E. (1998). 'Deutschlands europäische Diplomatie', in Werner Weidenfeld (ed.), *Deutsche Europapolitik*. Bonn: Europa-Union, 11–102.

Capelli, Fausto (1997). 'La notifica preventiva di una legge nazionale alla Commissione come condizione di applicabilità delle regole tecniche in essa contenute', *Diritto comunitario e degli scambi internationali*, 36/4: 713–22.

Council of the European Union (2001/2002). *Council's Rules of Procedure*. Luxembourg: Office for Official Publications of the European Communities.

Craig, Paul (1999). 'The Nature of the Community', in Paul Craig and Gráinne de Búrca (eds.), *The Evolution of EU Law*. Oxford: Oxford University Press, 5–81.

Curtin, Deirdre and Meijers, Herman (1995). 'The Principle of Open Government in Schengen and the EU', *Common Market Law Review*, 32/1: 391–442.

de Schoutheete, Philippe (1992). 'The European Community and its Sub-Systems', in William Wallace (ed.), *The Dynamics of European Integration*. London: Pinter, 106–24.

de Tocqueville, Alexis (1978). *Der alte Staat und die Revolution*. München: Deutscher Taschenbuch Verlag.

DellaCananea, Giacinto (1990). 'Cooperazione ed integrazione nel sistema amministrativo delle Comunità Europee: la questione della "comitologia" ', *Rivista trimestrale di diritto pubblico*, 4: 655.

Diekmann, Knut (1998). 'Die Vertretung spezifischer deutscher Interessen in der Europäischen Union', in Werner Weidenfeld (ed.), *Deutsche Europapolitik*. Bonn: Europa-Union, 209–65.

Dreier, Horst (1991). *Hierarchische Verwaltung im demokratischen Staat*. Tübingen: Mohr.

Due, Ole (1991). 'Article 5 du traité CEE. Une disposition de caractère fédéral?', *Collected Courses of the Academy of European Law*, II/1: 15–36.

European Commission (1993a). 'An Open and Structured Dialogue between the Commission and Special Interest Groups', *Official Journal of the European Communities*, C 63/02, 5.3.1993: 2–7.

—— (1993b). 'Openness in the Community. Communication to the Council, the Parliament and the Economic and Social Committee', *Official Journal of the European Communities*, C 166/04, 17.6.1993: 4–10.

—— (1998). *Maintaining the Single Market. Directive 83/189/EEC—A Commentary. A Guide to the Procedure for the Provision of Information in the Field of Technical Standards and Regulations*. Luxembourg: Office for Official Publications of the European Communities.

Everling, Ulrich (1993). 'Überlegungen zur Struktur der Europäischen Union und zum neuen Europa-Artikel des Grundgesetzes', *Deutsches Verwaltungsblatt*, 108/16: 936–47.

—— (1998). 'Folgerungen', in Armin von Bogdandy and Claus-Dieter Ehlermann (eds.), *Konsolidierung und Kohärenz des Primärrechts nach Amsterdam* (Beiheft zu Europarecht, Vol. 2). Baden-Baden: Nomos, 185–94.

Falke, Josef and Winter, Gerd (1996). 'Management and Regulatory Committees in Executive Rule-Making', in Gerd Winter (ed.), *Sources and Categories of European Union Law*. Baden-Baden: Nomos, 541–82.

Friesenhahn, Ernst (1958). 'Parlament und Regierung im modernen Staat', *Veröffentlichungen der Vereinigung der Deutschen Staatsrechtler*, 16: 58–9.

Fronia, Joachim (1996a). 'Transparenz und Vermeidung von Handelshemmnissen bei der Produktspezifikation im Binnenmarkt', *Europäische Zeitschrift für Wirtschaftsrecht*, 7/4: 101–9.

—— (1996b). 'Annotation', *Europäische Zeitschrift für Wirtschaftsrecht*, 7/12: 383–4.

Glatthaar, Christiane (1992). 'Einflussnahme auf Entscheidungen der EG durch die Ausschüsse der EG-Kommission', *Recht der Internationalen Wirtschaft*, 38/3: 179–82.

Grewe, Wilhelm G. (1988) 'Auswärtige Gewalt', in Paul Kirchhof and Josef Isensee (eds.), *Handbuch des Staatsrechts der Bundesrepublik Deutschland* (Vol. 3). Heidelberg: C. F. Müller, 921–75.

Häberle, Peter (1995). 'Die Europäische Verfassungsstaatlichkeit', *Kritische Vierteljahresschrift für Gesetzgebung und Rechtswissenschaften*, 78/1: 298–312.

Hallstein, Walter (1979). 'Some of our "Faux Problèmes". Stevenson Lecture im Royal Institute of International Affairs, "Chatham House", London, 04.12.1964', in Walter Hallstein (ed.), *Europäische Reden*. Stuttgart: Deutsche Verlags-Anstalt, 503–16.

Hartley, Trevor C. (1998). *The Foundations of European Community Law*. Oxford: Oxford University Press.

Hayes-Renshaw, Fiona and Wallace, Helen (1997). *The Council of Ministers*. Houndmills: Macmillan and New York, NY: St. Martin's Press.

Héritier, Adrienne, Mingers, Susanne, Knill, Christoph, and Becka, Martina (1994). *Die Veränderung von Staatlichkeit in Europa*. Opladen: Leske + Budrich.

Hermes, Georg (1998). 'Art. 65', in Horst Dreier (ed.), *Grundgesetz-Kommentar* (Vol. 2). Tübingen: Mohr-Siebeck, 1224–47.

Hoffmann-Riem, Wolfgang (2000). 'Strukturen des Europäischen Verwaltungsrechts—Perspektiven der Systembildung', in Wolfgang Hoffmann-Riem and Eberhard Schmidt-Aßmann (eds.), *Verwaltungsrecht in der Informationsgesellschaft*. Baden-Baden: Nomos, 317–82.

Hufen, Friedhelm (1999). 'Verwaltungskooperation in der EG: Lebensmittel- und Veterinärrecht', in Eberhard Schmidt-Aßmann and Wolfgang Hoffmann-Riem (eds.), *Strukturen des Europäischen Verwaltungsrechts*. Baden-Baden: Nomos, 99–122.

Ipsen, Hans-Peter (1972). *Europäisches Gemeinschaftsrecht*. Tübingen: Mohr.

Jachtenfuchs, Markus (1997). 'Die Europäische Union—ein Gebilde sui generis?', in Klaus-Dieter Wolf (ed.), *Projekt Europa im Übergang?* Baden-Baden: Nomos, 15–35.

Janning, Josef and Meyer, Patrick (1998). 'Deutsche Europapolitik—Vorschläge zur Effektivierung', in Werner Weidenfeld (ed.), *Deutsche Europapolitik*. Bonn: Europa-Union, 267–93.

Joerges, Christian (1991). 'Markt ohne Staat? Die Wirtschaftsverfassung der Gemeinschaft und die regulative Politik', in Rudolf Wildenmann (ed.), *Staatswerdung Europas? Optionen einer europäischen Union*. Baden-Baden: Nomos, 225–68.

—— and Falke, Josef (2000). *Das Ausschußwesen der Europäischen Union*. Baden-Baden: Nomos.

—— and Neyer, Jürgen (1997). 'Transforming Strategic Interaction into Deliberative Problem-Solving', *Journal of European Public Policy*, 4/4: 609–25.

Kapteyn, Paul (1996). *The Stateless Market*. London: Routledge.

Kaufmann, Marcel (1997). *Europäische Integration und Demokratieprinzip*. Baden-Baden: Nomos.

Kirchhof, Paul (1992). 'Der deutsche Staat im Prozeß der europäischen Integration', in Josef Isensee and Paul Kirchhof (eds.), *Handbuch des Staatsrechts der Bundesrepublik Deutschland* (Vol. 7). Heidelberg: C. F. Müller, 103–63.

Kohler-Koch, Beate (1996). 'Die Gestaltungsmacht organisierter Interessen', in Markus Jachtenfuchs and Beate Kohler-Koch (eds.), *Europäische Integration*. Opladen: Leske + Budrich, 193–222.

—— (1998). 'Bundeskanzler Kohl—Baumeister Europas?', in Göttrik Wewer, Nils C. Bandelow, and Hans-Hermann Hartwich (ed.), *Bilanz der Ära Kohl. Christlich-liberale Politik in Deutschland 1982–1998* (Special Issue of Gegenwartskunde, Vol. 10). Opladen: Leske + Budrich, 283–311.

—— (1999). 'The Evolution and Transformation of European Governance', in Beate Kohler-Koch and Rainer Eising (eds.), *The Transformation of Governance in the European Union*. London and New York: Routledge, 14–35.

Kühn, Jürgen (1994). *Die Koordinierung der deutschen Europapolitik* (ZEW Working Paper, No. 33). Bonn: Zentrum für Europäisches Wirtschaftsrecht.

Ladeur, Karl-Heinz (1997). 'Towards a Legal Theory of Supranationality: The Viability of the Network Concept', *European Law Journal*, 3/1: 33–53.

Louis, Jean-Victor (1997). 'Le traité d'Amsterdam: une occasion perdue?', *Revue du Marché Unique Européen*, 2: 5–18.

Luhmann, Niklas (1995). *Das Recht der Gesellschaft*. Frankfurt a. M.: Suhrkamp.

Majone, Giandomenico (1998). 'Europe's "Democratic Deficit": The Question of Standards', *European Law Journal*, 4/1: 5–28.

Mancini, Federico (1998). 'Europe: The Case for Staathood', *Harvard Jean Monnet Working Papers*. www.law.harvard.edu/Programs/Jean Monnet/papers/98/98-6-.html.

Meier, Gert (1989). 'Europäische Amtshilfe—Ein Stützpfeiler des Europäischen Binnenmarktes', *Europarecht*, 24/3: 237-48.

Mentler, Michael (1996). *Der Ausschuß der Ständigen Vertreter bei den Europäischen Gemeinschaften*. Baden-Baden: Nomos.

Mény, Yves, Muller, Pierre, and Quermonne, Jean-Louis (1996). 'Introduction', in Yves Mény, Pierre Muller, and Jean-Louis Quermonne (eds.), *Adjusting to Europe. The Impact of the European Union on National Institutions and Policies*. London: Routledge, 1-22.

Moravcsik, Andrew (1993). 'Preferences and Power in the European Community', *Journal of Common Market Studies*, 31/4: 473-524.

—— (1997). 'Warum die Europäische Union die Exekutive stärkt', in Klaus-Dieter Wolf (ed.), *Projekt Europa im Übergang?* Baden-Baden: Nomos, 211-69.

Moreau Defarges, Philippe (1998). 'Welche institutionelle Zukunft für die Europäische Union? Der französische und deutsche Standpunkt im Vergleich', in Werner Weidenfeld (ed.), *Deutsche Europapolitik*. Bonn: Europa-Union, 152-65.

Nettesheim, Martin (1994). 'Antidumping- und Antisubventionsrecht in der Gemeinschaft', in Eberhard Grabitz, Armin von Bogdandy, and Martin Nettesheim (eds.), *Europäisches Außenwirtschaftsrecht*. München: Beck, 197-235.

Pernice, Ingolf (1998). 'Art. 23', in Horst Dreier (ed.), *Grundgesetz-Kommentar* (Vol. 2). Tübingen: Mohr-Siebeck, 325-400.

—— (1999). 'Multilevel constitutionalism and the Treaty of Amsterdam', *Common Market Law Review*, 36: 703-50.

Pitschas, Rainer (1993). 'Allgemeines Verwaltungsrecht als Teil der öffentlichen Informationsordnung', in Wolfgang Hoffmann-Riem, Eberhard Schmidt-Aßmann, and Gunnar F. Schuppert (eds.), *Reform des Allgemeinen Verwaltungsrechts*. Baden-Baden: Nomos, 219-305.

—— (1999). 'Strukturen des europäischen Verwaltungsrechts—Das kooperative Sozial- und Gesundheitsrecht der Gemeinschaft', in Eberhard Schmidt-Aßmann and Wolfgang Hoffmann-Riem (eds.), *Strukturen des Europäischen Verwaltungsrechts*. Baden-Baden: Nomos, 123-69.

Priebe, Reinhard (1999). 'Die Aufgaben des Rechts in einer sich ausdifferenzierenden EG-Administration', in Eberhard Schmidt-Aßmann and Wolfgang Hoffmann-Riem (eds.), *Strukturen des Europäischen Verwaltungsrechts*. Baden-Baden: Nomos, 71-131.

Reflexionsgruppe (1996). *Bericht der Reflexionsgruppe. Regierungskonferenz 1996*. Luxembourg: Amt für amtliche Veröffentlichungen der Europäischen Gemeinschaften.

Röhl, Hans Christian (1994). 'Die Beteiligung der Bundesrepublik Deutschland an der Rechtsetzung im Ministerrat der Europäischen Union', *Europarecht*, 29/4: 408-44.

Schaber, Thomas (1997). 'Transparenz und Lobbying in der Europäischen Union', *Zeitschrift für Parlamentsfragen*, 28/2: 266-78.

Scharpf, Fritz W. (1997). 'Introduction. The Problem Solving Capacity of Multi-Level Governance', *Journal of European Public Policy*, 4/4: 520-38.

—— (1999). *Regieren in Europa. Effektiv und demokratisch?* Frankfurt a. M.: Campus.

Scheuing, Dieter (1994). 'Europarechtliche Impulse für innovative Ansätze im deutschen Verwaltungsrecht', in Wolfgang Hoffmann-Riem and Eberhard Schmidt-Aßmann (eds.), *Innovation und Flexibilität des Verwaltungshandelns*. Baden-Baden: Nomos, 289–354.

Schlink, Bernhard (1982). *Die Amtshilfe*. Berlin: Duncker & Humblot.

Schmidt-Aßmann, Eberhard (1998). *Das allgemeine Verwaltungsrecht als Ordnungsidee*. Berlin: Springer.

Schreckenberger, Waldemar (1997). 'Von den Schengener Abkommen zu einer gemeinsamen Innen- und Justizpolitik', *Verwaltungsarchiv*, 88/3: 389–415.

Selmer, Peter (1998). *Die Gewährleistung der unabdingbaren Grundrechtsstandards durch den EuGH: zum 'Kooperationsverhältnis' zwischen BverfG und EuGH am Beispiel des Rechtsschutzes gegen die Bananenmarkt-Verordnung*. Baden-Baden: Nomos.

Slot, Piet Jan (1996). 'Annotation', *Common Market Law Review*, 33/4: 103–5.

Steinberg, Rudolf (1998). *Der ökologische Verfassungsstaat*. Frankfurt a. M.: Suhrkamp.

Timmermans, Christian (1996). 'The Effectiveness and Simplification of Decision-Making', in Jan A. Winter, Deirdre M. Curtin, Alfred E. Kellermann, and Bruno de Witte (eds.), *Reforming the Treaty on European Union*. The Hague: Kluwer Law International, 133–46.

VerLoren van Themaat, Piet (1996). 'The Internal Powers of the Community and the Union', in Jan A. Winter, Deirdre M. Curtin, Alfred E. Kellermann, and Bruno de Witte (eds.), *Reforming the Treaty on European Union*. The Hague: Kluwer Law International, 249–63.

Vesting, Thomas (1990). *Politische Einheitsbildung und technische Realisation*. Baden-Baden: Nomos.

—— (1992). 'Erosionen staatlicher Herrschaft', *Archiv des öffentlichen Rechts*, 117/1: 4–45.

von Bogdandy, Armin (1995). 'Sittlicher Interventions- oder vermittelnder Supervisionsstaat? Begegnungs-, Kampf- und Leerplätze in der aktuellen Staatsdiskussion', *Archiv für Rechts- und Sozialphilosophie*, 81/1: 102–11.

—— (1999). *Supranationaler Föderalismus als Wirklichkeit und Idee einer neuen Herrschaftsform*. Baden-Baden: Nomos.

—— (2000a). 'The European Union as a Supra-national Federation', *The Columbia Journal of European Law*, 6/1: 1–27.

—— (2000b). *Gubernative Rechtsetzung*. Tübingen: Mohr-Siebeck.

—— (2000c). 'Information und Kommunikation in der Europäischen Union: föderale Strukturen in supranationalem Umfeld', in Wolfgang Hoffmann-Riem and Eberhard Schmidt-Aßmann (eds.), *Verwaltungsrecht in der Informationsgesellschaft*. Baden-Baden: Nomos, 133–94.

—— and Nettesheim, Martin (1993). 'Strukturen des gemeinschaftlichen Außenhandelsrechts', *Europäische Zeitschrift für Wirtschaftsrecht*, 4/15: 465–74.

Weiler, Joseph H. (1991). 'The Transformation of Europe', *Yale Law Journal*, 100/8: 2405–83.

Wessels, Wolfgang (1996). 'Verwaltung im EG-Mehrebenesystem: Auf dem Weg zur Megabürokratie?', in Markus Jachtenfuchs and Beate Kohler-Koch (eds.), *Europäische Integration*. Opladen: Leske + Budrich, 165–92.

Wuermeling, Joachim (1996). 'Streicht die Räte und rettet den Rat! Überlegungen zur Reform des EU-Ministerrats', *Europarecht*, 31/2: 167–78.

Zuleeg, Manfred (1997). 'Art. 5', in Hans von der Groeben, Jochen Thiesing, and Claus-Dieter Ehlermann (eds.), *Kommentar zum EU-/EG-Vertrag* (5th edn). Baden-Baden: Nomos, 1/263–1/277.

4

National Systems' Adaptation to the EU System: Trends, Offers, and Constraints

Andreas Maurer, Jürgen Mittag, and Wolfgang Wessels

4.1 National systems turn European: The focus of research

The interrelationship between the European Union (EU) and its member states attracts growing attention of academics and politicians alike. The 'Europeanization' of institutions and systemic features of national political systems is a key element for conceptualizing the changes of political systems during the process of interaction, cooperation, and integration between various forms of collective entities within the realm of the EU (Andersen and Eliassen 1991; Ladrech 1994; Goetz 1995; Pappas 1995; Mény, Muller, and Quermonne 1996; Olsen 1996; Wessels 1996; Hanf and Soetendorp 1997; Carter and Scott 1998; Knill and Lehmkuhl 1999; Wessels, Maurer, and Mittag 2003).

The EU is increasingly seen to be a central arena for transnational cooperation and supra-national problem-solving. Its institutions regulate policies with a wide range of differentiated policy instruments and procedures on an ever-wider scope of policy fields. Against this background, we consider a set of fundamental trends of the Brussels arenas:

(1) the dynamic evolution of new and refined treaty provisions leading—in a typical model pattern—to an ever-increasing set of communitarized frameworks for policy-making;
(2) the subsequent widening of the functional scope of integration: sectoral differentiation concerning an increasing variety of policy fields and thus involving more and more actors;
(3) the creation of institutions by successive treaty amendments: institutional differentiation, which increases the number of interaction styles in relevant arenas of the policy cycle;

(4) the set-up and cross-institutional combination of different kinds of procedures, which provide the actors with several opportunity structures of taking binding decisions: procedural differentiation, which increases the complexity and the need of national actors to improve their procedural skills. With the majority rule as an acceptable mode of decision-making and with an increasing speed of the co-decision procedure, national actors cannot adopt an attitude of 'wait and see';
(5) the activation of policy networks, procedural and working mechanisms, which allow a growing set of actors outside the 'official' array of institutions to participate in European Community (EC)/EU policy-making: This specific kind of actor differentiation establishes structures building up the need to take an ever-increasing number of interests and preferences into account;
(6) the increase in scope and density of legal obligations: the doubling of the acquis communautaire from the early 1980s to 1998 indicates both the rise of the para-constitutional set-up as well as the 'invasion' of the legal space of member states.

Looking at the emerging and evolving realities of the European polity we are fascinated by the way member states (re-)act in and adapt to a dynamic institutional and procedural arrangement. Our major puzzle is: how do governmental and non-governmental actors in different national settings corresponding to different national traditions adapt to common challenges, constraints, and opportunities, for which they are mainly responsible themselves?

In view of several ways of conceptualizing Europeanization, we define this term as a process by which governmental, parliamentary, and non-governmental actors shift their attention to the Brussels arena, involve their resources and invest 'time' (Wessels 1997: 36; Maurer 2001: 36–7). With this definition, we indicate a change in relative terms of using limited and scarce resources. The levels from where actors gain access might be national, European, or regional. We, therefore, look at different forms of 'travelling actors'. While national and regional actors orient their capacities towards the EU legislative process, EU policy-making triggers constant institutional adaptation in the member states, alters the domestic rules and the inter-institutional distribution of means for complying with the requirements for an effective participation in European governance. In the extreme, Europeanization by orientation and integration could lead to a synchronization of national politics with self-made EC/EU 'imperatives' or—at the other end of the spectrum—to the successful instalment of policy-making structures and constitutional norms which bring the member states in clear and structural opposition to the EC/EU system. However, empirical research on the participation of member states in the EU (Maurer and Wessels 2001b; Wessels, Maurer, and Mittag 2003) indicates that those elites involved in the policy cycle seem to develop specific—non-accidental—and original attitudes which lead to a general acceptance and support of the system; in any case, they are ready to spend a considerable amount of energy and hope to achieve substance out of it.

Fifteen traditional systems and their variations might be better explained when compared in view of their reactions to the same challenges. We discuss how core institutions of the West-European nation state are shaped by becoming part of a new and different polity. We might witness a 'further stage in the history' of the West-European state (Rokkan 1975). The EU is considered to make a marked difference to its constituent units. In this way, the 'masters of the treaties' (German Constitutional Court 1994) shape also their roles of masters of their own constitution.

Do the common challenges of managing the Brussels 'system' push national systems into one direction of organizing the essential constitutional and institutional dimensions of their polity? Are the member states becoming more similar or do the reactions to the same demands stress national traditions in a way that national specificities are becoming more relevant than the similarities? Will such an adaptation be asymmetrical? Will the point of convergence be dominated by specific structures of one member state or one (core) group of member states, overall or in specific cases? Have institutional arrangements like the role of the Danish parliament, the UK cabinet system or the strategies of the German *Länder* served as a model for other member states? Can we also grasp the dynamics of this transformation? These questions are not only of academic interest. If the constituent backbones of the EU system—the member states and the EU institutions—become more heterogeneous, the structures, processes, and networks which link the different branches and layers of governance will turn out to be even more complex. Heterogeneity of institutional adaptation also raises the issue of 'fitness'. We should discuss the range and desirability of improvements not only for the next round of newcomers to the Union but also for founding members. Do we identify an optimal model? We might conclude that old or new members should refrain from simply importing or implanting an institutional and procedural device, which will not work as planned in a different environment.

We will investigate the patterns of cooperation and adaptation in view of fusion theory (Wessels 1996, 2000; Maurer 2001a: 31-7), which regards EU institutions and procedures as core channels and instruments by which national governments and administrations as well as other public and private actors increasingly pool and share public resources from several levels. Institutional and procedural growth and differentiation mirror a growing participation of several actors from different levels, which is sometimes overshadowed by cyclical ups and downs in a political conjuncture. However, each 'up' leads to a ratchet effect by which the level of activities in the valley of day-to-day politics will have moved to a higher plateau. The major feature of this process is a 'fusion' of policy instruments from several institutional levels. Treaty building is a typical product of the attempt to improve the capacity for an effective solving of problems which are pressing at the time and for keeping and even improving a large 'national say'.

In the first part of our chapter, we will describe the dynamics of European integration as well as the impacts of the remarkable and persistent shift of attention, of individual and institutional resources to the Brussels level. Subsequently, the second part of our contribution will deal with the strategies of national actors to adjust to the challenges of the ever closer and more complex European multi-level system and their success in doing so. Our analysis will demonstrate that each member state pursues its own way into the Brussels space. Nevertheless, some general trends can be shown with regard to different types of national actors who will be attached to the four categories of multi-level players, European players, national players, and feeble players in the European policy cycle.

4.2 Growth and differentiation: Challenges from a dynamic system?

4.2.1 *The impact of constitutional changes*

If we look at the 'longue durée' perspective of the EU's evolution, the West-European states have created a unique and hybrid kind of political system (Coombes 1999: 7-15; Hix 1999: 2-5; Wallace 2000: 8-9). Within the EU, common institutions take decisions, which are binding for the fifteen member states and their citizens. The dynamics of the last decades are considerable: in amending the original treaties via the Single European Act, the Maastricht, the Amsterdam, and the Nice versions of the Treaty on European Union (TEU), the member states have enlarged

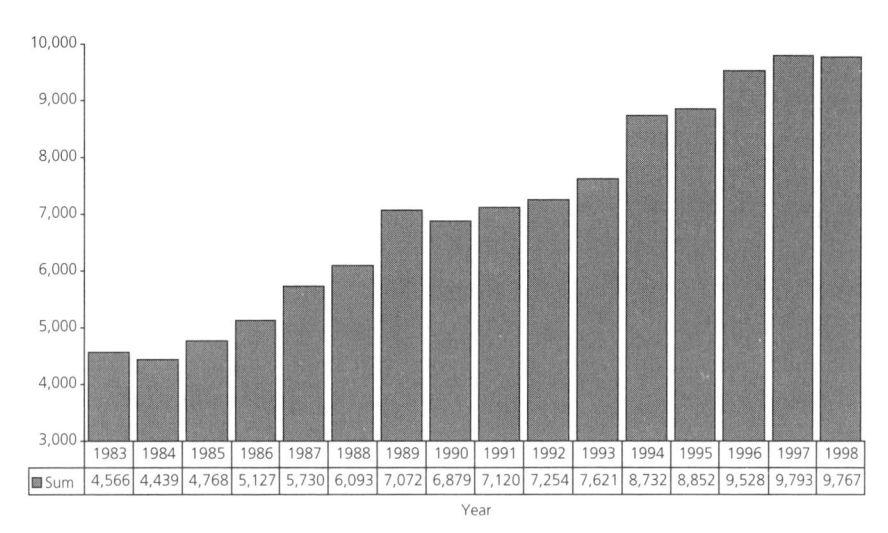

Fig. 4.1 European legislation in force, 1983–1998

Source: Maurer and Wessels (2001b), based on the Directory of Community Legislation in Force, Luxembourg, 1984–99 (December issues)

Year	1983	1984	1985	1986	1987	1988	1989	1990	1991	1992	1993	1994	1995	1996	1997	1998
Sum	4,566	4,439	4,768	5,127	5,730	6,093	7,072	6,879	7,120	7,254	7,621	8,732	8,852	9,528	9,793	9,767

the scope of the policy fields by adding new articles which define specific competencies and procedures (from 86 articles in 1957 under the European Economic Community (EEC) Treaty to 254 articles in 2001 under the Treaty of Nice) and thereby revised the institutional and procedural framework. The output of decisions—taking various forms from regulations and directives towards legislative programme decisions and non-binding recommendations—has evolved over the last decades towards 52,799 in December 1998. A high amount of these decisions is set for relatively short time periods or is regularly replaced by new legislation. However, during the last decade the acquis communautaire—the legislation in force at a given moment—more than doubled from 4,566 in 1983 towards 9,767 legal acts in 1998 (Fig. 4.1).

Do para-constitutional[1] acts like treaty revisions and similar fundamental amendments matter for the emerging multi-level system and its component parts? Do they affect major characteristics of the policy processes which link de-nationalized forms of governance with national and sub-national systems or are they peripheral? Relations between treaty reform and treaty implementation are not one-directional (see for the conventional view on treaty development: Moravcsik 1998; Moravcsik

---

[1] Using the term constitution for the European Union Treaties does not necessarily imply a normative statement (Weiler 1999).

and Nicolaïdis 1998, 1999). Treaty reforms do not come out of the blue as a 'deus ex machina' from some distant masters, but they are reactions to prior trends, reflecting the complex day-to-day machinery at all relevant levels of participation. Quite often these contractual treaty foundations rubberstamp institutional evolutions, which have been developed within (inter-institutional agreements, institutional rules of procedure and codes of conduct) or outside (bi- or multilateral agreements between EU members) the existing treaty provisions (Genco 1980; Christiansen 1998; Sverdrup 1998; Christiansen and Jorgensen 1999; Maurer and Wessels 2001*b*). These modifications aim at addressing some institutional and procedural weaknesses identified during the implementation of previous adjustments of the rules of the game. Treaty revisions are thus endemic parts of the process. They are not just independent variables affecting the nature and the evolution of the system, but they are themselves objects of the dynamism they might have shaped themselves. Institutions (Riker 1982; Hall 1986: 19; March and Olsen 1989: 167) are creations and creators at the same time.

To describe these developments in a historical–institutionalist perspective we offer an ideal three-step evolutionary pattern for the installation of policy fields, competencies, and respective procedures, which reflect governmental strategies for dealing with common problems. To achieve some objectives of joint interest and to reduce transaction costs, member states agree first to cooperate in one or more areas of common concern. In this phase, governments realize the usefulness of cooperation. They rely on some kind of loose intergovernmental procedures—of course without any major interference of any non-national body such as the Commission. Transaction costs might be reduced, but the member states learn fast that when pooling their resources they cannot escape the decision-making dilemma. Free-rider positions give incentives for defection and non-compliance. Negative experiences mean that national actors have to face up to the same lesson repeatedly: the favoured intergovernmentalism, which would merely work under the improbable dominance of enlightened self-interests, is insufficient if effective measures are really to be pursued by this group of states.

In a second phase, they include the new policy area(s) expressis verbis into the treaty, perhaps with formulas limiting the roles of EC/EU bodies or securing member states' veto powers (unanimity in the Council), since they remain hesitant to give too much power to non-national actors or to risk being outvoted by majority decisions and restrictive rule interpretations. This—ideal—second step is to move a given policy field into the 'single institutional framework' of the Union. Actors look for a better organizational framework and establish some kind of rationalized intergovernmentalism. Treaty architects grant a limited role to the Commission, a symbolic right of inquiry to the European Parliament (EP) but no power to the European Court of Justice (ECJ). Unanimity in the Council is an essential element of this phase. Again, the limits to this kind of arrangement lie in the fact that meeting in the Council does not change the rules and the respective patterns of behaviour. The capacity to deal effectively with problems remains insufficient.

In a third phase, governmental actors are bound to commit themselves to qualified majority voting instead of unanimity in the Council for the sake of efficiency. As indicated above, member states are rather reluctant to provide power to another actor in the first phase of institution building. Therefore, the EP is granted with more extensive rights of participation only in the subsequent phases—ideally consultation in the second phase and cooperation, co-decision or assent in the third step of constitutional revision. At this third critical juncture of treaty revision the 'masters of the treaty' convince themselves that they have to make the leap to a more efficient set of rules with a stronger role for supra-national bodies to get at least some kind of productive output. 'Credible commitments to delegate sovereignty' (Moravcsik and Nicolaïdis 1999: 59) are taken, albeit with doubts about what might be hidden in the shadow of the future concerning the real effects of these changes to the legal constitution. To keep some kind of control, member governments install committees of national civil servants to ensure careful observation of what supra-national bureaucracies are doing (Wessels 2000).

Illustrative cases for these step-by-step trial and error processes are abundant in the EU evolution although there is some variation within them: the evolution from the TREVI group[2] towards the area of freedom, justice, and security or the move from the European Monetary System (EMS) towards Economic and Monetary Union (EMU). As for justice and home affairs, governments were reluctant to cross the third hurdle in the Nice Treaty: majority voting would have been a qualitative jump going too far.

Using this three-step evolutionary model, we capture a strong centripetal trend towards 'communitarization': a push and pull of provisions towards the EC Treaties or, within the treaties, towards supra-national procedures[3]

---

[2] TREVI is a forum created in 1975 for intergovernmental cooperation on matters relating to internal security, organized crime, terrorism, and drug trafficking, and is forming the basis of JHA established by the TEU.

[3] Qualified majority voting instead of unanimity; co-decision instead of cooperation.

or towards EC-like rules within the intergovernmental pillars of the Union[4] (Monar 1998), where 'dirty' communitarizations (Wessels 1997) and institutional anomalies[5] take place.

We conceive these treaty revisions and amendments as offers and constraints to actors in the EU institutions. In this multi-level and multi-actor governance framework, treaties create incentives and disincentives to use or to refrain from using the specific provisions set over time (Scharpf 1997a; Olsen 1998). The character of treaty provisions is reinforced by a specific legal feature: a trend towards procedural 'ambiguity' over time. Whereas the original treaties had included a restricted (clear-cut) set of rules and competencies for each policy field, subsequent treaty amendments led to a procedural differentiation with a variety of 'offers'. In other words, different procedural blueprints and inter-institutional codes 'compete' for application and raise the potential for conflict between the actors involved.

4.2.2 *The evolution of the EU system's treaty provisions: The opportunities and their use*

Concentrating on the evolution of the EC/EU's legal empowerments between 1952 (ECSC Treaty) and 1999 (Amsterdam Treaty), the total number of treaty articles dealing with specific competencies and decision-making rules in a growing amount of policy areas has considerably developed towards 219 cases. The substantial scope of the EC/EU action is further illustrated by the following: the expansion of the number of Commission DGs (from 9 in 1958 to 25 in 1998) and of autonomous executive agencies (from 2 in 1975 to 14 in 1998), the agendas of the EP at its plenary sessions and especially the presidency conclusions published after sessions of the European Council, and finally the respective composition of the sectoral Council formats (from 4 in 1958 to 23 in 1998; Westlake 1995: 164–7) including the extension of its administrative substructure. As for the provisions governing the decision-making system within the Council, Fig. 4.2 shows the absolute proportion of the Council's rules between 1952 and 2001. It can be clearly demonstrated that the total number of rules providing for unanimity and qualified majority voting (QMV) has considerably increased over time. We also notice an over-proportional growth of QMV voting until Amsterdam.

[4] See, for example, Article 34 TEU as amended by the Treaty of Amsterdam.
[5] 'Institutional anomaly' is the term used by the Portuguese Council Presidency within the framework of the IGC 2000 (Conference of the Representatives of the Governments of the Member States 2000).

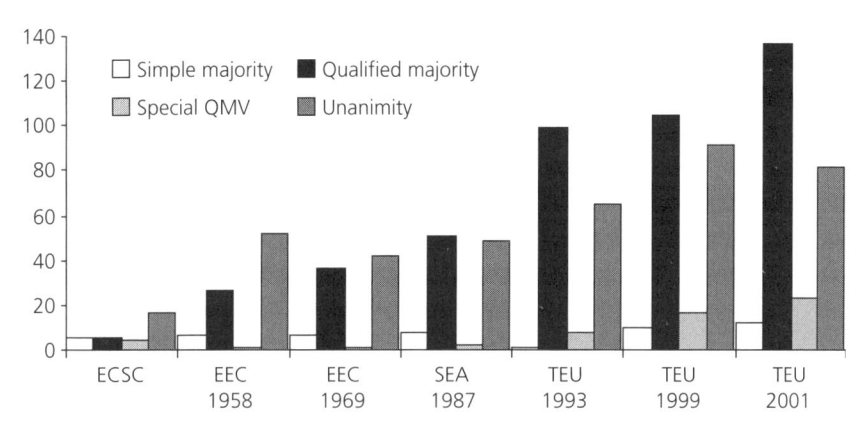

Fig. 4.2 Decision-making modes in the Council of Ministers 1952–2001 (absolute numbers)

Source: Maurer and Wessels (2001b), calculation based on EC/EU Treaties 1952–2001

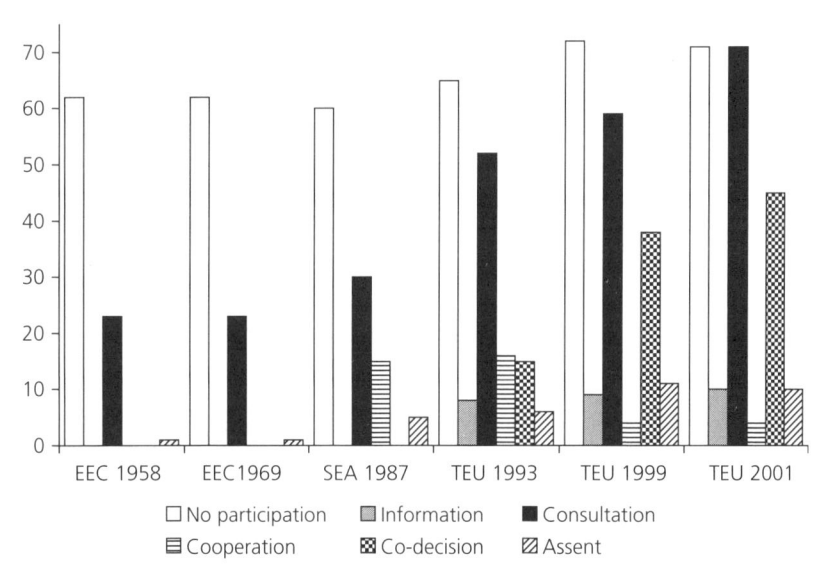

Fig. 4.3 Evolution of decision-making procedures, 1957–2001 (absolute numbers)
Source: Maurer (2002), calculation based on EC/EU Treaties 1952–2001

With regard to the roles of the EP provided by the treaties, the relative proportion of its 'exclusion' from the EC/EU policy-making process has considerably diminished (Fig. 4.3). However, the absolute rates of the treaty-based decision-making procedures show that the growth in consultation, cooperation, and co-decision procedures is balanced by a small augmentation of the 'non-participation' procedure of the EU. The main

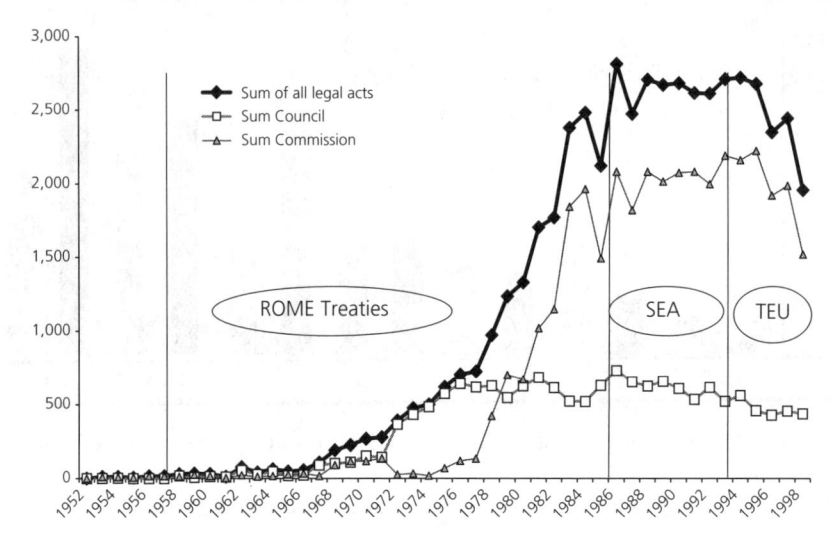

Fig. 4.4 Legal output of the Council and the Commission, 1952–1998
Source: Maurer (1999), calculation based on CELEX database

reason for this development is the dynamic of subsequent treaty reforms. In this respect, it is of particular interest to look at the combination of the respective powers of the two bodies, which show a remarkable increase in procedural complexity over time.[6]

After recapitulating the evolution of procedures of EU decision-making we look at the output of their use in an aggregated form (Fig. 4.4). Altogether, we can list a total sum of 52,799 legal acts adopted between 1952 and December 1998.[7]

These legal acts, however, are not of equal ranking in terms of their legal relevance and political importance. Besides regulations, directives, decisions, and recommendations, the EU's databases also include a set of acts which are less binding. Figure 4.4 indicates a quasi-linear growth in

---

[6] For a presentation of the relative numbers of the use of decision-making modes in the Council and with respect to the EP's involvement see Maurer and Wessels (2001a).

[7] If we refer to the printed Communitatis European Lex (CELEX) version—the 'directory of Community legislation in force' (DCL)—the overall number is much smaller. According to the annual reports of the Commission the number is much higher. The reason for this discrepancy is that the annual reports also list all internal administrative acts including appointments, decisions regarding salaries, etc. The methodological problem is that 'legislation in force' does not take into account the very process of decision-making and legal output over time. Since the DCL is updated twice a year, it has to be understood as a snapshot of EC/EU output at a given time. What cannot be derived from these data is the dynamic of the system which produces legislation across the time.

original secondary legislation from 1961 onwards until 1987 and a constant step-by-step decrease from 1987 onwards. The output of the Council of Ministers shows a steady decline from 1986/87 onwards; also the Maastricht provisions did not have a positive impact. Hence, the legal acts which arose from the new Maastricht pillars—common foreign and security policy (CFSP) and justice and home affairs (JHA)—have not changed the overall trend. The EC's output started to grow from 1976 onwards, although the relative growth—that is, the growth rate in relation to the Council's 'original' output—remained stable between 1980 and 1993. With the coming into force of Maastricht, the legal output decreased dramatically, reflecting the decline in Council legislation from 1986/1987 onwards. The reduction of the Council's output from 1987 onwards mainly originates from three major policy areas of the EC—the common agricultural policy (CAP)/fisheries policy, external trade, and customs policy—which constitute 41,886 legal acts (79.3 per cent) of all decisions produced until December 1998. Given their 'age' one can assume a saturation of these policies. In fact, the overall decline in the production of EC legislation is almost exclusively due to these policy areas (Fig. 4.5).

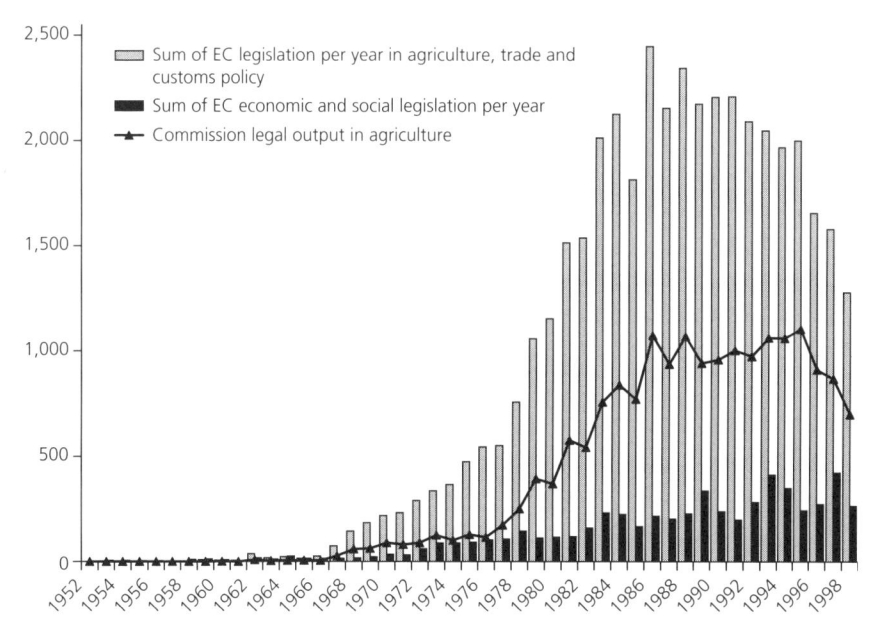

Fig. 4.5 Legal output of policy fields in comparison—agriculture, trade, and customs policy against economic and social legislation

Source: Maurer (1999), calculation based on CELEX database

As to the effective exploitation of qualified majority voting in the Council, statistical data have only been published since the coming into force of the Maastricht Treaty in late 1993. Among the 561 legal acts of the Council in 1994 64 (11.40 per cent) were subject to real voting. The relative share of 'real votes' increased slightly in 1995 to 54 (11.79 per cent). In 1996, the Council referred 45 times to QMV for a total of 429 cases (10.48 per cent), and in 1999 'real voting' occurred 31 times on a total of 327 acts (9.78 per cent). Altogether, the rather small share of 'real voting' indicates the underlying 'culture of consensus' (Hix 1999: 73) of the Council and its component members. Voting may cause problems in the later stages of the policy cycle. Given that since 1993 voting results are published by the Council, outvoted member states are on show for all sides of interest groups—governmental as well as non-governmental ones. Thus, member states which have failed to gain a majority for their point of view may come under pressure from domestic actors to oppose the transposition of EU directives into national legislation and then to block the timely enforcement of the legal act in question. However, one should not attach too much significance to the small share of 'real voting'. The idea behind QMV is not its routine practice but its potential power as a 'sword of Damocles' that pushes member state actors to negotiate 'under the shadow of the majority vote' (Scharpf 1997b: 191–3), that is to concede in order to reach agreement.

As regards the exploitation of the EP's roles, we notice that between 1987 and December 1993 more than 30 per cent of those Commission's legislative proposals which addressed the EP fell under the cooperation procedure. Since Maastricht, the share of the cooperation procedure decreased towards 13.6 per cent (1995) whereas the share of co-decision rose to 21.8 per cent (Maurer 1999). Around 65 per cent of the 274 co-decision procedures concluded between November 1993 and July 2001 fell under Article 95. In spite of the fact that co-decision was conceived only for 9.25 per cent of all EC Treaty provisions containing procedural specifications, nearly 25 per cent of the EU's legislative proposals submitted to both the Council and the Parliament until April 2001 fell under this procedure (Maurer 2002). This is not only motivated by a parliament-friendly attitude but also due to the fact that these provisions are mainly ruled by QMV (except for cultural policy and research policy programmes). The 'demand' for this kind of legislation was much higher than the original—treaty-based—'supply' would have suggested.

The growth in the number of policy fields and relevant treaty provisions invite member states to orient their own legal frameworks for policy-making accordingly. In this regard, treaty reforms of the EC's legal framework and its set of competencies may induce a re-allocation and restructuring of related legal provisions in the member states. Moreover, scope enlargement in the EU theatre affects a growing number of governmental and non-governmental bodies dealing with public policy-making. Decision-making methods differ across the areas of application and across the institutions and bodies involved. Maastricht introduced new bodies (Committee of the Regions, European Central Bank, Employment Committee, and Political and Security Committee) and procedures ('enhanced cooperation clauses' and 'open method of co-ordination'). 'New institutions are not established in order to swell even further the institutional structure of the EU, but because they are thought to be required to deal with new policy duties of the Union, to give the EU a single voice or interface for dealing with third countries and organizations or to become the EU's formalized feedback towards the specific geographical or functional levels of governance' (Maurer 1999: 43). Institutions do not operate in a political vacuum, but in a closely connected system of power distribution in which the treaty architects have implanted them. Whenever new institutions gain autonomy, they do not use it in isolation, but in a framework of already established rules and bodies of political power. Concomitantly, this process of institutional growth attains a higher degree of complexity, potentially mirrored by new structures and processes in the member states.

Do the EU's para-constitutional revisions matter—and how do they matter—for the evolution and the functioning of national, sub-national and non-governmental policy-making structures? What are the challenges to the member states and their politico-administrative systems?

4.3 National institutions and the EC/EU system: Europeanization under scrutiny

The evolution of the institutional and procedural system of the European Union has created considerable challenges for all European Union member states (Rometsch and Wessels 1996: 328–65; Cowles, Caporaso, and Risse 2000; Goetz and Hix 2000) and their institutions (Maurer and Wessels 2001*b*). The fifteen national systems face an increasing salience of the EU as well as an increasing complexity of the EU system.

To guide our analysis, we focus on the extent and intensity of participation by national institutions in the process of preparing, making, taking, implementing, and controlling EC/EU generated decisions. Within this

Brussels arena		National arena	
		Strong	Weak
	Strong	Multi-level players (with highest performance at both levels) (1)	European players (with high performance at the EU level) (2)
	Weak	National players (with high performance at the national level) (3)	Feeble players (with lowest performance at both levels) (4)

Fig. 4.6 Typology of member states' 'adaptation' modes

framework, we offer a typology (Fig. 4.6) which differentiates between strong and feeble actors both at the national and at the 'Brussels' level (Maurer 2001: 33–5; Mittag and Wessels 2003). These models are heuristic and ideal archetypes, but to classify the role of national institutions and bodies within the context of the EU's multi-level nature, these models might prove helpful. Forms of participation are related to the formal provisions of national constitutions and the EU Treaty. However, beyond the 'legal constitution' (Olsen 2000) we need to explore the real patterns of how actors use the EU's 'opportunity structures' (Bulmer 1996; Scharpf 1997b; Knill and Lehmkuhl 1999) and develop additional channels of influence.

Multi-level players (field 1) are considered as the most-performing actors, since they are able to work across the various levels of the EU and the member states. The logic of multi-level governance means that actors need to allocate personal and financial resources to different levels and various loci of interaction (such as working groups, Comité des Représentants Permanents, COREPER etc.). Adaptation to the EU's evolution can be translated into effective reorientations of policy instruments and resources. Multi-level players are able to instrumentalize the access on one level for increasing their influence on the other level. Their investments allow them to mobilize a virtuous circle of involvement.

European players (field 2) could be defined as bodies such as the EP which are primarily located in and focused on the Brussels/Strasbourg arenas. Given a rather low rate of direct access to the national arenas of EU governance, they are not as highly competitive as the multi-level players. They adapt to the EU's system by revising and focusing their instruments vis-à-vis the other EU actors at this level without explicitly considering the roles of national or sub-national actors.

A national player (field 3) would be a body able to effectively voice its interests within the national arena. Adaptation would be focused at the national level without considering the possibility of shifting or pooling the existing resources in order to reach out to the EU level. Within the EU policy cycle, these actors are present during the preparation and implementation phases, but not in the crucial arenas of EU joint decision-making.

The feeble players (field 4) would then be considered as bodies with the same—national—orientation. They are not capable of keeping the status quo ante of prerogatives at the domestic EU-linked level. They are likely to suffer in a vicious cycle from a continuous fall in influence. A low investment in resources leads to an ever-decreasing rate of participation.

4.3.1 *Governments and administrations: National gatekeepers in the European machinery?*

No matter whether prime ministers have a strong or a weak position in 'their' national policy arena, they have become real multi-level players in EU affairs. In all member states of the EU, the heads of government have turned into key actors in EU affairs. Principally through their role as members of the EC, they are able to top internal procedures and perform in leading the decision-making process. As a result of the need to act forcefully and coherently at vital decisions by the EC, prime ministers gained influence vis-à-vis their ministerial colleagues. The EC and bilateral summits have even reinforced the role of heads of government whose formal status in the member states had traditionally been that of a primus inter pares. Frequently, the shift of coordinating capabilities in the national implementation of EC policy is linked with a less powerful role of the foreign affairs ministries, which dominated the European theatre for decades (see for the case of Germany, Bulmer, Maurer, and Paterson 2001; for Italy, Gallo and Hanny 2003). This is due to a number of factors, such as the EU pressure towards an equal standing of members of Council meetings and the prime ministers' wish to be in charge of matters that are politically sensitive. Thus, the EC/EU process has even changed the balance inside governments.

Depending on the policy field and the issue at stake in the Council, national ministries are more or less involved in the EC/EU decision-making process. We can roughly differentiate between 'pioneer ministries' (foreign affairs, finance, economics, and agriculture) and 'newcomers' (environment, education, justice, and internal affairs). Ministries with a long-standing involvement in European affairs and special EU-related units have consolidated their position and acquired a substantial role. Yet almost every national ministry in each member state has activated a separate unit responsible for EU affairs. Due to this process the need for hierarchical or cooperative coordination across the various policy sectors has grown considerably (Scharpf 1997a; Wessels 2000: 252). Without any exception, all member states have substantially increased their internal coordination efforts in the 1990s. Since the coming into force of the Maastricht Treaty the foreign ministers have partly lost their traditional high influence. Particularly the competition between foreign ministries and economic/financial ministries has led to a more differentiated structure. As a result of the growing importance of the EMU, this shift is accompanied by a more outstanding role of the ministers for finance. The sectoral differentiation at the EC/EU level had, therefore, a notable effect and has increased the number of experienced and skilled multi-level players.[8] Government ministries and, in many cases, administrative units within departments have established their own EU resources and networks. Sectoral differentiation of the EU's legal sphere has had remarkable effects. This fragmentation of policies and policy arenas is also evinced by the increase in the number of committees operating on the same level as COREPER (Westlake 1995; Hayes-Renshaw and Wallace 1997). Moreover, it has promoted coordination between the departments and ministries (Kassim et al. 2001; Council of the European Union 2001). The more the ministries were concerned by EU procedures, the more they were driven to introduce effective mechanisms for inter- and intra-ministerial coordination.

All member states have increased their internal coordination efforts in the 1990s. The number of different policy fields at the EU level has, thus, promoted more sophisticated coordination between ministries and different inter-ministerial coordination bodies. As ministries have been

---

[8] With the initiative for 'military crisis management' (European Council 1999) even defence departments are becoming involved: the General Affairs Council in November 1999 brought together for the first time the ministers of foreign affairs and defence.

Horizontal coordination	Functional decentralization	
	Low	High
Low	Unified Ireland (1)	Pluralist-fragmented Germany, Italy (3)
High	(2) Centralized UK, France	(4) Horizontal agreement Netherlands

Fig. 4.7 Models of horizontal coordination and vertical hierarchy

increasingly affected by European policies and as their desire to participate has grown, it has become necessary for governments to establish an effective system of inter- and intra-ministerial coordination and cooperation in order to reach common viewpoints and to develop a coherent negotiation strategy.

However, the ways single member states have chosen reveal quite dissimilar patterns (Fig. 4.7). A number of member states[9] have adopted the practice of establishing special informal or *ad-hoc* cabinet committees (E, F, I, NL, UK) while in other countries the cabinet as a whole takes on the task of formal coordination and decision-making (A, B, DK, IR, S, SF). While in Ireland we can detect a 'relatively light co-ordination' (Laffan 2000: 136), other member states which have developed 'elaborate co-ordination mechanisms' (Laursen 2003) are known for their streamlined coordination machinery (UK, DK, F, P, SF). Developments after the coming into force of the TEU show that hierarchical methods of coordination are decreasingly able to cope with all issues, actors, and information in the European sphere. They have not prevented the 'subtle trend towards more independent approaches to the EC/EU affairs on the part of certain ministries' (Lloréns 2003), that is, a tendency towards sectoralization and decentralization. In Spain, the existence of a central coordination

---

[9] The following abbreviations are used: A, Austria; B, Belgium; D, Germany (Deutschland); DK, Denmark; E, Spain (España); F, France; SF, Finland; GR, Greece; I, Italy; IR, Ireland; LUX, Luxembourg; NL, Netherlands; P, Portugal; S, Sweden; UK, United Kingdom.

body has not prevented inter-ministerial conflicts and difficulties in defining positions in COREPER and the Council of Ministers. This tendency is still relevant after the internal reform of the 'Secretariat' in 1998. Other countries such as Germany or Belgium are characterized by fragmented policy-making and have developed more complicated internal coordination mechanisms with the result that their positions in Brussels are not always free of contradictions.

Given the broad functional scope and the political salience of the EU, it is remarkable that a strongly centralized approach becomes less representative. It is obvious that in all member states, prime ministers have discovered the political importance of getting involved. By an early and strong centralization some governments have tried to reduce the potential negative effects of functional decentralization. However, this remedy proved not to be particularly successful. The most interesting case is another one: the strategy to coordinate units which find their own channels to Brussels.

Two sub-types can be identified in this context: a strong hierarchy based on a central agency, which is permanently supported by the political masters, and horizontal coordination among equals based on consensus. The French and the UK arrangements are normally cited as examples of the first case, the Dutch and the Danish as examples of the second. In the light of developments of the 1990s, the differences, though clearly still existent, might be less prominent than often stated. Furthermore, horizontal coordination seems to become overshadowed by an increasingly involved political hierarchy. Of course, this indirect effect only works when there is a sufficiently clear and stable political leadership. Hierarchy, on the other hand, needs broad inputs from the specialized ministries and units.

The clearest indicator of conceptualizing the EU as a dynamic system can be seen in the creation and subsequent development of EU institutions as well as in the increasing differentiation of procedures within the policy cycle. An important characteristic of this institutionalization is the comprehensive and intensive participation of national governments and administrations in all phases of the policy cycle. The use of related bodies for cooperation and coordination has increased quite considerably. Taking together the various kinds of bodies, we can list for 1997 at least 700 expert groups and *ad-hoc* advisory committees of the Commission, roughly 300 working groups and approximately 400 comitology committees: altogether the administrative infrastructure in Brussels includes at least around 1,500 bodies. Assuming that each member state sends an average of at least two civil servants or experts, there may be about 40,000 national officials involved in the EU's policy cycle. Finally, the salience of EU decision-making for national governments and administrations is not only highlighted by the number of EU bodies and national civil servants participating in them, but also by the number of EU-related organs at the national level such as inter-ministerial coordination bodies for European policy.[10]

4.3.2 *The national parliaments: Latecomers in European Union affairs?*

Until Maastricht, in a large number of member states the national parliaments were regarded as the losers of the integration process (Pöhle 1992). They were perceived as weak players at both levels as they had lost power nationally and got no additional power at the EU level. Due to the growing supremacy of the national governments in the European decision-making process on the one hand and because of the governments' capability to use the knowledge and powers of administrations on the other, national parliaments were left outside of the decision-making process or they were only marginally involved. Neither their financial nor their human resources could cope in any way with the still increasing amount of EU legislation—though in all national systems the formal legislative competencies are traditionally in the hands of the parliaments. Though EC directives allow the member states room for manoeuvre, parliaments were not capable of modifying the content of the respective acts due to their limited resources. In addition, some national parliaments did not even show a notable interest in EU affairs, which can be explained to a certain extent by the disinterest of national voters in EU-related political questions. Moreover, it can be explained by the complex internal structure of the respective parliaments as, for example, in the case of Germany or France and the Netherlands.

Since the coming into force of the TEU, this perception has changed significantly.[11] National parliaments have started to recognize that not only new policy fields and competencies have become a subject matter of the

---

[10] For Germany's involvement in EU affairs and especially national coordination mechanisms see Bulmer, Maurer, and Paterson 2001: in particular 196.

[11] The role of national parliaments in the legislative process of the EU has received special attention in the post-Maastricht period. For comparative research, see especially the contribution of Arthur Benz (this volume). See also Laursen and Pappas 1995; Norton 1995; Weber-Panariello 1995; Bergman 1997; Maurer 2002.

European Union, but also that they themselves are losing their traditional control and legislative functions. Besides their traditional instruments of parliamentary questions and debates, parliaments in all member states have addressed their call for more influence to their national governments. Referring to the EC/EU policy cycle, one special demand has always been in the centre of the national parliaments' pleadings: parliaments asked to be informed earlier and more comprehensively about legislative proposals. Those parliaments which have succeeded in establishing their right to see and to express their views on policy documents and legislative proposals at the early stages of the EU policy cycle have been more capable in influencing the policy of their governments (Carter 2001; Hölscheidt 2001; Raunio 2001; Maurer and Wessels 2001b; Laursen 2003).

The forms and implications of parliamentary attempts differ largely. Overall, the picture we get from the national systems suggest that national parliaments have learned from their failures and try to cope with the European challenge by means of a better management and self-organization, that is, by improving the intra-parliamentary sifting of EU documents or by effectively constraining their governments through so-called parliamentary scrutiny reserve mechanisms. Moreover, parliaments have attempted to play a more effective part by strengthening the role of specialized standing committees in EU affairs. Other national parliaments, such as the Finnish *Eduskunta* or the Swedish *Riksdag*, are following in the footsteps of Denmark where the *Folketing* is regarded as a strong policy-making assembly, which has retained its position after entering the Community.

Yet these developments remain restricted to the national level. The relative weakness of national parliamentary institutions within the European multi-level system cannot be overlooked. The overall trend of reinforcing the role of national parliaments since 1991/1993 might also be explained as a consequence of popular discontent. In this regard, parliaments have not turned into a systematic opposition force offering a public voice to an overall critical population. The logic of parliamentary government with the basic cleavage between the cabinet and the parliamentary majority on the one hand and parliamentary minority on the other has not been replaced by a return to the classical division of power between cabinet and parliament. The incentives of the European arena have even strengthened the governmental actors. The increased activities of some parliaments and their constitutive units (parliamentary groups, committees, etc.) have not shifted the overall institutional (dis-)equilibrium. National parliaments have not been willing and/or able to gain a decisive voice.

Furthermore, clear deficits in their resources to play a multi-level game still reduce the effective say of national deputies. The Conference of

Community and European Affairs Committees (COSAC) has not been an effective channel for access and influence. The links with the EP remain rather weak and largely designed by the MEPs' rolling agenda. Due to the voluminous number of draft legal acts from Brussels members of national parliamentary committees are only able to take a very selective approach. Thus, the involvement of parliaments in EU policies remains limited in the national policy cycle. Parliaments are still reactive institutions.

4.3.3 The regions: New but efficient players in the multi-level game?

Beyond a fundamental attempt of governmental actors to play an active role in the European policy-making process we can identify different directions. The European sphere is particularly matched by the national governmental level in centralized countries (DK, F, GR, IR, LUX, P, S, SF, UK) where national governments have a powerful grip on external and EU affairs and where the bureaucracy dealing with EU matters is directly linked to the government—developing effective means of participation in the EU decision-making process. The more decentralized (E, I, and NL) and the federal countries (A, B, and D) are characterized by a stronger involvement of the regional level. In Belgium and Germany, even regional ministers can and do actively participate in the Council's decision-making.

The EU has had an ambiguous impact on territorial politics in the member states. Due to the federal structure of some member states, regions were strongly concerned in Belgium, Germany, Austria, and—varying considerably— in Spain (Keating and Jones 1995; Jeffery 1996; Keating and Hooghe 1996). In these countries, prior to and especially after Maastricht, formalized rules and structures have been developed in order to assure participation rights on both levels—particularly with regard to financial matters. Money from the EU has created a new kind of politics which encouraged people to look both below and beyond the state. Moreover, new instruments have been established with regard to the way EU policy is dealt with.

As a result of the incentives from the European level, several experiments with new regional authorities have been undertaken. For example, in Finland the regions set up for EU purposes are not identical with the formal state districts (Hrbek 1997; Tillikainen 2003). To a certain extent, the EU has incited a process of regionalization or decentralization in the member states. Regional and local authorities have adapted their structures to the EC policy-making process. Particularly, they urge central governments for more competencies and a better involvement in EU affairs. Therefore, the changes in the more federally organized countries converge rather around the participation of the regional bodies through the influence and cooperation channels in the central state than with the European institutions. Although no formal constitutional changes have taken place to reinforce regional levels in the member states, the effects of the European integration process have led to a partial institutional adaptation and some kind of an institutional learning. Thus, traditional patterns or at least conventional views of national policy-making are being eroded, but to a limited degree as far as regions are concerned. Where regions have got own resources at their disposal, they turn into effective multi-level players. Some have, however, remained solely national or European performers—or feeble players.

4.3.4 The national courts: Relevant actors in the European policy cycle?

Though national courts have generally not received a great deal of press, they can be qualified as political institutions since they are involved in the institutional interaction within the EU system. They come in at the end of the policy cycle, during the phase of implementing and controlling Community law. Courts become active when a case is brought before them and they pronounce their judgment on the basis of the national law, the EC Treaties, previous judgments, or established legal rules and principles. Thus, also in an anticipatory view, they have an important indirect influence on the shaping of Community law and the institutional system as such, provided they do not 'stay away from politics' (Laursen 2002) due to the supremacy of other bodies as the national parliament in the Danish case. In some member states, the courts were 'rather straight forward in accepting the mainstream principles of Community law'—'even before accession', as has been the situation in Greece (Frangakis and Papayannides 2003).

The most radical impact on the sovereignty of the member states results from the gradual establishment of the supremacy of Community law. Alter (1996) elaborates that during the 1960s and 1970s the question of EC law supremacy was fervently debated. During this time, many of the high courts rejected the European Court of Justice's (ECJ's) claim to this supposed right. Later the relationship between Community and national law ceased to be a major issue of legal dispute among national high courts. Some states have never even made any attempts to interpret the character of the EU in order to judge the compatibility of national and European law.

In the meantime, the supremacy of Community law has generally been accepted (Hirsch 1996). National courts have apparently accepted the primacy of EC law without any serious resistance and when needing to interpret the latter, they have referred to the ECJ. Lower courts, especially in an attempt to gain influence themselves, actively forwarded many cases to the ECJ, thereby circumventing their own rights. Though EC law 'remains a domain of specialists and a certain elite' (Franck, Leclercq, and Vandevievere 2003), the growing amount of EC legislation and the number of cases involving Community law has increased the requirement in all member states to familiarize themselves with EC law. The unspectacular but persistent involvement of national courts in the EC system is one of these basic trends which, to an increasing degree, link the EU and the national systems. Thus—with all reservations in view of the specific character of national variations—the court system might be characterized as belonging to the group of active multi-level players.

4.4 Interaction with the Brussels institutions—from independence to interdependence

Fundamental challenges to all EU member states arise from European integration and the growing differentiation at the Brussels level that pertain to the sectoral and procedural dimension as well as to actor constellations. Confronted with these substantial challenges national governments, administrations, parliaments, and regions reacted with a remarkable and persistent shift of attention. More and more actors, becoming aware of the salience of European integration strive to participate in the EU policy cycle at both the national and the Brussels level. Thereby, national actors have to adjust themselves to a multiplicity of different and continuously changing rules as well as to the inclusion of an increasing number of governmental and non-governmental actors. However, the requirement of adaptation has not led to dramatic modifications with regard to the overall systemic designs of the member states. Thus, comparing the changes at the European level to those in the fifteen national systems, a clear asymmetry becomes obvious. The rate, frequency, and cumulative effects of changes in the Brussels arena are larger and faster than those at the national level. Traditional national patterns are resistant and apparently flexible enough to be sufficiently capable of coping with the challenges from the European level. Thus, we note that the reactions to the EC/EU system on the national level have reached a certain prominence, but they do not constitute a dramatic turnaround from traditional patterns of policy-making. Typically, we observe a mobilization of established actors within the existing constitutional and institutional framework.

Even if the grown attention to the Brussels level can be spotted as a common feature of the fifteen member states, this overall trend does not lead to any uniform pattern of reaction with regard to the constitutional, institutional, and administrative nation state systems. The patterns of member state policy-making have not converged into one specific or standardized model. The EU remains an organization with fifteen-plus-one quite different component units. But even if European integration does not lead to the development of a uniform type of policy-making, the historical differences of the member states may lose their enduring strength and the new EU polity may become the force dominating national structures. In the long run, these dynamics could work as a push towards convergence within a corridor of smaller variations. In view of national characteristics, it is extremely difficult to make any serious and valid statements about which players are more or less successful. If we take the rate of implementation of EC law as a sign of successfully adapting national systems to the legal output of the EC/EU, we get a different rating than if we look at similarities of constitutional features or at the substantial national, regional, or local outputs on specific EC/EU policies. Specific characteristics, such as size or degree of centralization, may exert some influence, but they are not at all determinant. Although the availability of different power resources is of importance, this does not imply that smaller states are not competitive. Thus, systems which look rather fragmented at the national level might turn out to be quite strong on certain European issues where leadership can be mobilized on the basis of a large national or sectoral consensus.

As to individual institutions, some actors, particularly administrations and several regions, have been more successful in adapting to the changed environment than others. The intensity of the success changes considerably within and between member states. Profits and losses depend mainly on whether national actors have found their own channels to Brussels. In the older member states, parliaments and regions have reacted to the TEU and adapted their access by mixing two parallel strategies: on the one hand, they search for formalized access—via national governments at the beginning as well as at the end of the EC policy cycle. On the other hand, these participants also go beyond the national arena and search for direct access to the Brussels institutions and become part of the EC/EU network. Thus, several regions have become effective multi-level players, while national parliaments remain predominantly national players even though their position has been strengthened since the coming into force of the TEU. Moreover, the increased involvement of national courts in the EC/EU system has led them to position themselves within the group of active multi-level players. Hence, generalizations about governments and especially foreign ministries being the masters or at least the gatekeepers of the European polity are now only valid to a very limited extent.

The process of differentiation and Europeanization, the increasing patterns of institutional co-operation and also the limited systemic convergence between the member states can be explained more persuasively by the logic of the fusion approach (Wessels 1996, 2000; Maurer 2002: 31–7) than by the logic of other approaches. The fusion theory highlights the efforts of national actors taking part in an irreversible process of pooling and merging policy instruments. The EU's multi-level system clearly features a persistent trend towards setting up and living with a multitude of institutional interaction and cooperation mechanisms without always considering a hierarchy of layers and actors. The fusion theory stresses the 'checks and balances' between the national and the European institutions in preparing, making, taking, implementing, and controlling EC/EU binding decisions. It also emphasizes the frequently observed mixture of national and EU competences as well as the—now and then consciously veiled—spreading of responsibility for the use of decision-making instruments. Finally, the fusion thesis highlights ongoing trends and a likely future development which is characterized by ever-closer transnational communication and cooperation.

References

Alter, Karen (1996). 'The European Court's Political Power', *West European Politics*, 19/3: 458–87.
Andersen, Svein S. and Eliassen, Kjell A. (1991). 'European Community Lobbying', *European Journal of Political Research*, 20/2: 173–87.
Bergman, Torbjörn (1997). 'National Parliaments and EU Affairs Committees. Notes on Empirical Variation and Competing Explanations', *Journal of European Public Policy*, 16/3: 373–87.
Bulmer, Simon (1996). 'The Governance of the European Union: A New Institutionalist Approach', *Journal of Public Policy*, 16/4: 351–80.
——, Maurer, Andreas, and Paterson, Williams (2001). 'The European Policy-Making Machinery in the Berlin Republic: Hindrance or Handmaiden?', in Douglas Webber (ed.), *New Europe, New Germany, Old Foreign Policy? German Foreign Policy Since Unification*. London and Portland: Frank Cass, 177–206.

Carter, Caitríona (2001). 'The Parliament of the United Kingdom: From Supportive Scrutiny to Unleashed Control?', in Andreas Maurer and Wolfgang Wessels (eds.), *National Parliaments on their Ways to Europe: Losers or Latecomers?* Baden-Baden: Nomos, 395–424.

—— and Scott, Andrew (1998). 'Legitimacy and Governance Beyond the European Nation State: Conceptualizing Governance in the European Union', *European Law Review*, 4: 437–45.

Christiansen, Thomas (1998). 'Bringing Process Back In: The Longue Durée of European Integration', *Journal of European Integration*, 21/1: 9–121.

—— and Jorgensen, Knud E. (1999). 'The Amsterdam Process: A Structurationist Perspective on EU Reform', *European Integration online Papers*, 3/1.

Conference of the Representatives of the Governments of the Member States (2000). *Possible Extension of Qualified Majority Voting—Articles which Could Move to Qualified Majority Voting as they Stand* (Presidency Note on IGC 2000, CONFER 4706/1/00, Brussels, 11 February 2000).

Coombes, David (1999). *Seven Theorems in Search of the European Parliament*. London: Kogan Page.

Council of the European Union (2001). *Preparing the Council for Enlargement*. POLGEN 12 ADD 1 REV 1, 9518/01, 7 and 19 June 2001. Brussels.

Cowles, Maria Green, Caporaso, James A., and Risse, Thomas (eds.) (2000). *Transforming Europe, Europeanization and Domestic Change*. Ithaca: Cornell University Press.

European Council (1999). Presidency Conclusions. Helsinki European Council, 10 and 11 December 1999. www.consilium.eu.int/en/Info/eurocouncil/index.htm.

Franck, Christian, Leclercq, Hervé, and Vandevievere, Claire (2003). 'Belgium: Europeanisation and Belgian Federalism', in Wolfgang Wessels, Andreas Maurer, and Jürgen Mittag (eds.), *Fifteen into One? The European Union and its Member States*. Manchester: Manchester University Press, 169–91.

Frangakis, Nikos and Papayannides, Antonios (2003). 'Greece: a Never-ending Story of Mutual Attraction and Estrangement', in Wolfgang Wessels, Andreas Maurer, and Jürgen Mittag (eds.), *Fifteen into One? The European Union and its Member States*. Manchester: Manchester University Press, 166–83.

Gallo, Flamminia and Hanny, Birgit (2003). 'Italy: Progress Behind Complexity', in Wolfgang Wessels, Andreas Maurer, and Jürgen Mittag (eds.), *Fifteen into One? The European Union and its Member States*. Manchester: Manchester University Press, 271–97.

Genco, Stephen J. (1980). 'Integration Theory and System Change in Western Europe: The Neglected Role of System Transformation Episodes', in Ole R. Holsti (ed.), *Change in the International System*. Boulder: Westview, 55–80.

German Constitutional Court (1994). *Decisions* (Vol. 89). Tübingen.

Goetz, Klaus (1995). 'National Governance and European Integration. Intergovernmental Relations in Germany', *Journal of Common Market Studies*, 3/1: 91–116.

—— and Hix, Simon (eds.) (2000). *Europeanised Politics? European Integration and National Political Systems* (Special Issue of West European Politics, Vol. 23, no. 4). Ilford: Cass.

Hall, Peter (1986). *Governing the Economy: The Politics of State Intervention in Britain and France*. New York: Oxford University Press.

Hanf, Kenneth and Soetendorp, Ben (1997). 'Small States and the Europeanization of Public Policy', in Kenneth Hanf and Ben Soetendorp (eds.), *Adapting to European Integration, Small States and the EU*. London: Longman, 1–13.

Hayes-Renshaw, Fiona and Wallace, Helen (1997). *The Council of Ministers*. New York: St Martin's Press.

Hirsch, Günther (1996). 'Europäischer Gerichtshof und Bundesverfassungsgericht— Kooperation oder Konfrontation?', *Neue Juristische Wochenschrift*, 49/2: 2457–66.

Hix, Simon (1999). *The Political System of the European Union*. New York: St Martin's Press.

Hölscheidt, Sven (2001). 'The German Bundestag: From Benevolent "Weakness" Towards Supportive Scrutiny', in Andreas Maurer and Wolfgang Wessels (eds.), *National Parliaments on their Ways to Europe: Losers or Latecomers?* Baden-Baden: Nomos, 123–56.

Hrbek, Rudolf (1997). 'Die Auswirkungen der EU-Integration auf den Föderalismus in Deutschland', *Aus Politik und Zeitgeschichte*, 24: 12–21.

Jeffery, Charlie (ed.) (1996). *The Regional Dimension of the European Union, Towards a Third Level in Europe?* (Special Issue of Regional and Federal Studies). London: Routledge.

Kassim, Hussein, Menon, Anand, Peters, Guy B. and Wright, Vincent (eds.) (2001). *The National Co-ordination of EU Policy. The European Level*. Oxford: Oxford University Press.

Keating, Michael and Jones, James Barry (1995). *The European Union and the Regions*. Oxford: Clarendon.

—— and Hooghe, Liesbet (1996). 'By-passing the Nation State? Regions in the European Union', in Jeremy J. Richardson (ed.), *European Union: Power and Policy Making*. London: Routledge, 216–29.

Knill, Christoph and Lehmkuhl, Dirk (1999). 'How Europe Matters. Different Mechanisms of Europeanization', *European Integration online Papers*, 3/7.

Ladrech, Robert (1994). 'Europeanization of Domestic Politics and Institutions. The Case of France', *Journal of Common Market Studies*, 32/1: 69–88.

Laffan, Brigid (2000). 'Rapid Adaptation and Light Co-ordination', in Rory O'Donnell (ed.), *Europe, The Irish Experience*. Dublin: Institute of European Affairs, 125–47.

Laursen, Finn (2003). 'Denmark: in Pursuit of Influence and Legitimacy', in Wolfgang Wessels, Andreas Maurer, and Jürgen Mittag (eds.), *Fifteen into One? The European Union and its Member States*. Manchester: Manchester University Press, 92–114.

—— and Pappas, Spyros A. (eds.) (1995). *The Changing Role of Parliaments in the European Union*. Maastricht: European Institute of Public Administration.

Lloréns, Felipe Basabe (2003). 'Spain: the Emergence of a New Major Actor in the European Arena', in Wolfgang Wessels, Andreas Maurer, and Jürgen Mittag (eds.), *Fifteen into One? The European Union and its Member States*. Manchester: Manchester University Press, 184–215.

March, James and Olsen, Johan P. (1989). *Rediscovering Institutions: the Organizational Basis of Politics*. New York: Free Press.

Maurer, Andreas (2001). 'National Parliaments in the European Architecture: From Latecomers' Adaptation towards Permanent Institutional Change?', in Andreas Maurer and Wolfgang Wessels (eds.), *National Parliaments on their Ways to Europe: Losers or Latecomers?* Baden-Baden: Nomos, 27–76.

—— (1999). *What next for the European Parliament?* London: Kogan Page.

Maurer, Andreas (2002). *Parlamentarische Demokratie in Europa. Der Beitrag des EP und der nationalen Parlamente* Baden-Baden: Nomos.
—— and Wessels, Wolfgang (eds.) (2001a). *National Parliaments on their Ways to Europe: Losers or Latecomers?* Baden-Baden: Nomos.
—— —— (2001b). 'National Parliaments after Amsterdam: From Slow Adapters to National Players?', in Andreas Maurer and Wolfgang Wessels (eds.), *National Parliaments on their Ways to Europe: Losers or Latecomers?* Baden-Baden: Nomos, 425-76.
Mény, Yves, Muller, Pierre, and Quermonne, Jean-Louis (eds.) (1996). *Adjusting to Europe— The Impact of the European Union on National Institutions and Policies*. London: Routledge.
Mittag, Jürgen and Wessels, Wolfgang (2003). 'The "One" and the "Fifteen"? The Member States Between Procedural Adaptation and Structural Revolution', in Wolfgang Wessels, Andreas Maurer, and Jürgen Mittag (eds.), *Fifteen into One? The European Union and its Member States*. Manchester: Manchester University Press, 413-54.
Monar, Jörg (1998). 'Ein Raum der Freiheit, der Sicherheit und des Rechts: Die Innen- und Justizpolitik nach Amsterdam', in Mathias Jopp, Andreas Maurer, and Otto Schmuck (eds.), *Die Europäische Union nach Amsterdam. Analysen und Stellungnahmen zum neuen EU-Vertrag*. Bonn: Europa Union Verlag, 127-54.
Moravcsik, Andrew (1998). *The Choice for Europe. Social Purpose and State Power from Messina to Maastricht*. London: Cornell University Press.
—— and Nicolaïdis, Kalypso (1998). 'Federal Ideals and Constitutional Realities in the Treaty of Amsterdam', *Journal of Common Market Studies* (Annual Review), 36/1: 13-38.
—— —— (1999). 'Explaining the Treaty of Amsterdam: Interests, Influence, Institutions', *Journal of Common Market Studies*, 37/1: 59-85.
Norton, Philip (ed.) (1995). *National Parliaments and the European Union*. London: Frank Cass.
Olsen, Johan P. (1996). 'Europeanization and Nation–State Dynamics', in Sverker Gustavsson and Leif Lewin (eds.), *The Future of the Nation–State*. Stockholm: Routledge, 245-85.
—— (1998). *The Many Faces of Europeanization* (ARENA Working Papers, 1/2) Oslo: ARENA.
—— (2000). *Organizing European Institutions of Governance* (ARENA Working Papers, 00/2). Oslo: ARENA.
Pappas, Spyros A. (ed.) (1995). *National Administrative Procedures for the Preparation and Implementation of Community Decisions*. Maastricht: European Institute for Public Administration.
Pöhle, Klaus (1992). 'Die Parlamente in der EG, Formen der praktischen Beteiligung', *integration*, 15/2: 72-82.
Raunio, Tapio (2001). 'The Parliament of Finland: A Model Case for Effective Scrutiny?', in Andreas Maurer and Wolfgang Wessels (eds.), *National Parliaments on their Ways to Europe: Losers or Latecomers?* Baden-Baden: Nomos, 173-98.
Riker, William H. (1982). 'Implications from the Disequilibrium of Majority Rule for the Study of Institutions', in Peter Ordeshook and Kenneth A. Shepsle (eds.), *Political Equilibrium*. Boston: Kluwer Nijhoff Publishing, 3-24.
Rokkan, Stein (1975). 'Dimensions of State Formation and Nation-Building: A Possible Paradigm for Research on Variations within Europe', in Charles Tilly (ed.), *The

Formation of National States in Western Europe. Princeton: Princeton University Press, 562–601.

Rometsch, Dietrich and Wessels, Wolfgang (eds.) (1996). *The European Union and Member States. Towards Institutional Fusion?* Manchester: Manchester University Press.

Scharpf, Fritz W. (1997a). 'Economic Integration, Democracy and the Welfare State', *Journal of European Public Policy*, 4/1: 18–36.

—— (1997b). *Games Real Actors Play. Actor-Centered Institutionalism in Policy Research*. Boulder: Westview.

Sverdrup, Ulf (1998). *Precedents and Present Events in the European Union—An Institutional Perspective on Treaty Reform* (ARENA Working Papers, 98/21). Oslo: ARENA.

Tillikainen, Teija (2003). 'Finland: Smooth Adaptation to European Values and Institutions', in Wolfgang Wessels, Andreas Maurer, and Jürgen Mittag (eds.), *Fifteen into One? The European Union and its Member States*. Manchester: Manchester University Press, 150–65.

Wallace, Helen (2000). 'The Institutional Setting. Five Variations on a Theme', in Helen Wallace and William Wallace (eds.), *Policy-Making in the European Union*. Oxford: Oxford University Press, 3–38.

Weber-Panariello, Philipe A. (1995). *Nationale Parlamente in der Europäischen Union*. Baden-Baden: Nomos.

Weiler, Joseph H. H. (1999). *The Constitution of Europe. 'Do the New Clothes Have an Emperor' and Other Essays on European Integration*. Cambridge: Cambridge University Press.

Wessels, Wolfgang (1996). 'Institutions of the EU System: Models of Explanation', in Dietrich Rometsch and Wolfgang Wessels (eds.), *The European Union and Member States. Towards Institutional Fusion*. Manchester: Manchester University Press, 20–36.

—— (1997). 'Der Amsterdamer Vertrag—Durch Stückwerksreformen zu einer immer effizienteren, erweiterten und föderalen Union?', *Integration*, 20/3: 17–35.

—— (2000). *Die Öffnung des Staates*. Opladen: Leske + Budrich.

——, Maurer, Andreas, and Mittag, Jürgen (eds.) (2003). *Fifteen into One? The European Union and its Member States*. Manchester: Manchester University Press.

Westlake, Martin (1995). *The Council of the European Union*. London: Cartermill.

5

Compounded Representation in EU Multi-Level Governance

Arthur Benz

5.1 The EU as a compounded representative polity[1]

The debate on democracy in the European Union (EU) has produced a great variety of evaluations of the democratic deficits and proposals for their solution. While the general public mainly talks about the still limited power of the directly elected European Parliament (EP) in comparison to the power of the EU bureaucracy (Riehl-Heyse 1998), the arguments which political scientists have developed are based on their specific theories of democracy and on their understanding of the nature of the EU (summarized in Grande 1996; Wolf 1997, 2000: 177–211; Abromeit 1998; Føllesdal and Koslowski 1998; Kohler-Koch 1998; Lord 1998; Benz 1998a). Given these divergent points of departure it is hardly surprising that despite differentiated reasoning, disputes remain unsettled.

It seems more promising to start the analysis with a rather general conception of democratic legitimacy. In a large polity, the constitution of a government has the inevitable consequence that those who hold power are not identical with those who are affected by the use of that power.[2]

---

[1] This article summarizes findings of a research project on 'Democratic Legitimacy of Regional Policy in EU Multi-Level Governance' funded by the German research council (*Deutsche Forschungsgemeinschaft*) and carried out with the assistance of Katrin Auel and Thomas Esslinger. During the first stage of our research work, Gerhard Lehmbruch joined our team. His approach to the study of the German federal system deeply influenced our perspective on multi-level governance in the EU. I would also like to thank Nikola Jung, Beate Kohler-Koch, Rainer Eising, and Nathalie Behnke for helpful comments on draft versions of this article.

[2] There may be good reasons to consider referendums as a form of democracy in a multi-level polity (Grande 1996; Zürn 1996; Abromeit 1998). They may stimulate cooperation among actors in multi-level governance and serve as a method to overcome blockades. In practice, they play a certain role in the ratification of important decisions in some member states. However, referendums are procedures for very specific matters. Even if we accept that

As a consequence, basic criteria for evaluating democratic legitimacy have to conform to a representative government. They concern the relationships between citizens and their representatives, in particular their government (Pitkin 1972). These relations can be characterized as democratic as far as they conform to three criteria, formulated in the theory of a complex democracy (Naschold 1968; Scharpf 1970, 1998; Schmidt 2000a: 204-14):

1. Institutions and procedures have to bring about *effective solutions of political problems*.
2. A political system must enable an *unbiased transmission of citizens' interests* into the process of governance. The interests of citizens should be decisive both with respect to the agenda of a government and with respect to the decisions on alternative solutions (Dahl 1989: 109-14).
3. Office-holders have to be *accountable* for their decisions. 'Political accountability depends on institutional arrangements that create a circular relationship between governors and the governed' (Scharpf 1997: 183). In structures of public communication, representatives have to give reasons for their decisions and the represented have to be able to protest or vote against their representatives if they are not convinced by the decisions or the reasons given for them.

Even if we leave aside the societal preconditions essential for fulfilling these criteria,[3] such a normative framework does not yield any indication on how democratic institutional structures should be designed. Yet the

---

they should be used more often than is presently the case, they can only be regarded as a supplementary element. The EU is in its basic structure a representative form of government.

[3] To be sure, representative democracy does not work without a specific societal basis. First of all, citizens have to be capable of formulating and enunciating their interests (Dahl 1989: 110-11). Second, power structures in a society must not privilege specific groups or exclude individuals or groups from influencing policy-making. Third, patterns of communication should allow for unbiased information of citizens and facilitate open discussion among citizens on matters of public policy. Finally, members of a society should be guided by a minimal standard of solidarity, which motivates each one of them to accept outcomes of democratic procedures even if they do not agree with them (Offe 1998). However, the following sections will solely deal with the institutions of a democratic government. These institutions are regarded as structures that provide *opportunities* for citizens or groups to influence policy-making, create and limit political power, and hold governments responsive and accountable to citizens. As far as the societal basis of democracy in the EU is concerned, I realize that there are problems concerning communication and solidarity, but I do not consider them to be insurmountable. Moreover, the pluralistic character of a multi-ethnic society and the chances that open frontiers generate for improving education, information, and values (tolerance) should not be underestimated. On balance, the multi-national character of the European political space is not necessarily an obstacle for democratizing the EU (Abromeit and Schmid 1998; Eder, Hellmann, and Trenz 1998).

specific features of an existing institutional framework determine the quality of democracy. Since we apparently cannot expect the EU to develop into a fully fledged state with a parliamentary system of government, democracy has to match the structural features of an interpenetrated system and multi-level governance that vary between policies (Jachtenfuchs and Kohler-Koch 1996; Jachtenfuchs 1998; Hix 1999: 2–5; Hooghe and Marks 2001). From this point of view, democratization of the EU appears not only as a problem of European institutions, but also of linking national and European institutions of democracy.

In the EU multi-level system, citizens are represented in different institutions. Therefore, it is promising to regard the EU as a compounded representative government of a new type (Kincaid 1999; Tuschhoff 1999). At the first glance, the conception of a compounded representation, stemming from the theory of federalism, resembles Arend Lijphart's definition of a consociational democracy (Lijphart 1999), which is also applied to the EU (Lord 1998: 46–54; Schmidt 2000b; Schmitter 2000). However, in contrast to Lijpart's use of the term, a compounded polity does not constitute an integrated system in which decisions are based on consensus and cooperation.[4] As I will show later, the multi-level system of the EU constitutes a political system which fuses incompatible components of competitive and consociational democracies. Such a combination of 'rule systems' (Lehmbruch 2000) is characteristic of multi-level governance. In the EU, 'incongruities' mainly exist in the interplay between the Council, the EP, and the national parliaments, that is, between those institutions constituting the core of the representative system. My hypothesis is that both the linkage of these institutions and the practice of dealing with the mentioned incongruities mainly cause the democratic deficit of the EU.

In the following sections, I will start by describing the EU as a compounded representative polity. Based on this concept I will reformulate the often-criticized 'democratic deficit' of the EU by drawing attention to the fusion of incompatible institutional settings. Assuming that actors in a political system are forced to deal with incompatibilities, it is appropriate to look at how the system really works in practice, that is, which 'escape routes' (Héritier 1999) are chosen and how they affect democratic governance. A case study on the reform of regional policy in the context of the Agenda 2000 will illustrate the theoretical analysis.

---

[4] The concept of compounded representation is also not identical with the notion of a mixed or a composite polity both of which focus on the division of power and institutional balance (Héritier 2001).

5.2 The problem of democracy in the EU reconsidered

5.2.1 *The institutionalization of representative democracy in the EU*

The following structures of representation constitute the compounded system of democracy in the EU, as far as supra-national policies are concerned:[5]

1. The *European Parliament* (EP) represents the peoples of the EU (Article 189 TEC). Although elections are organized by member states, the EP does not constitute an assembly of national representatives. In practice, members of the EP more often than not advocate and promote transnational concerns (Bailer and Schneider 2000).[6] Therefore, the characteristic of the EP mentioned is not merely a normative statement (Ernshaw and Judge 1996; Shephard 1998).
2. In the *Council*, ministers from member state governments represent the 15 nations of the EU. These governments are accountable to their national parliaments.
3. Given this duality of representation in the multi-level structure of the EU, *national parliaments* are important institutions for transmitting and representing citizens' interests in European politics. It is the community of citizens in the nation state, which is represented in this fashion.

These three institutions constitute the core of the representative government of the EU. Legislative decisions are taken by the Council or by the Council and the EP with the power of the EP depending on the issue concerned. National parliaments are intermediaries between the EU and the citizens of the member states.

As regards the representation of interests, other institutions are relevant, too. First of all, the Committee of the Regions (CoR) representing regional and local communities deserves attention. Institutional structures of sub-national governments in Europe vary, and so do the modes of representation and accountability of the members of the CoR

---

[5] The vertical and horizontal inter-organizational relations in the multi-level system of the EU vary between policies. Therefore, we have to be careful when drawing general conclusions. I do not claim that the general argument outlined in the following section is valid for policies adopted through intergovernmental procedures.

[6] Particularly those members who have been serving more than one term in the European Parliament consider themselves rather 'a European team' than a conference of representatives from different member states (Franklin and Scarrow 1999). This, of course, does not prevent national or regional governments from attempting to make 'their' EP members an instrument for promoting single national or regional interests on the European level.

(Schöbel 1995; Tauras 1997). Some of them are accountable to regional parliaments, some are accountable to local councils; most are, however, members of the executive with a limited number being nominated by associations of regional or local governments. Since the committee has only consultative powers, it cannot veto decisions, but it can influence policy-making by raising its voice. A similar role is played by the Economic and Social Committee (ESC), an institution designed to represent societal groups. However, in reality its members have acted more as experts than as representatives of associations.

The complexity of multi-level governance has its virtues, but also its vices. From a theoretical point of view, the differentiated structures promise that there would be a sufficient consideration of citizens' interests regarding European, national, regional, and local concerns. These structures also provide multiple access points for interest groups. On the other hand, the interplay between European and national institutions is subject to two dilemmas of a democratic policy. They arise due to the divergence and negative interference of the decision modes in the three core arenas of the European polity (Benz 1998a,b; Lehmbruch 2000: 15-30).

5.2.2 The 'divided government problem' in the interplay between the EP and the Council

During several reforms of the treaties, the EP was able to extend its veto power to a considerable range of policies. In the co-decision and assent procedures, the relationship between the Council and the EP resembles the two-chamber legislature in the German federal system (Hix 1999: 98) with the EP being a veto player (Tsebelis 1995). From the perspective of a theory of multi-level governance, the EP as well as the Council constitute internal veto players, which are directly involved in the process of decision-making. Internal veto players can block decisions, while they can influence policy-making by their negotiation strategies at the same time. Therefore, it is not the existence of veto power that obstructs the harmonization of policy-making in the EP and the Council, but the different structures of interests and the different modes of operation in both institutions that have repercussions on negotiations.

The Council assembles national representatives who, in general, are interested in joint policy-making at the European level when issues are concerned which cannot be dealt with in the context of a nation state. However, in specific policies, member state governments also pursue national interests. Governments participating in European policy-making have to deal with a collective choice dilemma: even if all member state governments agree that a European policy is better than individual national or regional policies, a joint policy may fail to materialize due to distributive bargaining strategies of governments. To overcome this 'negotiator's dilemma' (Lax and Sebenius 1986), governments have to adopt cooperative strategies and evaluate issues not only from a national point of view, but also from a 'European perspective' (Scharpf 1997: 124). They have to reflect their national interests in the light of transnational consequences.[7] This is more likely if isolated policies are at stake, while in cross-sectoral issues, negotiations mostly end by package deals balancing divergent national interests.

The aggregate of these interests, resulting from bargaining or policy-specific compromises among Council members, is not necessarily identical with the European interest as defined by a majority of the members of the EP. As a body, the EP, like the Council, represents European interests. Each member of the EP finds himself or herself in a minority position if he or she intends to pursue particular national or regional goals. Therefore, it is more attractive to them to advance the general goal of European integration (Thomassen and Schmitt 1999). Despite this, inter-institutional coordination and cooperation may fail due to the pluralistic nature of the EP. As conflicts and the aggregation of interests are shaped by parties only with respect to few particular issues (e.g. those concerning social affairs), decision-making is not predictable as is the case in systems of 'party government' like Great Britain or Germany. In the EU, the associations of national parties are heterogeneous and rather weak. A majority in the EP is usually not fixed by factions but has to be negotiated for each particular policy (Lord 1998: 65). Since the EP's position is not reliable, the negotiation of a compromise or the agreement on a package deal is rendered difficult.

Under these conditions, policy-making can end in a deadlock if decision-making in the Council and the EP evolves in different directions and if the approval of the EP is necessary. This situation is all the more problematic as 'divided government' exists independently of electoral

---

[7] This mixed orientation is supported by the regular rotation of the presidency. Those governments which have the responsibility of the presidency or vice-presidency (the so-called 'troika') cannot openly pursue national interests which would contradict the president's task of moderating between contrasting positions of the member state governments and finding a compromise. Moreover, institutional structures and procedural rules contribute to moderate 'nation-centred' orientations of participants (Hayes-Renshaw and Wallace 1997: 99; Eising 2000).

outcomes. It constitutes a structural feature of the EU's compounded representative system.

5.2.3 The 'negotiation-accountability dilemma' of the Council and the national parliaments

The Council is the institution that links the European with the national arena. It is a central European institution, but its members are part of national governments and accountable to their parliaments. This is the reason why the directly elected national parliaments are rightfully regarded as core arenas of representative democracy in the EU. However, not only members of national parliaments but also political scientists complain about the declining influence of these parliaments in EU multi-level governance (Moravcsik 1997; Beyme 1999: 541).

Yet members of the Council are not entirely free from pressure by their national parliaments. By and large, there is a clear trend in the parliaments of the EU member states towards substituting their loss of sovereignty with powers to issue opinions and proposals (Weber-Panariello 1995; Norton 1996a; Kamann 1997). At first sight it seems as if this might contribute to holding members of the Council accountable to citizens and thus to making European governance more democratic. This conclusion, however, seems to be premature if we look at the inter-institutional relations between the national and the European level. By taking into account the logic of the 'two-level game' (Putnam 1988) that is played in the European and the national parliamentary arenas, we again realize that two modes of incompatible representation collide (Benz 1998b).

As outlined above, members of the Council have to deal with a mixed-motive situation at the European level. At the national level, they are in a different constellation. Their action orientations are shaped by the fact that they are accountable to parliaments. The policy of a parliament is decided by the majority. While parties forming the majority are in principle willing to support the government, they also have to consider that they compete with the opposition parties for the support of electors. This competition concerns the question of who is better in supporting the interests of the national citizens. Even if a Europeanized policy is accepted, parties compete on how national interests should be pursued at the European level. A majority faction in parliament loyal to its government has to avoid being blamed by the opposition parties for giving up essential national objectives. Therefore, the best it can do is to encourage the government to support the national rather than European concerns. For this reason, party competition in the national parliamentary arenas induces competitive bargaining strategies in the Council.[8]

As a rule, parliaments can issue non-binding statements. Such *ex ante* decisions mainly influence action orientations of Council members, if they have not to be considered, for political reasons, as *de facto* binding policy proposals of the respective parliaments. The dilemma of multi-level governance is much more acute if parliaments can credibly threaten to apply veto power. Among the EU member states, the Austrian, Danish, Finnish, and Swedish parliaments have formal rights to issue binding propositions on EU matters to their government. In most other parliaments *de facto* vetoes are possible although they can only be applied *ex post* (by a vote of non-confidence, by not ratifying decisions on the treaties, or by obstructing the transposition of EU law into national law). Even if such vetoes are not very likely, the mere possibility has an effect on European policy-making. While *ex ante* vetoes can be detrimental to multi-level governance as they reduce the flexibility of governments in negotiations, *ex post* vetoes may block a decision and may cause a crisis in the multi-level system by undermining the mutual trust of governments (Auel and Benz 2000). A government will do all it can to avoid such a situation.

From an institutionalist point of view, national parliaments participate in European policies as 'external veto players', if they have to ratify or transpose European law. They are able to disturb policy-making in arenas outside their jurisdiction, but they cannot immediately shape policies. Moreover, factions in national parliaments are not exposed to the mixed-motive situation of the European negotiation process but compete for the support of the national electorate. Nothing induces them to accept disadvantages for their constituency in order to achieve the joint profits of a European solution which governments negotiating in the European policy process work for. For this reason, the collective choice dilemma of joint policy-making, which the governments are exposed to in the Council, is intensified due to the accountability of governments to national parliaments (Benz 1998*b*; Lehmbruch 2000).

The impact of veto powers of parliaments varies with the decision rules in the Council and the stages of EU policy-making. In processes of

---

[8] Depending on the structure of the party system and the institutional structure of the national parliamentary system, the competition among parties and its repercussion on action orientations of representatives in the Council vary between member states. In principle, however, in all member states national preferences are formed in a competitive interplay between the majority and opposition parties.

```
┌─────────────────────────────────────┐  ┌─────────────────────────────────┐
│        European Parliament          │  │            Council              │
│                                     │  │                                 │
│   Negotiation of majorities         │  │  Negotiation among actors       │
│   among participants oriented       │◄─'divided government'─►│  linked to national frames of   │
│   to political parties, national    │  │          reference              │
│   interests, and regional           │  │                                 │
│   interests                         │  │                                 │
└─────────────────────────────────────┘  └─────────────────────────────────┘
                                                         ▲
                                            │ Effectiveness in            │
                                            │ negotiations vs.            │
                                            │ accountability              │
                                                         ▼
                                          ┌─────────────────────────────────┐
                                          │      National parliaments       │
                                          │       Party competition         │
                                          └─────────────────────────────────┘
              ▲                                          ▲
              │                                          │
           Citizens                                    Citizens
```

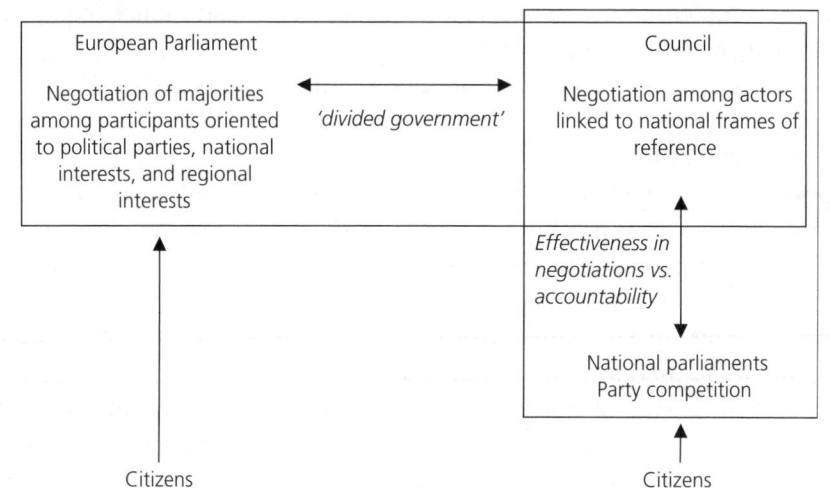

Fig. 5.1 Basic problems in the compounded representative system of the EU

EU legislation, vetoes of national parliaments can block a European decision, if the Council has to decide with unanimity. In case of majority decisions in the Council, parliamentary vetoes can impede the individual national representatives from settling a compromise that at least partially conforms to interests of the respective member state. In this situation, the national parliament risks that its position may finally be defeated by the majority of the other Council members (Fig. 5.1)[9].

5.2.4 Institutional politics leading towards strict coupling of incompatible decision rules

These dilemmas arise only if the arenas are strictly coupled. The term 'strict coupling' designates an inter-organizational relationship in which one organization can effectively interfere with the policy-making processes of another. One potential consequence of strict coupling is that patterns of conflicts and the modes of dealing with them spread from one arena of policy-making to another: Distributive bargaining can supersede

---

[9] In the process of implementation, national parliaments have effective veto rights. If these are applied, the individual national executive is forced to enter into new negotiations with European institutions or with parties in the national parliament in order to find a solution conforming both to the European framework and to preferences of a majority in parliament—otherwise the member state concerned may be punished by the EU. Therefore, vetoes in the implementation process do not cause stalemate but induce new dynamics of intergovernmental policy-making.

integrative deliberation, competition and confrontation among parties can influence negotiations, minorities can be supported from outside and can gain veto power against a legitimate majority. On the other hand, the coordination of decisions in strictly coupled institutions operating according to different modes of decision-making may fail. In the worst case, policy-making may end in deadlock. A strictly coupled compounded polity generates joint-policy traps (Scharpf 1988).

The dynamics of the EU's institutional development tends to foster the strict coupling of arenas. These dynamics were, for a long time, mainly driven by the logic of functionalism. Behind this, a process driven by a 'logic of influence' emerged: the more the EC/EU extended its power to a greater range of policy fields, the more the European institutions were addressed by sub-national governments and interest groups. This process has led to increasing demands for democratizing institutions. It, thus, has instigated a further source of dynamics which follows the 'logic of institutional politics' characterized by efforts of actors in elected institutions to extend their guaranteed power. The more the EU has developed into an ever-closer Union, the more the powers of the EP have been increased, and the correlation of these two processes can be expected to persist in the future. As a consequence, the linkages between the EP and the Council became more intense. Moreover, national parliaments tried to gain rights to participate in European policy-making. This was pursued in particular by establishing special committees on European affairs, which improved their capacities to issue statements (to raise their voice) on EU policies. They presumably realized their responsibility for policies of their government, even if these policies were made at the European level. For this reason, they reacted to the criticism of the executive predominance in the EU, despite the fact that in reality they are not more powerful in national policy-making (Norton 1996*b*).

Thus, the compounded polity is tending towards a more strictly coupled fusion of powers in decision-making. Both the logic of influence and the logic of institutional politics seem to persist in the future. In the course of the 'post-Nice process', the role of national parliaments shall be improved with all the potential consequences described earlier. Proposals for a constitutional reform designed to turn the EU into a two-chamber system with the Council becoming a second chamber representing national citizens or representing the member states (if the model of the German Federal Council (*Bundesrat*) shall be realized) may increase the problem of a divided government.

The following section should clarify whether the problems inherent in the multi-level structures of the EU are dealt with in practical policy-making.

As both theoretical studies on collective choice (Ostrom 1998) and empirical studies on policy-making in the EU multi-level governance have shown, actors confronted with looming deadlocks are strongly motivated to search for strategies or new patterns of interaction, if not new rules which promise to avoid negative outcomes. In case this can be proven, a second question arises: If actors are able to successfully make decisions in the compounded polity, is European politics and policy-making still in accordance with the standards of democratic legitimacy? In order to answer these questions, we have to study processes of policy-making.

5.3 Compounded representation in practice: The case of structural policy

The following case study refers to the regional policy of the EU. Representing a redistributive policy, regional policy in particular raises the issue of democratic legitimacy. The focus of the study is on the reform of regional policy during the Agenda 2000 process. In this process, it was apparent from the outset that in the face of the enlargement of the EU, a far-reaching change in the allocation of regional policy funds would be necessary. Therefore, the EU was challenged with the difficult problem of redistribution among member states and regions. In March 1999, shortly before the decisive Berlin Summit, two experts declared that 'there is a real danger that the matter may not be closed within the current year, or that the final agreement may be perceived as unfair by a significant minority of states, thereby weakening the legitimacy of EU institutions' (Fuente and Doménech 1999: 16). However, after a process of two years (the main stages are summarized in Table 5.1), a rather satisfying result was found.

5.3.1 *Regional policy reform: A satisfying solution?*

The reform of the structural funds, finally negotiated at the Berlin summit under the German presidency, altered the EU regional policy both with regard to the substance of the policy and the allocation of the funds (European Council 1999). Several measures aim at increasing efficiency of the regional policy of the EU. By reducing the number of objectives, it became more transparent and will be more focused on regions in need. At the same time, the scope of issues that can justify funding under the objectives was further extended. National and regional institutions implementing the funds obtained more discretion, while the Commission partly gave up controlling power in the implementation process. Together with the introduction of incentives for best practices, this decentralization

Table 5.1 The Agenda 2000 process

July 1997	Commission	Proposals for the Agenda 2000
December 1997	European Council (Luxembourg)	First discussion on the Commission's proposals
December 1997	EP	First resolutions on the Commission's proposals
March 1998	Commission	Proposals of legal acts necessary to implement the Agenda 2000
May 1998	European Council (Cardiff) EP	Discussion on the budgetary consequences of the Agenda 2000, resolution to pass the Agenda as a package deal in spring 1999, debate on the reform package
October 1998	Commission	Report on the 'own resources' of the EU after enlargement
November 1998	EP	First reading on the regulations, proposals for amendments
March 1999	Commission	Revised proposals; resignation of the Santer Commission
March 1999	European Council (Berlin)	Final decision on the Agenda 2000
May 1999	EP	Approval of inter-institutional agreement on the Agenda 2000
June/July 1999	Council/EP	Approval of the structural funds regulations
July 1999	Commission	Publication of objective 1-regions

should improve the implementation of the structural funds. As regards the enlargement of the EU, cuts in the financial resources are of considerable importance. In the face of rising regional disparities in an enlarged EU, the funds for the 'old' member states were reduced. While they had covered regions with about 51 per cent of the population before the reform, they now include regions with only about 41 per cent of the population. Moreover, structural policy is now focused more on promoting employment in the EU than it was in the past (Jessen 1999).

The Agenda 2000 process did not end up in a comprehensive renovation of the institutional and financial framework of regional policy, as was the case in previous reforms. Nevertheless, it brought about changes that are significant compared to, say, the much more incremental joint policy-making in the German regional policy (Nägele 1996; Benz 2000).

The EU showed considerable skill in dealing with the difficult problem of the redistribution of its structural funds in the face of the EU enlargement (Lang 2001). It goes without saying that the new framework for regional policy is not without flaws, and it is confronted with criticisms from economists as well as political scientists. Moreover, none of the relevant actors in the EU's political system could accomplish his or her whole agenda. The reform of regional policy was part of a larger package deal including agricultural and budgetary issues. And the decision comprised elements designed to reduce the level of conflicts: The Commission had to grant a rather long period of 6 years for 'phasing out' the funding for those regions that are no longer eligible under the new rules. That the EU gives the member states and regions more leeway in the implementation of the structural funds can also be regarded as a concession to governments criticizing EU intervention. The Council postponed a decision on the 'objective' criteria for defining the objective 2 regions and left this to the Commission. Finally, contrary to the goal of efficiency, the Council accepted several additional grants to individual regions and member states.

Although the result of the Agenda 2000 process did not meet the expectations of those who pleaded for a substantial renovation of regional policy, it adjusted the financial framework to the challenge of the accession of East European countries to the EU. As is typical of redistributive policies, the process showed all signs of bargaining and finally ended with a package deal and a compromise. In this respect, the performance of multi-level politics in the EU is not much superior compared to interlocking politics in nation states. But it is also not inferior. Despite taking into account all reasons for critique (Mittendorfer 1999), one must accept that the reform of regional policy marks a step towards increased efficiency.

Whatever the evaluation of this material outcome might amount to, its quality in terms of democratic legitimacy has yet to be scrutinized. A democratic deficit would exist if we discovered that an effective result has been achieved by a policy-making process which was dominated by executives or bureaucrats while parliaments or representatives of public or private interests were powerless. In fact, this has not been the case.

5.3.2 Linking negotiations among executives to the parliamentary arenas: The EP and the national parliaments

Taken as a normative concept, the notion of compounded representation makes the interplay between the Council and parliaments at the national and the European level the crucial element for determining the democratic quality of EU multi-level governance. On the other hand, empirical studies usually justify a more sceptical view of the role of parliaments. The EP has often been described as a weak institution representing in fact national interests rather than the European community of peoples (Lodge 1996). While recent studies point out its power to influence the agenda of the EU, it is often emphasized that the EP either merely reinforces the predominance of national governments or that it can only react to initiatives of the Commission (Rudzio 2000). National parliaments are often labelled as powerless institutions with their role being reduced at best to the ratification and transposition of European law.

Our empirical study on the reform of regional policy reveals a different picture. It is particularly telling if we take the findings on the power of national parliaments in domestic politics as the standard for evaluation. In general, parliaments constitute policy-influencing rather than policy-making institutions (Norton 1990a: 5). Only when it cooperates with the executive during the elaboration of a bill or a resolution is a parliament able to shape policies. This is exactly the way the EP has gained its influence on the Agenda 2000. Beyond its involvement in the formal proceedings according to the rules of the assent procedure, the EP participated in the very early stages of policy-making, when the Commission drafted proposals for the reform of the structural funds. It made its voice heard by issuing so-called initiative reports on particular subjects. Such initiative reports are regularly used devices for expanding the EP's influence on the agenda and the negotiations between the Commission and representatives from member state governments. Moreover, the plenary debated on regional policy several times before the first reading of the directives.

The influence of the EP on the reform of European structural policy was based primarily on the continuous participation of two in-house committees, the Committee on Regional Policy and the Committee on Budgets. As one person interviewed during our study put it: 'The contacts are daily [...] There is constant negotiation going on between the different institutions' (Interview BRR 080798). The corresponding members in the cabinet of the Commission and the DG 'Regional Policy' (formerly DG XVI) had a vital interest in contacting the speakers of the Parliament's committees.[10]

---

[10] The resignation of the European Commissioners before the Berlin summit doubtlessly strengthened the EP. However, during this affair the reform proposals, which had been worked out mainly at the level of the Commission's services, were never called into question. Whether the time pressure resulting from the intention to have the Agenda 2000 ratified before the election of a new parliament in June 1999 had a positive effect on the cooperation between the EP and the Commission, is an open question.

For the Commission, the contact with the EP has a legitimizing effect on its policy. Moreover, these early contacts serve to push through the Commission's resolutions more effectively by integrating potential opposition. The Parliament's committees are informed simultaneously with the Council. During the first and second reading of the reform proposals they nominate spokesmen who are the contact partners for the Commission services.

This interaction between the EP, the Council, and the Commission can be characterized as an ongoing communication rather than a bargaining process (Westlake 1994). It is linked to internal negotiations among groups of members of the European Parliament (MEPs) aimed at finding a majority supporting a policy. In regional policy, one could expect national or regional coalitions to prevail. However, the situation is more complicated. MEPs have to reconcile interests of their home regions with national concerns as well as the European goal of concentrating the resources provided by the structural funds on regions in need (Interview BRP 080798). Surely, contacts to lobbyists from their region have become daily business for the members of the regional committee of the EP. During the sessions of the committee, a considerable amount of time has been spent on hearings where delegates from affected regions (non-governmental organizations: NGOs, local civil servants, mayors, and leading members of regional governments) presented their views on selected topics. On the other hand, MEPs regard themselves as both representatives of their regions' interests and regional educators on prevalent European issues. Even if some national groups of MEPs (e.g. the Spanish group) act more coherently than others, they also have to realize that they are in a minority position if they pursue specific national interests. This was quite obvious in the policy-making process on the Agenda 2000, when the EP, despite conflicts at the outset, turned into a supporter of the structural funds reform as suggested by the Commission.

The Commission carefully scrutinized if, how, and what kind of majorities developed on essential questions in the Committee on Regional Policy of the EP and, even more important, in the plenary, especially when the EP possessed co-decisive power. Certainly, this practice of mutual adjustment of policies did not prevent confrontations between the Council and the EP. When, for example, the German presidency argued strongly in favour of eliminating the Cohesion Fund, the Spanish MEP Gil-Robles expressed the warning that without the preservation of the fund the consent of the Parliament would be all but self-evident. However, such events are more the exception than the rule. More important than its veto power was the

Parliament's contribution to setting the agenda of the European structural funds reform.

Therefore, we can conclude that the EP contributed significantly to the transmission of interests into the policy process. At the same time, the situation of a 'divided government' did not emerge because policy coordination between the Council and the EP was achieved through efforts of mediation by the Commission. The EP and the Commission had a joint interest in mutually supporting one another in defining the agenda and the policy alternatives the Council had to deal with. While the EP provided legitimacy for the Commission's proposals, the EP gained information and influence in the decisive stage of policy-making. The early involvement of the EP in the agenda-setting process led to a sequential coordination of the decisions in the EP and the Council which proved rather successful.

Compared to the EP, national parliaments are much less influential in the EU multi-level governance. Nevertheless, the hypothesis of a 'deparliamentarization', that is a decline of national parliaments resulting from Europeanization, must be differentiated. There are three reasons for this:

First, the role of national parliaments depends on the national institutional setting. In our empirical research we selected France and Germany as contrasting cases. In comparative research, the French *'Assemblée Nationale'* is characterized as a weak parliament (Norton 1990b: 146). The term 'rationalized parliamentarism' (Duverger 1990) illustrates the fact that the constitution of the Fifth Republic strengthened the executive at the expense of a parliament that had been hampered by a fragmented and volatile party system. In the German Federal Republic, a strong parliamentary system emerged after the Second World War. The power of the first chamber, the *Bundestag*, rests in well-organized political parties and a dualistic party system while the second chamber, the *Bundesrat*, is the arena in which the powerful governments of the German *Länder* participate in legislation.

Second, as mentioned above, national parliaments reacted to the European integration by adjusting their institutional structures. The German *Bundestag* and the *Bundesrat* established European affairs committees that can formulate statements on EU matters instead of the whole House. In this way, the parliament can react more quickly and more effectively to the challenges of European policy-making. In France, the *Délégation de l'Assemblée Nationale pour l'Union européenne* was created by an amendment of the constitution. Like the German *Bundestag* committee, it is open to the participation of French members of the EP.

The French *Sénat* deals with European policies in a corresponding committee. Moreover, parliaments obliged their governments to inform them on issues and decisions related to the EU. Finally, they tried to extend their powers to participate in European politics. The German Basic Law stipulates that the federal government 'shall take account of the opinion of the *Bundestag*' in the legislative process of the EU (Article 23 section 3) and similar powers are given to the *Bundesrat* in issues affecting the *Länder* (Article 23 sections 4–6). In France, the *Assemblée* and the *Sénat* can, by their committees or in plenary sessions, issue an opinion on drafts of European regulations, before the EU Council of Ministers starts its negotiations.

Third, as our interviews revealed, members of the national parliaments have learned to deal with the negotiation-accountability dilemma in multi-level governance. They realize that propositions forcing the government into distributive bargaining may bring about outcomes that are problematic even from the national point of view. Therefore, they formulate statements that give the government a wide scope for action. At the same time they use informal channels in order to get information on policy-making at the European level and to influence European policies of their national government.

This can particularly be observed in the 'strong' German parliament. Although the plenary and the responsible committee discussed potential consequences of EU enlargement and passed statements in the very early stage of the Agenda 2000 process, members of the *Bundestag* no longer exclusively rely on formal proceedings. They started to establish informal contacts[11] with colleagues from associated committees in the EP as well as with colleagues of the corresponding party organizations in other national parliaments. Because members of the European affairs committee—although it was affiliated to the majority factions—felt inadequately informed by the federal government in the past, they have also reacted by looking for direct communications with officials in the Commission.

On the other hand, as it became evident during the negotiations on the Agenda 2000, the differentiated committee structure of the German *Bundestag* counteracted this strategy. The Agenda 2000 package dealt with very specific matters related to different policy aspects that were, therefore,

---

[11] An attempt to formalize and stabilize these contacts failed, however. The institutionalized participation of MEPs in the European affairs committee of the *Bundestag* does not work very well due to problems of coordination of the session times.

assigned to the corresponding special committees (in the case of the reform of the structural funds to the committees of economics, agriculture, and social affairs) and only later summed up by the European affairs committee. Members of the special committees do not maintain as many external relations with European actors as members of the European affairs committee. In the face of the multi-level decision structure, these special committees reacted by a certain self-restraint in European policy, above all in policies concerning financial issues. For this reason, the influence of the *Bundestag* on the reform of the structural funds remained limited.[12]

The French parliament played, until recently, a rather passive part in European policy-making, quite in accordance with its rating as weak parliament in comparative research. This changed in part with the Agenda 2000. Disunity arose when the government passed the first proposals to the *Assemblée Nationale*. The parliament indicated that it wanted to state its opinion on these documents on the basis of Article 88.4 of the constitution, which the government refused. The *Assemblée* argued that it could not wait until the government would hand over the final proposals because then it would be too late to declare its opinion. The controversy was settled by an amendment of the constitution, induced by the Treaty of Amsterdam. Article 88.4 now obliges the government to transmit all European drafts of legislative nature (of all three pillars of the EU) and enables the government to transmit all other EU documents as well. The latter is decisive, since the parliament now has the opportunity to issue a proposition on all documents transmitted by government.

In practice, the parliament used its increased powers cautiously and mainly in informal relations with the government. In the Agenda 2000 process, the French *Assemblée Nationale* formulated explicit positions in parliamentary *rapports d'information* on the whole Agenda 2000, on the reform of structural policy and on agricultural policy, and the *Sénat* passed a resolution on the structural funds.[13] With these reports and ensuing

---

[12] See, in particular, BT-Drs. 14/514. This document includes the second and final statement of the European affairs committee on the Agenda 2000, which passed the *Bundestag* by 18 March 1999 with the votes of the coalition parties.

[13] Assemblée Nationale: Agenda 2000, Rapport d'information no. 425 (1997); Pour une politique régionale plus juste et plus efficace; Rapport d'information de la Délégation pour l'Union européenne no. 1280 (1998); Rapport d'information no. 1247, sur le projet de réforme de la politique agricole commune (1998); Résolution sur l'établissement de nouvelles perspectives financières pour la période 2000–2006 no. E 1049 (17 March 1999); Sénat: Agenda 2000: Quelle politique régionale pour une Europe élargie, rapport no. 157 (1997); Quelle réforme pour la politique agricole commune, rapport no. 466; Résolution sur la proposition d'acte communautaire relative à la réforme des fonds structurels no. E 1061 (1998).

resolutions, the French parliament made no serious attempt to coerce the government in the Council negotiations. Its reports on the Agenda 2000 mainly served for public communication on the relevant issues rather than as a critique of the French government's policy. However, as in Germany, members of parliament (in particular chairs of the relevant committees) exercised influence via informal negotiations and consultations with their government. Long before the plenary came to deal with the European issues, informal negotiations between ministers on the one side and the presidents of the involved parliamentary committees as well as the presidents of both chambers on the other side took place. When the plenary finally debated on the subject, usually decisions had already been taken and the coordination between the parliament and the executive completed.

In France as well as in Germany, the national parliament's participation in European negotiations apparently does not jeopardize the effectiveness of negotiations. National representatives in the Council know what their parliaments expect, but they are free to develop and implement their negotiation strategies. This is not to say that parliaments could not exert any influence. Even the French parliament brings more power to bear than expected. More than the German *Bundestag*, it proved able to distribute information and to initiate discussions on the issues at stake at the European level. Both national parliaments considered in our research have gained independent access to information by building up networks to national and European actors. Based on this, they are able to elaborate their positions and to transmit them into the European negotiation process, not by binding statements but by communication and cooperation with the executive. These activities, however, mostly depend on the engagement of individual members of the parliaments and are hardly visible to the public.[14]

5.3.3 De-institutionalization of decision-making

Our case study neither justifies the conclusion that the EU is predisposed to the situation of a divided government in the two legislative institutions, the EP and the Council, nor that the effectiveness of multi-level policy-making is seriously affected by the participation of national parliaments. The relations between the Council, the Commission, and the EP

---

[14] The structures of inter-parliamentary cooperation (Maurer 1996) are used to establish contacts, but the institutions of cooperation by themselves (e.g. the COSAC) are not very effective.

have evolved into a certain functional division of powers with the EP focusing more on influencing the definition of the agenda (i.e. the elaboration of policy proposals by the Commission) and the Council negotiating the final decision. Within this structure, the EP is able to introduce the interests of Europe's citizens. Thus, the quality of 'input legitimacy' is better than it is often assumed to be. Moreover, the cooperation between the European institutions works fairly well and does not prevent effective decisions. National parliaments are not utterly uncoupled from the European policy arenas, but they also do not interfere into the complicated European negotiation processes by vetoes or by binding their government to rigid positions.

What is more problematic is the fact that policy-making in EU multi-level governance is highly informal and that this is caused by the manner in which the problems of the compounded multi-level system are dealt with. We can observe this informalization in the relations between the Council and the EP where the Commission has adopted an intermediary role. Furthermore, policy-making at the interface between national parliaments and the Council is mostly informal. The mutual adjustment of decisions in the institutions of the compounded polity takes place mainly outside the formal institutions and established procedures. Apparently, the strategies of actors to deal with the intricacies of the system lead to a certain 'deinstitutionalization'. This results in opaque processes with the public being hardly able to control them. It makes accountability of representatives difficult and, hence, deteriorates the democratic quality of representative structures. Thus, despite (or because of) the important role of parliaments in EU policy-making, the system fails to conform to the standards of democratic accountability.

This process of policy-making outside the institutions becomes even more obvious if we consider the participation of regions and private interests groups. Policy proposals of the Commission to the Council and the EP regularly result from extensive consultations of the responsible DGs with experts from governments, public administrations, and associations. We know from policy studies that these consultations in formal and informal committees contribute quite substantially to the effectiveness of the EU (Héritier 1996, 2000; Joerges and Neyer 1997: 618; Neyer 2000: 299–301). Moreover, they are regarded as structures to improve the 'input legitimacy' as well (Héritier 2000; Kohler-Koch and Eising 2000).

During the reform of the structural funds in the course of the Agenda 2000 process, networks of contacts between the Commission and regional governments became particularly important. In the CoR, regional policy ranged at the top of the agenda. A special working group was installed in order to communicate opinions from the CoR to the Commission. The final statement of this group resulted in more than 300 requests for changing the original proposals. However, in the negotiations between the committee and the members of the regional policy commissioner's cabinet, tensions arose because of potential disadvantages individual regions would face with the new structural funds regulations. Finally, the Commission disapproved of the committee's effort to act as an independent negotiator, not in the least due to the fact that the propositions of the heterogeneous committee could not solve any problems discussed between the Commission, the Council, and the EP (Interview BRK100200). For this reason, concerted regional lobbying by the CoR had no significant effect on the final negotiations. For similar reasons, the Economic and Social Committee (ESC) could not gain any significant impact on the decisive negotiations.

As a consequence, regional and special interests were pursued mainly in informal consultations at different levels. At the national level, representatives of regions and associations actively lobbied their national executives and parliamentary political bodies. On account of such activities, these interests frequently made their way into the national positions. The patterns of contacts are influenced by national institutions and routines. In Germany, the *Bundesrat* gives the *Länder* an effective forum for issuing their concerns, provided that *Länder* governments find an agreement. Nevertheless, both in France and in Germany interests are transmitted mainly via the executive, that is, via contacts between individual regions or associations and the responsible ministries. This mode of operation makes the national parliaments more independent in formulating their policies, but deprives them of information and of contacts with regional representatives and social groups.

At the European level, the issue networks of the Commission constituted the most important points of access. After the Commission started the structural funds reform with internal discussions among actors from the political (commissioners and their cabinets) and the expert level (Directorate-Generals, DGs), the following consultation process attracted the attention of organizations that felt affected by the reform proposal. During this stage of policy-making, individual member state governments put forward their initial positions on the relevant subjects. At the same time sectoral and regional interests entered the process by stating their opinions, such as single regions or regional associations (e.g. the coastal regions), but also employers' associations, the unions, and the chambers of trade and commerce. These lobbyists directly contacted the DGs concerned with the reform process.

The evolution of these differentiated patterns of communication has positive effects, because the process of policy-making becomes more open to new interests, ideas, and perspectives (Peters 1995; Héritier 1999: 275). However, the informal character of the participation of different actors and the evolution of a maze of interaction reduce the transparency of decision-making. As a consequence, participants cannot be held accountable, even if they are subjected to formal procedures of control within the government or association they represent. The stabilization of informal policy communities turns representatives into autonomous experts and leaves those represented outside with the consequence that the political practice resembles the pre-democratic pattern of representative government (Mather 2001: 198), and if we recognize the importance of these patterns of interaction for European policy-making, we face a serious obstacle for the democratic legitimacy of multi-level governance.

5.4 Summary and conclusion

Referring to the normative criteria of democratic legitimacy presented at the outset, we can summarize the case study on the regional policy reform as follows: The EU was able to cope with a difficult problem of redistributive policy, namely the stabilization of its regional policy scheme in the face of the anticipated accession of East European countries with serious economic problems. Although future development must prove the effectiveness of this decision, both a stalemate in the integration process as well as an enduring cleavage among member states has been avoided. Regarding the transmission of citizens' interests, the compounded representative system of the EU proved to be open to a plurality of interests appearing in the multiple 'transnational demoi' (Abromeit and Schmidt 1998: 315) of Europe, just as much to those of different territories as well as to those of sectoral interests. Of course, not all interests found equal opportunities to be heard. What is important, however, is the fact that the decision on the redistributive issue of regional policy was not made by a closed elite of executives or 'Eurocrats'. It resulted from an open process of consultation, negotiation, and cooperation among a multitude of actors and institutions.

While this improves the intermediation of interests, policy-making has become increasingly burdened by transaction costs. Under these conditions, the policy outcome described earlier could not be expected. This outcome is even more surprising in a multi-level political system that, from a theoretical point of view, is prone to deadlocks. The regional policy reform was the result of a process of policy coordination among national and European institutions operating under different decision rules. The finding that the EU came to reach rather efficient decisions can be explained by the strategies which actors resorted to in order to evade potential ungovernability. They used committees as an arena for policy coordination or cooperated outside the formal procedures and institutions. However, this goes to the detriment of accountability of national governments representing citizens of member states in the Council. In the same way, informal and opaque procedures in the coordination between the Council and the EP and in the interplay between national governments and their parliaments deteriorate the accountability of elected members of parliaments to citizens.

Table 5.2 summarizes the findings of the analysis in more detail by distinguishing the different patterns of interlocking politics in the EU multilevel governance. It should explain the following:

1. While the effectiveness of policy-making and the transmission of interests in the EU are to a considerable degree achieved by policy networks and consultative committees, these patterns particularly reduce the transparency of policy-making essential for the effective control by those represented. Actors in these networks act as experts and not as representatives accountable to regional parliaments or to particular groups of society.
2. National parliaments have made great and not unsuccessful efforts to improve their rights to participate in European policy-making. But up to now they have not found adequate procedures to influence or control

Table 5.2 Effects of inter-institutional linkages on the quality of representative democracy

	Input of interests	Effectiveness of problem-solving	Accountability
Consultative committees and networks	++	+	−
Council—national parliaments	+/−	+	−
Council—EP	+	+	−

+ (++): (very) positive; − (−−): (very) poor; +/−: neither good nor poor

their governments' behaviour in European negotiations in a way that is compatible with the norm of accountability. Neither are governments utterly dependent on parliamentary decisions that are formulated in the competition among parties, nor are parliaments without powers to influence European policy-making. However, as our study reveals for Germany and for France, a critical dialogue between government and majority factions is practised informally, while in public arenas both sides avoid explicit debates on matters of potential conflict. The specific positions of parties in this political process are hardly transparent for citizens to whom members of parliament are responsible.
3. The EP, always denounced as a weak parliament, has obtained a significant role in its relationships with the Council and the Commission, despite the multitude of interest group intervention. Even in cases where the parliament does not have formal veto power, it successfully influences the agenda and the policy framework by participating in the early stages of the policy process. This success is to a considerable degree achieved by informal contacts of members of the EP's committees with the Commission and also the Council.

Thus, it is the accountability deficit, which is most serious. For two reasons this deficit does not concern the European institutions as much as it concerns the national institutions: First, European institutions, that is, the Council and the EP, finally make decisions open to public. However, citizens can only get knowledge about them if national parliaments transmit information to the public. In fact, however, the function of publicity is not fulfilled very well by national parliaments (and presumably not better in strong parliaments than in those labelled as weak). Second, national parliaments and representatives from regions and associations regularly do not openly formulate their positions on European affairs, which left citizens without a chance to become informed about their policy. Thus, even if we admit the accountability problems of the EP and the Council, the decline of citizens' power against their national parliaments in the process of Europeanization must raise concern. This is even more irritating as those problems of democratic legitimacy are the paradoxical result of an institutional upgrading of national parliaments and regions in European policy-making. It is, therefore, not astonishing that empirical studies show people's growing dissatisfaction with the existing structures of EU governance and a declining support by citizens (Niedermayer and Sinnott 1995; Scheuer 1999).[15]

---

[15] In the short run, citizens' satisfaction with EU governance is wavering as confirmed by recent Eurobarometer findings showing an increasing trust in EU institutions and bodies mounting from 37 per cent in 1997 to 53 per cent in autumn 2001 (European Commission 2002).

A policy of democratizing European multi-level governance has to cope with a 'trilemma' (Höreth 1999): In the differentiated structures of EU governance, efficiency of decision-making, intermediation of interests, and accountability have to be brought into a balance that seems hardly achievable. Institutional reforms of the past as well as those currently under discussion bear the risk of achieving one goal at the cost of another. Therefore, institutional solutions often advance the deinstitutionalization of politics. Presumably, linking EU and national governance in a democratic way does not require new institutions but a balanced system of division of competencies between existing institutions that impedes both the fusion of powers as well as the uncoupling of processes in the various arenas. The public deliberation on European policies in the parliaments at all levels seems most important. The teaching function of parliaments (Bagehot 1963) that declined in competitive party politics of national parliamentary governments has to be taken more seriously. Finally, given the importance of the agenda setting in EU policy-making, one should look for ways to democratize this stage of the process (Benz 1998). By these allusions I do not claim to know the solution of the trilemma of democracy in multi-level governance. What I do suggest, however, is that the concept of compounded representation taken as an analytical approach and a normative theory can help to clarify the causes of the democratic deficits as well as the consequences of new institutional designs which pretend to overcome the deficit.

References

Abromeit, Heidrun (1998). *Democracy in Europe. How to Legitimize Politics in a Non-State Polity*. Oxford: Berghan Books.

—— and Schmidt, Thomas (1998). 'Grenzprobleme der Demokratie: Konzeptionelle Überlegungen', in Beate Kohler-Koch (ed.), *Regieren in entgrenzten Räumen* (Special Issue of Politische Vierteljahresschrift, Vol. 29). Opladen: Westdeutscher Verlag, 293–320.

Auel, Katrin and Benz, Arthur (2000). *Strength and Weakness of Parliament in EU Multilevel Governance—Accountability in a Compounded Representative Democracy* (paper presented at the IPSA World Congress, 1–5 August 2000, Quebec).

Bagehot, Walter (1963). *The English Constitution*. London: Collins Fontane Edition.

Bailer, Stefanie and Schneider, Gerald (2000). 'The Power of Legislative Hot Air: Informal Rules and the Enlargement Debate in the European Parliament', *The Journal of Legislative Studies*, 6/2: 19–44.

Benz, Arthur (1998*a*). 'Ansatzpunkte für ein europafähiges Demokratiekonzept', in Beate Kohler-Koch (ed.), *Regieren in entgrenzten Räumen* (Special Issue of Politische Vierteljahresschrift, Vol. 29). Opladen: Westdeutscher Verlag, 345–68.

—— (1998b). 'Postparlamentarische Demokratie? Demokratische Legitimation im kooperativen Staat', in Michael Th. Greven (ed.), *Demokratie—Eine Kultur des Westens?* Opladen: Leske + Budrich, 201-22.

—— (2000). 'Two Types of Multi-level Governance: Intergovernmental Relations in German and EU Regional Policy', *Regional and Federal Studies*, 10/3: 21-44.

Beyme, Klaus von (1999). *Die parlamentarische Demokratie. Entstehung und Funktionsweise 1979-1999*. Opladen: Westdeutscher Verlag.

Dahl, Robert A. (1989). *Democracy and its Critics*. New Haven and London: Yale University Press.

Duverger, Maurice (1990). *Le système politique français*. Paris: Presse Universitaire de France.

Eder, Klaus, Hellmann, Kai-Uwe, and Trenz, Hans-Jörg (1998). 'Regieren in Europa jenseits öffentlicher Legitimation? Eine Untersuchung zur Rolle von politischer Öffentlichkeit in Europa', in Beate Kohler-Koch (ed.), *Regieren in entgrenzten Räumen* (Special Issue of Politische Vierteljahresschrift, Vol. 29). Opladen: Westdeutscher Verlag, 321-44.

Eising, Rainer (2000). *Liberalisierung und Europäisierung. Die regulative Reform der Elektrizitätsversorgung in Großbritannien, der Europäischen Gemeinschaft und der Bundesrepublik Deutschland*. Opladen: Leske + Budrich.

Ernshaw, David and Judge, David (1996). 'From Co-Operation to Co-Decision. The European Parliament's Path to Legislative Power', in Jeremy J. Richardson (ed.), *European Union. Power and Policy-making*. London and New York: Routledge, 96-126.

European Commission (2002). *Eurobarometer. Public Opinion it the European Union*. Brussels: Directorate-General Press and Communication. http://europa.eu.int/comm./public_opinio/archives/eb/eb56/eb56_en.pdf.

European Council (1999). *Presidency Conclusions. Berlin European Council, 24 and 25 March*. http://europa.eu.int/council/off/conclu/mar99_en.htm.

Føllesdal, Andreas and Koslowski, Peter (eds.) (1998). *Democracy and the European Union*. Berlin: Springer.

Franklin, Mark N. and Scarrow, Susan E. (1999). 'Making Europeans? The Socializing Power of the European Parliament', in Richard S. Katz and Bernhard Weßels (eds.), *The European Parliament, the National Parliaments and European Integration*. Oxford: Oxford University Press, 45-60.

Fuente, Angel de la and Doménech, Rafael (1999). *The Redistributive Effects of the EU Budget: An Analysis and Some Reflections on the Agenda 2000 Negotiations* (CEPR Discussion Papers, DP 2113). London: Centre for Economic Policy Research.

Grande, Edgar (1996). 'Demokratische Legitimation und europäische Integration', *Leviathan*, 24/3: 339-60.

Hayes-Renshaw, Fiona and Wallace, Helen (1997). *The Council of Ministers*. Houndmills: Macmillan.

Héritier, Adrienne (1996). 'The Accommodation of Diversity in European Policy-Making and its Outcomes: Regulatory Policy as a Patchwork', *Journal of European Public Policy*, 3: 149-67.

—— (1999). 'Elements of Democratic Legitimation in Europe: An Alternative Perspective', *Journal of European Public Policy*, 6/2: 269-82.

—— (2000). *Policy-Making and Diversity in Europe. Escaping Deadlock*. Cambridge: Cambridge University Press.

Héritier, Adrienne (2001). *Composite Democratic Legitimation in Europe: the Role of Transparency and Access to Information* (Preprints of the Max Planck Project Group on Common Goods: Law, Politics and Economics, 2001/6). Bonn: Max Planck Project Group. www.mpp-rdg.mpg.de.

Hix, Simon (1999). *The Political System of the European Union*. New York: St Martin's Press.

Höreth, Markus (1999). *Die Europäische Union im Legitimationstrilemma. Zur Rechtfertigung des Regierens jenseits der Staatlichkeit*. Baden-Baden: Nomos.

Hooghe, Liesbet and Marks, Gary (2001). *Multi-Level Governance and European Integration*. Lanham: Rowman & Littlefield.

Jachtenfuchs, Markus (1998). 'Democracy and Governance in the European Union', in Andreas Føllesdal and Peter Koslowski (eds.), *Democracy and the European Union*. Berlin: Springer, 37–64.

—— and Kohler-Koch, Beate (eds.) (1996). *Europäische Integration*. Opladen: Leske + Budrich.

Jessen, Christoph (1999). 'Agenda 2000: Das Reformpaket von Berlin, ein Erfolg für Gesamteuropa', *Integration*, 22/3: 167–75.

Joerges, Christian and Neyer, Jürgen (1997). 'Transforming Strategic Interaction into Deliberative Problem-Solving: European Comitology in the Foodstuffs Sector', *Journal of European Public Policy*, 4/4: 609–25.

Kamann, Hans-Georg (1997). *Die Mitwirkung der Parlamente der Mitgliedstaaten an der europäischen Gesetzgebung*. Frankfurt a. M.: Peter Lang.

Kincaid, John (1999). 'Confederal Federalism and Citizens Representation in the European Union', in Joanne B. Brzinski, Thomas D. Lancaster, and Christian Tuschhoff (eds.), *Compounded Representation in West European Federations* (Special Issue of West European Politics, Vol. 22). London: Frank Cass, 34–58.

Kohler-Koch, Beate (1998). 'Die Europäisierung nationaler Demokratien: Verschleiß eines europäischen Kulturerbes?', in Michael Th. Greven (ed.), *Demokratie—eine Kultur des Westens?* Opladen: Leske + Budrich, 263–88.

—— and Eising, Rainer (eds.) (2000). *The Transformation of Governance in the European Union*. London and New York: Routledge.

Lang, Jochen (2001). 'Dezentralisierung à la Kommission. Prozeß und Ergebnisse der Reform 1999', in Hubert Heinelt, Jochen Lang, Tanja Malek, and Bernd Reissert (eds.), *Die Entwicklung der europäischen Stukturfonds als kumulativer Politikprozeß. Zur Institutionalisierung und Veränderung von Politikinhalten im Mehrebenensystem der EU* (Report on a research project funded by the German Research Council (DFG) under the programme 'Governance in the European Union'). Darmstadt and Berlin, 114–54.

Lax, David A. and Sebenius, James K. (1986). *The Manager as Negotiator. Bargaining for Co-operative and Competitive Gain*. New York: The Free Press.

Lehmbruch, Gerhard (2000). *Parteienwettbewerb im Bundesstaat. Regelsysteme und Spannungslagen im Institutionengefüge der Bundesrepublik Deutschland* (3rd edn). Opladen: Westdeutscher Verlag.

Lijphart, Arend (1999). *Patterns of Democracy: Government Forms and Performance in Thirty-Six Countries*. New Haven and London: Yale University Press.

Lodge, Juliet (1996). 'The European Parliament', in Svein S. Andersen and Kjell A. Eliassen (eds.), *The European Union: How Democratic Is It?* London: Sage, 187–214.

Lord, Christopher (1998). *Democracy in the European Union*. Sheffield: Sheffield Academic Press.

Mather, Janet (2001). 'The European Parliament—A Model of Representative Democracy?', *West European Politics*, 24/1: 181–201.

Maurer, Andreas (1996). *Les Implications du Traité sur L'Union Européenne sur la Coopération Interparlementaire*. Brüssel: Presses Interuniversitaires Européennes.

Mittendorfer, Heinz (1999). 'Kritik der Agenda 2000', in Heinz-Jürgen Axt (ed.), *Agenda 2000—eine gute Grundlage für die Reform der EU-Strukturpolitik?* (Duisburger Materialien zur Politik- und Verwaltungswissenschaft). Duisburg: Gerhard-Mercator-Universität Duisburg GH, 94–101.

Moravcsik, Andrew (1997). 'Warum die Europäische Union die Exekutive stärkt: Innenpolitik und internationale Kooperation', in Klaus Dieter Wolf (ed.), *Projekt Europa im Übergang* 2. Baden-Baden: Nomos, 211–69.

Nägele, Frank (1996). *Regionale Wirtschaftspolitik im kooperativen Bundesstaat. Ein Politikfeld im Prozeß der deutschen Vereinigung*. Opladen: Leske + Budrich.

Naschold, Frieder (1968). 'Demokratie und Komplexität', *Politische Vierteljahresschrift*, 9/4: 494–518.

Neyer, Jürgen (2000). 'Risikoregulierung im Binnenmarkt: Zur Problemlösungsfähigkeit der europäischen politischen Verwaltung', in Christian Joerges and Joseph Falke (eds.), *Das Ausschußwesen der Europäischen Union*. Baden-Baden: Nomos, 257–328.

Niedermayer, Oskar and Sinnott, Richard (eds.) (1995). *Public Opinion and Internationalized Governance*. Oxford: Oxford University Press.

Norton, Philip (1990a). 'Parliaments: A Framework for Analysis', in Philip Norton (ed.), *Parliaments in Western Europe*. London: Frank Cass, 1–9.

—— (1990b). 'Legislatures in Perspective', in Philip Norton (ed.), *Parliaments in Western Europe*. London: Frank Cass, 143–52.

—— (ed.) (1996a). *National Parliaments and the European Union*. London: Frank Cass.

—— (1996b). 'Conclusion: Addressing the Democratic Deficit', in Philip Norton (ed.), *National Parliaments and the European Union*. London: Frank Cass, 177–93.

Offe, Claus (1998). 'Demokratie und Wohlfahrtsstaat: Eine europäische Regimeform unter dem Streß der europäischen Integration', in Wolfgang Streeck (ed.), *Internationale Wirtschaft, nationale Demokratie. Herausforderungen für die Demokratietheorie*. Frankfurt a. M. and New York: Campus, 99–136.

Ostrom, Elinor (1998). 'A Behavioral Approach to the Rational Choice Theory of Collective Action', *American Political Science Review*, 92/1: 1–22.

Peters, Guy B. (1995). 'Equilibria and Disequilibria in Agenda Setting in European Union', in Joachim Jens Hesse and Theo A. J. Toonen (eds.), *The European Yearbook of Comparative Government and Public Administration* (Vol. 1). Baden-Baden: Nomos, 141–59.

Pitkin, Hanna Fenichel (1972). *The Concept of Representation*. Berkeley: University of California Press.

Putnam, Robert (1988). 'Diplomacy and Domestic Politics: The Logic of Two-level Games', *International Organization*, 42/3: 427–60.

Riehl-Heyse, Herbert (1998). 'Diktatur der Bürokraten', *Süddeutsche Zeitung*, 24/25 January: 11.

Rudzio, Kolja (2000). *Funktionswandel der Kohäsionspolitik unter dem Einfluß des Europäischen Parlaments*. Baden-Baden: Nomos.

Scharpf, Fritz W. (1970). *Demokratietheorie zwischen Utopie und Anpassung*. Konstanz: Universitätsverlag.
—— (1988). 'The Joint-Decision-Trap. Lessons from German Federalism and European Integration', *Public Administration*, 66: 239-78.
—— (1997). *Games Real Actors Play. Actor-Centered Institutionalism in Policy Research*. Boulder: Westview Press.
—— (1998). *Governing Europe, Efficient and Democratic*. Oxford: Oxford University Press.
Scheuer, Angelika (1999). 'A Political Community?', in Hermann Schmitt and Jacques Thomassen (eds.), *Political Representation and Legitimacy in the European Union*. Oxford: Oxford University Press, 25-46.
Schmidt, Manfred G. (2000a). *Demokratietheorien* (3rd edn). Opladen: Leske + Budrich.
—— (2000b). 'Der konsoziative Staat. Hypothesen zur politischen Struktur und zum politischen Leistungsprofil der Europäischen Union', in Edgar Grande and Markus Jachtenfuchs (eds.), *Wie problemlösungsfähig ist die Europäische Union? Regieren im Europäischen Mehrebenensystem*. Baden-Baden: Nomos, 33-58.
Schmitter, Philippe C. (2000). *How to Democratize the European Union... and Why Bother?* Lanham: Rowman & Littlefield.
Schöbel, Norbert (1995). *Der Ausschuß der Regionen—eine erste Bilanz*. Tübingen: Europäisches Zentrum für Föderalismusforschung.
Shephard, Mark P. (1998). 'The European Parliament: Crawling, Walking and Running', in Philip Norton (ed.), *Parliaments and Governments in Western Europe*. London: Frank Cass, 167-89.
Tauras, Olaf (1997). *Der Ausschuss der Regionen: institutionalisierte Mitwirkung der Regionen in der EU*. Münster: Agenda-Verlag.
Thomassen, Jaques and Schmitt, Hermann (1999). 'Partisan Structures in the European Parliament', in Richard S. Katz and Bernhard Wessels (eds.), *The European Parliament, the National Parliaments and European Integration*. Oxford: Oxford University Press, 129-48.
Tsebelis, George (1995). 'Decision Making in Political Systems: Veto Players in Presidentialism, Parliamentarism, Multicameralism and Multipartyism', *British Journal of Political Science*, 25/1: 289-325.
Tuschhoff, Christian (1999). 'The Compounding Effect: The Impact of Federalism on the Concept of Representation', in Joanne B. Brzinski, Thomas D. Lancaster, and Christian Tuschhoff (eds.), *Compounded Representation in West European Federations* (Special Issue of West European Politics, Vol. 22). London: Frank Cass, 16-33.
Weber-Panariello, Philippe A. (1995). *Nationale Parlamente in der Europäischen Union*. Baden-Baden: Nomos.
Westlake, Martin (1994). *The Commission and the Parliament: Partners and Rivals in the European Policy-Making Process*. London: Butterworths.
Wolf, Klaus-Dieter (ed.) (1997). *Projekt Europa im Übergang 2. Probleme, Modelle und Strategien des Regierens in der Europäischen Union*. Baden-Baden: Nomos.
—— (2000). *Die neue Staatsräson—Zwischenstaatliche Kooperation als Demokratieproblem in der Weltgesellschaft*. Baden-Baden: Nomos.
Zürn, Michael (1996). 'Über den Staat und die Demokratie im europäischen Mehrebenensystem', *Politische Vierteljahresschrift*, 37/1: 27-55.

6

The Making of a European Public Space: The Case of Justice and Home Affairs

Klaus Eder and Hans-Jörg Trenz

6.1 From cooperation to integration: The case of justice and home affairs

European cooperation in the field of justice and home affairs[1] (JHA) has been marked by an overall dominance of national governance over Communitarian policy-making. The arbitrary intergovernmental practice of bundling together a plethora of issues—such as immigration control and admission policies, illegal trafficking of drugs and of humans, restrictive asylum and temporary protection, and the fight against racism and organized crime—might account for many of the controversies and internal struggles that have characterized cooperation in this field thus far. The diverse JHA framework was originally held together by common security concerns, which had till then induced governments to restrict policy cooperation to private negotiations among secret agents and police experts. In spite of its official status as a highly specialized and differentiated area of policy-making, the underlying 'security ideology' of JHA cooperation (den Boer 1994) could not easily be subsumed under the functional logic of European Union (EU) policy-making. Against official legitimation, which has always required that the strengthening of external controls

---

For helpful comments and intense criticism on earlier drafts of this paper, the authors wish to thank Adrian Favell, Nikola Jung, Beate Kohler-Koch, and Jürgen Neyer.

[1] Without further consideration of the procedural details, 'justice and home affairs' is used here with reference to tracks of intergovernmental cooperation within and outside the EU framework ('third pillar cooperation' and cooperation among the nine states which have fully implemented the 'Schengen acquis'). For details see den Boer and Wallace (2000), Pauly (1996), and Wiener (2000).

should be regarded as the functional prerequisite for expanding internal liberties, the implementation of the so-called 'flanking measures' has proven to increase, above all, discretionary administrative powers at the expense of European citizens (Kostakopoulou 2000).

In response, European integration literature has slowly begun to acknowledge that this new phenomenon of the 'securitization' of Europe requires a different framework of analysis (Buzan, Waever, and de Wilde 1998; Huysmans 1998; Lavenex 1999). The logics of JHA cooperation would have to be seen as consisting in withdrawing more and more policy sectors from public debate limiting available choices and alternatives and rights of participation by 'securitizing' them and considering them as a matter of governmental priority (Wolf 1999). As such, the common security agenda which emerges in the JHA cooperation, risks entering conflicts with the rule of law, with standard procedures of democratic decision-making and with international human rights principles. Critical observers have spoken of the emergence of a 'new authoritarian Europe', of the 're-emergence of the Leviathan', and of the building of a 'fortress Europe' (Bunyan 1991; Leuthardt 1994).

Despite such dark prophecy, JHA cooperation still remains one of the policy areas where the EU can hardly claim to be wielding substantial powers. Even critics find it difficult to point out where exactly the assumed allocation of powers has taken place. 'Fortress Europe' can certainly not be brought into connection with any substantial policies which are effective at the European level. After almost two decades of intergovernmental cooperation, the policy output in the form of binding decisions is still rather negligible. Decision-making has been blocked mainly as a consequence of apparently irreconcilable conflicts between governments or has taken place in the form of non-binding resolutions and recommendations characterized by notorious deficits of implementation.[2]

At the same time, the slowness of decision-making contrasts sharply with the strongly variable institutional dynamics that have characterized the evolution of JHA cooperation. The history of JHA cooperation is one of institution building and transformation, not one of successful decision-making and policy implementation.[3] The gradual formalization of procedures, in accordance with the standard model of multi-level governance, was meant to extend cooperation to a plurality of actors and institutions

[2] For an overview of the 'acquis intergouvernementale' before Amsterdam see Guild (1996).

[3] Despite one's first intuitive assumptions, institutional perspectives on JHA cooperation have proven indispensable for explaining the dynamics of expanding cooperation in these areas (Soysal 1993; den Boer 1994).

(Guiraudon 2000). Thus, little is left today of the privacy which governments wanted to maintain in this sensitive field of policy cooperation. With the Amsterdam amendments, the way has been opened towards a flexibility which is likely to influence further integration of the field (Wallace 2000; Wiener 2000).

Fragmentation and the maintenance of multiple forms of cooperation have also stimulated the search for new integrative formulas and constitutional guarantees for the representation of the different civic constituencies and electorates in the emerging multi-level arrangement. The delicate issues to be debated within JHA have turned into one of the most conflictual fields of policy-making within the EU. These issues open a debate about the fundamental norms and principles of cooperation and ultimately accelerate the process of establishing a kind of constitutional superstructure for the enforcement of civic rights and liberties. Not long ago, European governments proudly announced the creation of an 'area of freedom, security and justice'. This was to be based upon the principles of transparency and democratic control, as well as upon an open dialogue with civil society in order to strengthen the acceptance and support of citizens.[4] Here, the original object of critique and delegitimation has turned into an object of legitimation for further cooperation within this field. The closed 'European security community' has become the 'open Europe', the 'fortress Europe' a 'Europe of rights, justice and solidarity'. This is an astonishing development, which needs further explanation.

The principal aim of this contribution is to develop an analytical model that accounts for the institutional dynamics of expanding cooperation in these fields, slowly integrating the 'European security community' into an encompassing 'area of justice, freedom and rights'. In our view, the prevailing focus on the role of governments has difficulties in explaining this turn from the 'protective Union' (Kostakopoulou 2000) to a new multi-level governance arrangement (Guiraudon 2000). Drawing upon a theory of the public sphere we develop an integrative approach which relates intergovernmental politics, supra-national institution building and new emerging forms of transnational communication and contention. It will be argued that the 'fortress Europe' account neglects two significant factors: first, governments act within an expanding transnational field made up of norms, discourses, and institutions which increasingly constrain their action; second, competitive actors within the field also deliver performances

---

[4] Presidency Conclusions. Tampere European Council, 15 and 16 October 1999.

towards the outside in response to increasing public monitoring of their activities. This transforms the transnational field of communication and contention into a public space attended by different audiences with shifting attention and expectations. In the following, the term 'transnational resonance structures' will be introduced to account for the integration and legitimation of this new organizing principle of governance between international, European, and domestic politics.[5]

6.2 Explaining the integration of multi-level governance: An analytical model of transnational resonance

6.2.1 JHA cooperation as an emerging 'political field'

The first part of the explanatory model with which we want to account for the integrative dynamics of the multi-level networks of JHA cooperation is based on the concept of a 'political field'. This concept which draws on Bourdieu's conception of 'social fields' has been used by Favell (1998) to spell out the logic of European immigration politics as a distinctly legitimized dimension of social order, produced and reproduced by the competition among different groups of people and situated in a transnational context of collective action. Institution building within the multi-level governance system provides new opportunities for collective action and contentious politics (Greenwood and Aspinwall 1998). The emerging political opportunity structure at the European level changes the rules of the game from traditional hierarchically organized forms of claims making within the nation–state toward a multi-level game of interests and representation (Marks and McAdam 1996, 1999; Reising 1998). On the European level, this new opportunity structure for civic participation opens channels of formal or informal access and intensifies horizontal relations between associations and EU institutions (Nentwich 1996). The Commission and the Parliament supply the economic capital (financial supports) as well as the social capital (information, procedures, and channels for participation) needed to enter the field of European politics.

---

[5] This alternative perspective is indicated by the constructivist approach in International Relations, which argues for the structural situatedness of states in their social environments (Checkel 1998; Christiansen, Jørgensen, and Wiener 1999; Cowles, Caporaso, and Risse 2001). The assumption of a fortress reduces the explanation for self-binding effects of intergovernmental cooperation to strategic interstate and intra-state interaction. In contrast, constructivist approaches have emphasized a relational perspective which links norms, discourses, and institutions to actors situated at different levels of governance (Risse, Ropp, and Sikkink 1999).

Notably, this model goes beyond the analytical focus on bargaining situations among governmental actors with given interests (which would correspond to the intergovernmental logic of JHA cooperation). Collective action within the political field is rather studied as a struggle among different elite actors who have been socialized into a transnational environment developing particular practices, institutionalized behaviour, a logic of appropriateness, and symbolic representations (Favell 1998; Geddes 2000). This theoretical idea is linked to the neo-institutional assumption that the development of institutional arrangements of governance depends on visions of a legitimate political order (March and Olsen 1995; Jachtenfuchs 1999). Diffusion processes within the institutional fields of transnational governance networks are then understood less by focusing attention on agency than by incorporating framing processes into such an understanding (Kohler-Koch 2000). The 'social field' that situates actors and allows them to follow their particular interests has a structural property that goes beyond the utilitarian interests of the actors involved; it assumes that these actors rely on shared knowledge about the world in which they interact.

According to our own investigations collective mobilization in the political field of JHA depends to a significant degree on the common experience of fighting against intergovernmentalism and preventing supra-statism. While targeting these non-democratic forms of exercising political power, contentious action has widely accepted multi-level governance as the 'standard model' of EU policy-making. Within this new institutional context, multi-level governance is no longer regarded as incomplete or only preliminary in relation to the primary objective of European state and nation-building. It is rather vested with its own legitimacy for the constitution of a European political order. We conclude that the dynamics of the field are determined by a shared experience of and a shared belief in the appropriateness of the particular (though undetermined) form of multi-level governance. Multi-level governance assumes a *normative force* which impacts on actors' identities, interests, and behaviour, pushing them to further integration and to situating JHA cooperation somewhere between the 'closed fortress' and the 'open Europe'.

However, this self-understanding might actually be just wishful thinking. According to our own empirical findings we will speak of the horizontal integration of the political field of JHA which is constituted by a plurality of actors which are situated mainly on the supra-national level of governance. Vertical links which connect elite actors to their social constituencies are largely absent, or at best only exist virtually in the elite actors' cognitive self-understanding in order to validate claims for the representation of their alleged national or sub-national constituencies. How can we account for the reality of multi-level governance if vertical integration as a structured relationship between European and domestic politics is *not* provided by institutional performance?

We could stop our explanation at this point, and instead, continue to consider the absence of vertical links to be a basis for the democratic deficit of the EU. The practical task, then, would consist in remedying poor institutional performance by improving actors' opportunities for participation. It might well be the case, however, that the idea of coupling the different levels of governance through collective action and institutional performance is not the adequate answer given the dynamics of cooperation in the EU multi-level system. Following this intuition, we continue our theoretical search by taking into consideration the structural embeddedness of institutions in their social environment. This extended perspective turns from the institutional *Überbau* to the *social basis* of European integration. Shared beliefs about the appropriateness of European governance as they develop within the political field must be defended against the outside world where strategies of disillusionment about the appropriateness of institutions are to be expected. The following is such an attempt of extending institutionalist perspectives by bringing society back to Europe in our analytical model.

6.2.2 *The public monitoring of the emerging political field*

The second part of the explanatory model with which we want to account for the dynamics of the social field of JHA cooperation is to embed this political field in an encompassing space of communication where actors not only struggle for positions and hierarchies, but also present themselves to an observing public.[6] Distinctive and competitive practices within the field secure their appropriateness as long as they find positive resonance with a public. The presence of the public creates specific restrictions for policy actors who, in turn, must either anticipate public resonance or react upon it. With regard to our initial question of how different levels of international, European, and domestic politics are structurally integrated, we will argue that the dynamics of the emerging

---

[6] The use of the term 'space' in this context is intentional. A space is distinct from a field by its three-dimensionality. The public in this conceptual order constitutes, thus, the third dimension in a communicative space where European institutions and non-institutional actors compete with each other.

political field of JHA cooperation unfolds as a new *transnational resonance structure*. This structure provides a mode of integrating the differentiated architecture of multi-level governance as a particular dimension of social order beyond the national will.

The term *transnational resonance structure* refers to the structural requisites of monitoring the political field in which national and transnational policy actors interact. Three analytical elements are essential for public monitoring (Schudson 1989). The first element is 'retrievability' which measures the probability of being exposed to transnational communication. The second element is transnational 'communicability' which describes the degree to which material and ideational interests can be exchanged across languages and life-worlds. The third element is 'narrative fidelity' which measures the ease with which a public is able to recognize the meaning of what is communicated.

Transnational resonance structures transcend institutionalized responses to political issues and often result in surprises for the institutions involved. The 'people's voice' is different from the 'institutional voice', and it is uttered in a political field, in which public observation is linked back to social carriers outside the institutional confines, that is, to the people in Europe.

The emergence of transnational resonance structures is, first of all, an effect of the differentiated architecture of multi-level governance itself. The loose coupling between different arenas of policy-making in the compounded European polity (Benz, this volume) creates grey zones of partial overlap where the institutional grip of the different levels of decision-making is overdetermined. This is where non-institutionalized social action comes in. A semi-political class and a semi-public emerge, which occupy these spaces. The social relations (or networks) which emerge in these spaces go unnoticed by political institutions until the actors in these spaces go public. Thus, positions for observing institutions can be established (and even institutionalized) that are autonomous from the national as well as from the supra-national (i.e. European) institutional space. This is the structural basis of the evolving public space in Europe.[7]

---

[7] From such an analytical point of view it is no longer necessary to assume that a European public sphere is structurally similar to the national public sphere (Gerhards 1993). The coincidence of national society, political state, and public sphere characteristic for the nation state is in a historical–comparative perspective a transitory phenomenon, which probably even never existed. We neither expect a supra-national public sphere in Europe nor a public sphere made up of the sum of the publics of its member states. Therefore, we prefer the term 'transnational' for describing a public sphere in Europe (Eder 2000).

Another reason for the development of transnational resonance structures can be found in the changing relation of European political institutions to their social environment (March and Olsen 1995: 183–240). European institutions encounter a society, which makes claims for its return into the European institutional system (Eder 2000). The effects of this encounter can be described as the turn from institutional 'self-reference' to 'outside-reference', or as the turn from secrecy to publicity and transparency. Institutions observe and interpret their environment. At the same time, they are observed and interpreted by their environment. In this constellation political institutions anticipate and react to the public voice of society. They do so through public relations (PR) and symbolic politics. Institutions become responsive to external claims which create a particular institutional resonance and also absorb public resonance directed towards them.

To summarize, transnational resonance is the effect of an interactive process of claims making, contentious politics, protest, or consensus[8] on the one hand and institutional responsiveness (or non-responsiveness) on the other. The former is characterized by a series of claims, opinions, attitudes, and actions that sometimes follow national traditions, sometimes cut across them, and sometimes only apply to specific issues. The latter is shaped by supra-national and/or national actors who sometimes cooperate, and sometimes compete with regard to policy decisions that are to be taken on the European level. Transnational resonance structures are established at the crossroads between the performance of power measured as institutional resonance on the one hand, and the political contentions reacting to it as measured in public resonance on the other.[9] Thus, our first argument is that the encounter of the inside resonance and outside resonance shapes the logic of the political field. Our second argument is that we find in this encounter the core of an emerging European public sphere.[10] Public spaces develop—we claim—as a by-product of the multi-level expansion of political institutions.

---

[8] Furthermore, silence is a form of reaction to the social environment of political institutions. In the context of European integration this silence has been named 'permissive consensus' which already indicates that we are dealing here with a genuinely European resonance structure. In the following, we add to this form of reaction non-permissive reactions or dissensus as a mode of generating European resonance structures.

[9] Measurement problems can be solved by survey data as well as by data on the amount of public communicative events produced by political institutions.

[10] This idea of a public space is close to the functional–sociological understanding of an intermediary realm between state and society (Neidhardt 1994).

Table 6.1 Types of European public spheres

Civic voicing	Institutional responsiveness	
	+	−
+	(a) The 'postclassic modern public sphere' (cooperative games between institutions and civil society)	(b) The 'classic modern public sphere' (beleaguering of institutions by civil society)
−	(c) The 'manipulated public sphere' (civil society becoming the object of symbolic politics)	(d) The 'indifferent public sphere' (the permissive consensus of civil society)

6.2.3 Transnational resonance structures and the evolving public sphere in Europe

We assume that transnational resonance is shaped by two factors: (1) the communicative responsiveness of institutions and (2) the amount of claims making by social actors addressing these institutions. In the following, the interplay between institutional responsiveness and civic voicing provides the variables which account for the variation of the resonance structures in an emerging transnational public sphere in Europe.[11] The combination of both factors, defined as institutional responsiveness and civic voicing, results in four types of European public spheres (Table 6.1).

These four types of public spheres can be systematically linked to the dynamics of JHA cooperation. Type (d) largely reflects the situation of the permissive consensus before the institutional expansion of cooperation took place: non-responsive institutions and no claims for civic participation. The silence of the public is not only a potential source of opposition and resistance; but a silent public is also a breeding ground for anti-European affects. The political integration of JHA has once and for all broken with this tradition of silent integration. It represents a case in which political elites depend on public resonance of their activities[12] and public voice is likely to find expression.

---

[11] This question of how communication leads to integration calls for building on the tradition of early integration theory, in particular, that of Karl W. Deutsch (1953) who argued essentially that increasing transnational communication and transnational action would lead ultimately to European society and community-building.

[12] This is the irony of security politics. For governments who have tried to hide behind the walls of the fortress, secrecy itself becomes part of the performance in front of the public.

The cases covered by the types (b) and (c) refer to the unilateral expression of resonance. Both types are rather unstable and transitory, depending on the reaction of those who are addressed by the communication. Type (b) describes the situation, where active publics relate to arcane practices of domination which exclude citizens from participation in decision-making processes. This is the 'classic modern' public sphere. Non-responsive institutional settings are challenged by the active citizens who mistrust institutions. Regarding the field of JHA, informal intergovernmentalism is perceived as a 'fortress' to be assaulted from the outside. The experience of JHA shows that secrecy in the form of 'negative' institutional resonance can have positive effects upon the mobilization of the public as long as there are critical citizens who demand to be informed about what is going on behind the closed doors of the Council. When institutions start to become responsive, an expansion of the public space takes place: type (b) is likely to result in type (a).

Type (c) describes the case of anticipative action on the part of the institutions which try to mobilize public support for their activities. In the field of JHA, the underlying security ideology is used as a justificatory account. A good example is the staging of PR campaigns like the European Year Against Racism by the Commission. 'Negative' civic resonance gives elite actors the opportunity to improve their ideological responsiveness and to impress their electorates through public performances. Institutions try to outbid the silence of the public by taking initiatives which provoke public resonance. When the civic public becomes responsive also this case is likely to result in an expansion of the public sphere: type (c) turns into a case of type (a).

Finally, we expect type (a) to develop towards a competitive public sphere between civic voice and institutional responsiveness. The most likely result is not public deliberation of institutions or rational communication among enlightened citizens, but a 'mediatized' public sphere held together by symbolic politics. In response to anticipative legitimization campaigns, launched by political institutions in search of a supportive audience, critical citizens turn to symbolic counter-mobilizations (as the debate on the 'fortress Europe' has shown). Such symbolic struggles can be expected to penetrate the media. 'Dramatized' European politics becomes a media event followed by a media public.[13] This logic of symbolic contestation is grasped by the term of a 'postclassic modern' public sphere.

---

[13] See, for instance, the public conflict about the implementation of the Schengen Treaty and the control of external borders in the case of Italy. Any new arrival of refugees at Italy's southern coasts provokes a media campaign, playing off European security interests against international human rights (Trenz 2001).

This model proposes the following paths for empirical research. First, it requires to confront the social relations and carriers of public monitoring (the 'civic public') and the network of national and supra-national policy actors (the responsive or anticipative institutions). In addition, the model requires the analysis of the impact of transnational communication on domestic *and* supra-national politics. Transnational resonance has given legitimacy to supra-national institution-building and to the extension of Communitarian powers. At the same time, European politics permeates national governance—not in the sense of restricting it, but of making it more dynamic and enlarging the scope of action of domestic policy actors. Transnational resonance is utilized, then, on both sides by different actors with the effect of transforming the political field of European politics into a public space. Looking at the dynamics of JHA provides a first step toward the empirical substantiation of this proposed model.

6.3 The dynamics of 'justice and home affairs'

The primary assumption of the following analysis is that public monitoring fosters stronger cooperation between national governments, EU organs, and other kinds of institutionalized or non-institutionalized actors within the transnational political fields of European governance. From this follows the hypothesis that intergovernmental forms of policy-making will cede to more explicit and regulated forms of policy the more public monitoring gains ground in the policy area. Accordingly, the empirical exploration of the field of JHA will proceed as follows: First, it will be analysed how and to what extent transnational resonance structures provide new windows of opportunity and legitimation for national and sub-national actors which foster the Europeanization of national governance. Second, evidence will be provided for the assumption that the spread of transnational resonance in the case of JHA leads to the slow dismantling of intergovernmental forms of cooperation which stabilize the standard form of multi-level governance.

6.3.1 The Europeanization of domestic politics

The growing impact of EU governance on domestic politics can hardly be put into question. In this sense, European policies are open to support and approval, but also to suspicion and delegitimation by national publics in the member states. This reproduces the 'classic modern' situation of a public sphere where civic actors relate to institutions as their enemy. In the case of JHA this critical public is constituted by active citizens who are challenged by the suspicious secrecy of their governments to engage in *state-watching* activities[14] and who demand to be informed about what is going on behind the closed doors of the Council. The parallel Europeanization of different national publics and the interactive effects to be expected from spreading public discontent and dissent would then lead to the emergence of a European critical public sphere (type (b) of our matrix).

However, the harmonization of JHA also points into another direction. Over the last years, the 'framing' of security politics in the EU has established the image of the *protective Union* as a collective point of reference with the purpose of pleasing the collective feelings of threat and insecurity of the European citizens (Kostakopoulou 2000). From this perspective, the impact of EU governance on domestic politics can be explained in large part by the symbolic aspects of JHA cooperation. The ability of national governmental actors to create at least the myth of the importance of the EU seems to be of crucial importance for enlarging their scope of action in domestic politics (Wolf 1999). In such strategic two-level games a new European justificatory rhetoric emerges which links the formerly segmented national resonance structures together by the common reference to security as a thick signifier to make sense of the EU (Huysmans 1998). The parallel symbolic mobilization of different national publics would then be the case for the emergence of a manipulated European public sphere (type (c) of our matrix).

These effects are usually described (or criticized) in terms of a unilateral strengthening of governmental autonomy (Wolf 1999). National governmental actors as the only relevant two-level players in the EU governance system profit from their privileged access to the field of European politics in a number of ways: (a) the reference to Europe allows them to influence and control the national public and media agenda; (b) such reference reduces viable choices and policy alternatives in domestic politics; (c) it guarantees a privileged position extending their information and resource advantages toward the rhetorical opportunities of *blame avoidance*, *scapegoating* (to make others responsible for unpopular decisions), and *credit-claiming* (to profit from decisions taken by others);[15] (d) it opens a particular policy window for national decision-making (such as the restrictions of the German asylum law).

---

[14] See the emblematic name of one of the major monitoring and documentation centres on JHA in the EU (http://www.statewatch.org).

[15] For an elaboration on these discursive functions see Moravcsik (1994).

However, the subordinated domestic actors, the other party in the game, are in no way confined to falling back to particularistic attitudes or even nationalistic resentment. Due to their dependence upon the wider culture, domestic actors discover that their interests lie in defending policy arrangements not as locally legitimate, but rather as instances of more universal rules. In doing so, they can easily use the same strategy of symbolic reference to Europe to break the monopoly of governments in defining legitimate forms of a European order.[16] One way to do so, is to turn symbolic mobilization into symbolic counter-mobilization, that is, to replace the positive image of the 'European security community' by the negative image of the 'fortress Europe'. This would represent the case of a 'postclassic modern' public sphere in Europe (type (a) of our matrix).

This is what we observe to be the domestic response to governmental attempts at pushing the new security agenda in Europe (Trenz 2002). Transnational resonance structures are strengthened by making increasing use of the normative force of 'world models' to induce domestic change. Where national governments have not adopted such 'world-approved' politics, local units and other domestic actors carry out or enforce conformity (Meyer et al. 1997: 161). In the JHA case, the reference to Europe allows national and sub-national civic actors (a) to enlarge the domestic agenda, introducing new issues, ideas, and perspectives, (b) to improve their control capacities in adjusting national policies to conform to world models or specific European justificatory discourses,[17] (c) to gain authority and legitimacy as the moral voice of the people, and (d) to break up political stalemates and immobility, thus making domestic politics more dynamic and conflictive.

Of particular importance is the 'boomerang pattern' identified as an agenda-setting and lobbying strategy by sub-national actors (Keck and Sikkink 1998: 12; Risse, Ropp, and Sikkink 1999). When channels of public intermediation are blocked at the state level, the excluded domestic groups might bypass their respective governments and directly search international or European allies to try to pressure their states from outside. This can be regarded as a case of a direct linkage of supra-national and national politics through the effects of transnational resonance. In Europe, such

---

[16] Examples would be the 'Europe of freedom and justice', the 'open and tolerant Europe' or the 'European solidarity community'. In particular, the 'power of human rights' to introduce domestic change has become the focus of attention (Risse, Ropp, and Sikkink 1999).

[17] Even citizenship law and practice seem to obey the legitimating force of such global models. Particular attempts of nation states to stick to models which deviate from global trends (Germany) are doomed to failure.

boomerang patterns are part of the new opportunity structure for collective action which encourages the deviation of protest mobilization from the national to the supra-national level. In the case of JHA, the boomerang pattern is regularly used by migrant and ethnic minorities with regard to human rights enforcement (Soysal 1996). Basically all European institutions, including the Council, the Commission, the Parliament, and in the near future probably also the Court of Justice, have been mobilized for this purpose.

However, the reorientation of domestic actors proceeds at a slow speed. It is easier to kick off processes of adaptation in the open and flexible European environment than in the complex web of national politics. Therefore, linking European with national and sub-national politics encounters many hurdles. National and sub-national actors have difficulties moving within the European field. Contrary to what many movement activists claim, namely to 'think globally and act locally' (Rucht 1993), the new European opportunity structure is only rarely used by national or sub-national actors. Existing links between local and communitarian politics are weak and highly artificial. For many local activists, networking is more a question of prestige than of actual use. Similarly, the significance of transnational networking for national policy actors is often overestimated. Being part of a broader network does not necessarily imply fundamental changes in the logic of group action (Trenz 2001).

Migrant groups acting on the Community level, on the other hand, are largely detached from domestic constraints and alienated from their social base. They are enclosed in the small but privileged Brussels world of interpersonal relations, mutual favours, and shared experiences (Favell 1998). In addition, many civic actors tend to reproduce deficits of democratic performance within their intra-organizational context. All too often, networks conceal hidden hierarchies instead of achieving the mediation between the European and the local level and vice versa. The inclusion of civic associations has so far not contributed significantly to improving transparency and openness towards the public. Instead, informal cooperation is maintained and intensifies the rather opaque nature of the EU political process (Trenz 2001). In this context, mediation between the European and the local level is blocked by both sides or, at best, takes place through intermediate, that is, national institutions.

At this point, we resume our central theoretical argument which is to explain the Europeanizing effect on domestic politics not as the result of a rational game of power between European and national policy actors, but rather as the result of a transnational resonance structure constraining the interaction of these actors. Patterns of transnational discourse and communication are, as Snow and Benford (1999) have already argued, crucial for explaining cross-national diffusion effects. In the field of JHA, the framing of policy issues takes place within a set of highly moralized beliefs and practices. Europeanization is embedded in increasing communication over policy-making whereby the attribution of responsibility is no longer confined to internal communication between policy actors, but instead is shared with the political field integrated increasingly by transnational resonance structures.

The dynamics of symbolic mobilization and counter-mobilization proves to be of crucial importance as an integrative mechanism of the field of JHA across different national contexts. The symbolic struggle over Europe is principally carried out using (and even instrumentalizing) the domestic space. Through symbolic mobilization, the actors competing within the field can push their interests, establish public constituencies of support, expand their skills and, maybe less tangibly but just as importantly, stimulate shifts in loyalty and establish some sense of a common identity. Political campaigns are a way of channelling protest from the transnational into the national and the local and vice versa. The issues and claims of such campaigns often originate from collective action within the European political field, and campaigners try to push them into domestic as well as intergovernmental decision arenas. Anti-racism is a good case to corroborate this point: The campaigning activities of transnational anti-racist movement have unfolded between European and national politics setting the agenda for anti-discrimination and affirmative action policies all over Europe (linked to different claims such as dual citizenship, affirmative action, protection of minorities, religious education, etc.). At the same time, anti-racism has penetrated the intergovernmental arenas where new standards and procedures of protection at the European level are formulated (Trenz 1999; Ruzza 2000).[18]

Thus, symbolic mobilization over Europe moves the European public space toward the type (a) of postclassic public sphere (type (a) of our matrix). For the time being, the structure of transnational resonance in Europe is still limited to the reciprocal observation among different Europeanized national publics. But national publics in Europe are no longer fragmented. They can make sense of similar experiences and use common patterns of discourse. They make complaints and articulate protest. They open conflicts about burden sharing and compliance with

---

[18] See the newly established Article 13 TEU.

Community law (e.g. the allocation of refugees, the control of external borders, and the implementation of Schengen). The probable result is the emergence of European cleavage structures which manifest themselves in new modes of symbolic contestation. This turn from fragmentation to polarization, from dissonance to resonance is the first step toward the evolution of the postclassic public sphere in Europe.

6.3.2 From intergovernmental negotiations to multi-level governance

How does this evolution affect the logic of EU policy-making? Transnational resonance has pushed the closed box of JHA cooperation into the realm of the public. To put such emphasis on the effects of transnational resonance is not to ignore the reality of the 'protective Union' (Kostakopoulou 2000). It does not deny the growing control capacities of governments in the process of extending self-binding political cooperation (Wolf 1999). But it is important to note that intergovernmental cooperation develops a dynamic which slowly, but steadily leads to the demolition of its own structural prerequisites. The new security ideology, which is used by governmental power to legitimate itself before a national electorate, might result in many small Pyrrhic victories which are gained at the cost of succumbing to the logic of public discourse, thus, *reintroducing* its normative principles into public debate and *reopening* the game of power and legitimacy.

This is the basic mechanism underlying the institutional transformation of JHA cooperation. Forms of intergovernmental cooperation are difficult to maintain in a policy area which is of high public relevance and under continual public observation. From the standpoint of supra-national governance, the 'constitutionalization' of JHA can be regarded as the proactive and cooperative response to public demands for participation and institutional openness. From the standpoint of national governance, the slowing down of policy cooperation or the opt out choice, as in the British case, would be the alternative response to public resonance.[19]

A first indicator for such changes is the constitution of a transnational 'community' of critical publics. The experience of JHA shows that even secrecy in the form of 'negative' institutional resonance can have positive effects upon the mobilization of the public, as long as there are critical citizens who are willing to participate in European politics and engage in

---

[19] For the remarkable case of the British 'No' to Schengen despite the shared interests of cooperation expressed by the government see Wiener (2000).

transnational networking activities. Non-governmental organizations (NGOs) and social movements active within the European field have developed social capital in the form of personal acquaintances and channels of informal access. They have learned to see the EU as a field for privileged social relations that can be strategically occupied. They have also learned that moving within the European field, far away from home constraints and control by their constituencies, might result in strategic advantages. Movement activists gain more access to first-hand information and move more independently in Brussels than they probably could at home (Favell 1998). In doing so, they have become much more competent and professional players on the transnational level, able to grasp new opportunities for collective action and mobilization.

However, the horizontal integration of the emerging political field has also led to an increasing alienation of supra-national 'civic actors' from their home constituencies. Nonetheless, also associational actors have been increasingly forced by the critical European citizens they claim to represent to turn from lobbying to public claims-making and from private to public negotiations. Under these conditions, associational actors will have to produce their own resonance in order to foster their image as legitimate representatives of the interests of the diverse local, regional, or national publics. Over the last years, public claims-making and protest mobilization has become a central part of the lobbying strategies of EU associations and are especially prevalent in the fields of anti-discrimination, citizenship, and human rights (Marks and McAdam 1999; Geddes 2000).

The power of public discourse for the introduction of political change has been increasingly recognized by the different NGOs and associations and has been reflected in their strategic choices for collective action. Different NGOs active in the JHA sector have recently presented a strategy paper, in which they define it as their first aim to stimulate European *and* national 'policy debates' on the salient issues of asylum, free movement, and integration of third-country nationals (Niessen and Rowlands 2000). The presumed contribution of such debates to a process of collective will formation allows these associations to claim that they 'reflect civil society's high expectations' on these issues (Niessen and Rowlands 2000: 8). This reference to the general will of the public endows the particularistic lobbying activity of associational actors with legitimacy.

Institutional actors, in turn, have learned that the appropriation of associational claims and interests might improve their credibility and strengthen their position in the arenas of intergovernmental negotiation. Instead of domination and conflict, the governments and the

Commission have generally developed supportive and cooperative strategies towards these associations. In the case of the Commission, this also reflects its new corporate self-understanding as the coordinator, organizer, and protector of civic activities at the supra-national level (Eder, Hellmann, and Trenz 1998).

The increasing importance of anticipating public resonance has pushed the EU institutions, and in particular the European Commission, to assume a new role as an observatory of European society. It is not a secret-service type of observation, but social-scientific observation, which measures general and policy-specific reactions in Europe.[20] The goal of the Commission in the multi-level system of European governance is to anticipate and to recollect the reactions not only of national publics of the 15 member states (e.g. through public opinion surveys), but also of the different European public constituencies which critically observe its activities (e.g. through public hearings). Professional PR strategies within the Commission show how this knowledge is transformed strategically into claims for public legitimacy (Meyer 1999).

However, anticipatory strategies of legitimation risk turning into delegitimation if the promises and expectations raised cannot be fulfilled. Running against the threat of delegitimation, institutional actors give increasing importance to the symbolic representation of EU governance. 'European politics must be more dramatic' has recently become a motto of European top politicians, who try to achieve 'the popularization of the democracy in Europe'.[21] For EU policy actors, the ability to create myths and symbols which resonate within the public may have a significant impact on their position in the negotiation arenas and encourage their willingness to collaborate (Cram 1998: 77). The strategy consists now in addressing the European public directly (and not indirectly through the staging of security politics), taking into account its unpredictable reactions.

Lastly, governments are generally perceived to serve only the demands of their own national electorate. The old strategy of intergovernmental negotiations in the field of JHA consisted in serving primarily the audience's security concerns and only secondarily its moral consciousness. Council meetings became ideological battlefields attended by different governments, proving themselves to be the best guardian of law and order. Admittedly, this was nothing more than the return to old strategies

---

[20] A recent example is the European Observatory Against Racism set up in Vienna.
[21] Daniel Cohn-Bendit in *Die Zeit*, 22 July 1999: 7. The Commission's campaign against racism can be viewed as a first example of the popularization of Europe (Trenz 1999).

of evoking national security interests and the exploitation of European cooperation for electoral politics. However, our findings have also indicated that the contingency of public communication can severely restrict the governmental scope of action (Trenz 2002). To the extent to which intergovernmental cooperation expands into multi-level governance, governments are increasingly forced to 'serve different masters'. Most importantly, the new expanding transnational publics are discovered as an alternative source of legitimacy and are increasingly recognized as such by other actors within the field (in particular by the Commission and the Parliament). Governments must now stage their policy choices for the increasingly diversified national, sub-national, and transnational publics. Under these conditions, the subordination of human rights under national sovereignty and security is no longer taken for granted. In the new 'area of justice', the enforcement of rights and democracy becomes the prerequisite for the freedom and security of individuals and society.[22]

In this new context, the practices of venue shopping in the intergovernmental arenas of cooperation (Guiraudon 2000) and credit-claiming in front of the electorate become difficult, since other actors make quite different credit claims. Our media analysis regarding the delicate issues of border checks indeed reveals that the governmental monopoly in defining the security agenda is increasingly challenged by all kinds of external supra- or transnational actors (such as international NGOs (INGOs); the Commission; members of the European Parliament (MEPs); but also governments of other member states) (Trenz 2002). As the impartial 'moral voice' of the people, the statements and initiatives of these transnational actors find approval in the media and are frequently used by domestic actors to oppose their government. Most importantly, those governments which decide to block decision-making now have to account for their choices publicly. They propagate specific justificatory discourses, symbolic devices, and claims for legitimacy without knowing in advance how the addressed and non-addressed publics will react to it.

These phenomena point to a particular mechanism of integration of multi-level governance: the integrative force of transnational resonance structures. This specific resonance structure has been measured in terms of growing attentiveness as well as concerns and expectations that are

---

[22] For an illustration, see again the change of rhetoric in the Tampere European Council. At the occasion of a more recent meeting the 'security ministers' of the EU have started to reflect on their future role in steering an active immigration policy for the EU and in preparing European citizens to live in 'multiethnic communities' (Presidency Conclusions. Informal Council Meeting on Justice and Home Affairs. Marseilles, 28 and 29 July 2000).

directed from the public towards the policy process within the emerging European field of JHA. The intensity of this resonance is measured by the growth of networks of collective action and contention.

In this field the distinction between domestic and European (foreign) affairs becomes blurred. The model of the two-level game, which identifies national governments as the relevant players between national and international politics, must therefore be replaced with a model which considers the intermediary structures of the emerging public sphere in Europe as the crucial mechanism which transforms JHA into true European affairs.

6.4 Transnational resonance structures and the symbolic integration of justice and home affairs

The analysis presented is certainly biased towards particular aspects of the policy process. However, this bias has made visible elements of a novel mode of political integration through transnational resonance that enables the recognition of positive-sum links between national and European levels of governance. Such positive-sum links are the simultaneous increase of power on both the national and the European level, the simultaneous increase of identity and loyalty on both levels, and the simultaneous increase in capacities of institutional reform on both levels. Our case study has led us to a central theoretical proposition that can be summarized as follows: *The more transnational resonance structures develop, the more positive sum games between the EU and the member states can be expected to develop.*

The programme for rebuilding JHA cooperation—as laid down in the Amsterdam Treaty and even more pronounced in the conclusion of the European Council of Tampere—clearly reflects the changing attitude of the governments in dealing with these issues. The new integrative formula of an 'area of freedom, security and justice' was welcomed by the Commission in its role as the advocate of a common good that belongs to all Europeans. In the public presentation by the newly established Directorate-General 'Justice and Internal Affairs' this is expressed as follows: 'The AFSJ concept[23] is not an invention of the Amsterdam Treaty but based on values and long-standing principles of the democracies of the EU.' As such it shall enshrine at the EU level 'the essence of what we

---

[23] EU parlance for 'area of freedom, security and justice'.

derive from our democratic traditions and what we understand by the rule of law'.[24] Clearly, these appeals for shared responsibilities have a bearing on the self-binding both of the member states and of the public. The new strategy entails presenting the new images and promises of European integration before turning to policy-making. The 'Europe of justice and of rights' is a projection, but a projection with resonance all over of Europe working against negative integration and particularistic interests.

In terms of institutional transformation, it can be expected that increasing transnational resonance will stabilize multi-level governance in Europe. Under conditions of public monitoring, multi-level governance is equipped with a normative force. As such, it is accepted as the standard model of EU governance that all actors within the field have to follow. For governments, this implies the necessity of making intergovernmental negotiation arenas transparent and opening them for participation. For civic actors, this implies the necessity of engaging in networking and of adapting their mobilization strategies to the logics of the emerging transnational political field. Multi-level governance does not necessarily result in an increase in decision-making (since the output in terms of binding policies is still small). It rather results in an increase in communication, collective action, and participation. In these terms the legitimacy of JHA cooperation will be evaluated.

We do not claim that this will bring about the sudden democratization of European politics. It is easy to criticize the importance given to PR and image campaigns as ideology and as a hidden form of power politics. What we claim, instead, is that European institutions become increasingly reflexive on the contingency of their interaction with the public. European institutions learn that the resonance of the public creates resistance and constraints that cannot be handled strategically. They learn that the pursuit of interests is only possible on the basis of arguments and the performance of public debates. It is not participation that counts here. What counts is that European institutions take on the normative premises of the public sphere as a framework for collective will formation. From this perspective, the public monitoring of the emerging European field of collective action may have contributed at least to some extent to the development of shared assumptions and expectations about transparency, democracy, and rights to which the institutional structure of EU governance can no longer remain unresponsive.

---

[24] This is the wording used in the presentation of JHA by the Commission on its website (http://europa.eu.int/comm/dgs/justice_home/mission/resp_en.htm). See also Commission of the European Union (1998).

References

Bunyan, Tony (1991). 'Towards an Authoritarian European State', *Race & Class*, 32: 19-27.
Buzan, Barry, Waever, Ole, and de Wilde, Jaap (1998). *Security: A New Framework of Analysis*. Boulder: Lynne Rienner Publishers.
Checkel, Jeffrey (1998). 'The Constructivist Turn in International Relations Theory', *World Politics*, 50/2: 324-48.
Christiansen, Thomas, Jørgensen, Knud E., and Wiener, Antje (1999). 'The Social Construction of European Integration', *Journal of European Public Policy*, 6/4: 528-44.
Commission of the European Union (1998). *Toward an Area of Freedom, Security and Justice*. Com (1998) 459 final. Luxembourg: Office for Official Publications of the European Communities.
Cowles, Maria Green, Caporaso, James, and Risse, Thomas (eds.) (2001). *Transforming Europe. Europeanization and Domestic Change*. Ithaca: Cornell University Press.
Cram, Laura (1998). 'The EU Institutions and Collective Action: Constructing a European Interest?', in Justin Greenwood and Mark Aspinwall (eds.), *Collective Action in the European Union. Interests and the New Politics of Associability*. London: Routledge, 63-80.
den Boer, Monica (1994). 'The Quest for European Policing. Rhetoric and Justification in a Disorderly Debate', in Malcolm Anderson and Monica den Boer (eds.), *Policing across National Boundaries*. London: Pinter Publisher, 174-96.
—— and Wallace, William (2000). 'Justice and Home Affairs: Integration through Incrementalism?', in Helen Wallace and William Wallace (eds.), *Policy Making in the European Union*. Oxford: Oxford University Press, 493-519.
Deutsch, Karl W. (1953). *Nationalism and Social Communication: An Inquiry into the Foundations of Nationality*. Cambridge: MIT Press.
Eder, Klaus (2000). 'Zur Transformation nationalstaatlicher Öffentlichkeit in Europa. Von der Sprachgemeinschaft zur issuespezifischen Kommunikationsgemeinschaft', *Berliner Journal für Soziologie*, 10/2: 167-284.
——, Hellman, Kai-Uwe, and Trenz, Hans (1998). 'Regieren in Europa jenseits öffentlicher Legitimation? Eine Untersuchung zur Rolle von politischer Öffentlichkeit in Europa', in Beate Kohler-Koch (ed.), *Regieren in entgrenzten Räumen* (Special Issue of Politische Vierteljahresschrift, Vol. 29). Opladen: Westdeutscher Verlag, 321-44.
Favell, Adrian (1998). 'The Europeanisation of Immigration politics', *European Integration online Papers*, 2/10.
Geddes, Andrew (2000). *Immigration and European Integration*. Manchester: Manchester University Press.
Gerhards, Jürgen (1993). 'Westeuropäische Integration und die Schwierigkeiten der Entstehung einer europäischen Öffentlichkeit', *Zeitschrift für Soziologie*, 22/2: 96-110.
Greenwood, Justin and Aspinwall, Mark (eds.) (1998). *Collective Action in the European Union: Interests and the New Politics of Associability*. London: Routledge.
Guild, Elspeth (1996). *The Developing Immigration and Asylum Policies of the European Union*. The Hague: Kluwer.
Guiraudon, Virginie (2000). 'European Integration and Migration Policy: Vertical Policy-Making as Venue Shopping', *Journal of Common Market Studies*, 38/2: 251-71.

Huysmans, Jef (1998). 'Security! What Do You Mean? From Concept to Thick Signifier', *European Journal of International Relations*, 4/2: 226-55.

Jachtenfuchs, Markus (1999). *Ideen und Integration. Verfassungsideen in Deutschland, Großbritannien und Frankreich und die Entwicklung der EU* (Habilitationsschrift). Mannheim: Universität Mannheim.

Keck, Margaret E. and Sikkink, Kathryn (1998). *Activists Beyond Borders: Advocacy Networks in International Politics*. Ithaca: Cornell University Press.

Kohler-Koch, Beate (2000). 'Framing. The Bottleneck of Constructing Legitimate Institutions', *Journal of European Public Policy*, 774: 513-31.

Kostakopoulou, Theodora (2000). 'The "Protective Union": Change and Continuity in Migration Law and Policy in Post-Amsterdam Europe', *Journal of Common Market Studies*, 38/3: 497-518.

Lavenex, Sandra (1999). *The Europeanisation of Refugee Policies. Between Human Rights and International Security* (doctoral thesis). Florence: European University Institute.

Leuthardt, Beat (1994). *Festung Europa: Asyl, Drogen, 'organisierte Kriminalität': die innere Sicherheit der 80er und 90er Jahre und ihre Feindbilder. Ein Handbuch*. Zürich: Rotpunktverlag.

March, James G. and Olsen, Johan P. (1995). *Democratic Governance*. New York: Free Press.

Marks, Gary and McAdam, Doug (1996). 'Social Movements and the Changing Structure of Political Opportunity in the European Union', *West European Politics*, 19/2: 249-78.

—— and McAdam, Doug (1999). 'On the Relationship of Political Opportunities to the Form of Collective Action. The Case of the European Union', in Donatella della Porta, Hanspeter Kriesi, and Dieter Rucht (eds.), *Social Movements in a Globalizing World*. London: Macmillan, 97-111.

Meyer, Christoph Olaf (1999). 'Political Legitimacy and the Invisibility of Politics. Exploring the European Union's Communication Deficit', *Journal of Common Market Studies*, 37/4: 617-39.

Meyer, John W., Boli, John, Thomas, George M., and Ramirez, Francisco O. (1997). 'World Society and the Nation-State', *American Journal of Sociology*, 103/1: 144-81.

Moravcsik, Andrew (1994). *Why the European Community Strengthens the State: Domestic Politics and International Cooperation* (Working Paper Series, No. 52). Cambridge: Centre for European Studies.

Neidhardt, Friedhelm (1994). 'Öffentlichkeit, öffentliche Meinung, soziale Bewegungen', in Friedhelm Neidhardt (ed.), *Öffentlichkeit, öffentliche Meinung, soziale Bewegungen* (Special Issue of Kölner Zeitschrift für Soziologie und Sozialpsychologie, Vol. 34). Opladen: Westdeutscher Verlag, 7-41.

Nentwich, Michael (1996). 'Opportunity Structures for Citizens' Participation. The Case of the European Union', *European Integration online Papers*, 0/1.

Niessen, Jan, and Rowlands, Susan (2000). *The Amsterdam Proposals or How to Influence Policy Debates on Asylum and Immigration*. Brussels: European Network against Racism (ENAR), Immigration Law Practitioners' Association (ILPA) and Migration Policy Group (MPG).

Pauly, Alexis (ed.) (1996). *De Schengen à Maastricht: Voie royale et course d'obstacles*. Maastricht: Institut Européen d'Administration Publique.

Reising, Uwe K. H. (1998). 'Domestic and Supranational Political Opportunities: European Protest in Selected Countries 1980-1995', *European Integration online Papers*, 2/5.

Risse, Thomas, Ropp, Stephen C., and Sikkink, Kathryn (eds.) (1999). *The Power of Human Rights. International Norms and Domestic Change*. Cambridge: Cambridge University Press.

Rucht, Dieter (1993). ' "Think Globally, Act Locally"? Needs, Forms and Problems of Cross-National Cooperation among Environmental Groups', in J. Duncan Liefferink, Phillip D. Lowe, and Arthur P. J. Mol (eds.), *European Integration and Environmental Policy*. London: Belhaven Press, 75-95.

Ruzza, Carlo (2000). 'Anti-Racism and EU Institutions', *Journal of European Integration*, 22/2: 145-72.

Schudson, Michael (1989). 'How Culture Works. Perspectives from Media Studies in the Efficacy of Symbols', *Theory and Society*, 18: 153-80.

Snow, David A. and Benford, Robert D. (1999). 'Alternative Types of Cross-national Diffusion in the Social Movement Arena', in Donatella della Porta, Hanspeter Kriesi, and Dieter Rucht (eds.), *Social Movements in a Globalizing World*. London: Macmillan, 23-39.

Soysal, Yasemin N. (1993). 'Immigration and the Emerging European Polity', in Kjell A. Eliassen and Svein S. Anderson (eds.), *Making Policy in Europe: The Europification of National Policy Making*. London: Sage, 171-86.

—— (1996). *Boundaries and Identity: Immigrants in Europe* (EUI Working Papers, EUF 96/03). Florence: European University Institute.

Trenz, Hans-Jörg (1999). 'Anti-Rassismus Kampagnen und Protestmobilisierung in Europa', *Forschungsjournal Neue Soziale Bewegungen*, 12/4: 78-84.

—— (2001). 'Global Denken—Lokal Handeln. Zur Mobilisierungslogik von Migranteninteressen in Europa', in Ansgar Klein, Ruud Koopmans, and Roland Roth (eds.), *Globalisierung, Partizipation, Protest*. Opladen: Leske + Budrich, 179-205.

—— (2002). *Zur Konstitution politischer Öffentlichkeit in Europa. Zivilgesellschaftliche Subpolitik oder schaupolitische Inszenierung?* Baden-Baden: Nomos.

Wallace, Helen (2000). 'Flexibility: A Tool of Integration or a Restraint on Disintegration?', in Karlheinz Neunreither and Antje Wiener (eds.), *European Integration after Amsterdam. Institutional Dynamics and Prospects for Democracy*. Oxford: Oxford University Press, 175-91.

Wiener, Antje (2000). *Forging Flexibility—the British 'No' to Schengen* (ARENA Working Papers, 00/1). Oslo: ARENA.

Wolf, Klaus Dieter (1999). 'Defending State Autonomy. Intergovernmental Governance in the EU', in Beate Kohler-Koch and Rainer Eising (eds.), *The Transformation of Governance in the European Union*. London: Routledge, 230-47.

7

Policy-Making in Fragmented Systems: How to Explain Success

Hubert Heinelt, Tanja Kopp-Malek, Jochen Lang, and Bernd Reissert

7.1 The capacity for reform of EU structural funds: A hypothesis and an empirical puzzle

Since the 1950s, the European structural funds (ESF) have been the most important policy instrument of redistribution between European regions and accordingly between people living in these regions. Today, about one-third of the Community budget is spent within the framework of the structural funds. Over the decades, the structural funds have not only grown dramatically in size, but have also undergone a series of wide-ranging reforms that have changed their objectives as well as their programming, funding, and implementation structures. The most important of these reforms can be characterized as follows (Benz and also Lang, this volume):

(1) the development of joint programming and implementation of regional interventions involving European Union (EU), national and sub-national actors;
(2) correspondingly, the institutionalization of the partnership principle, which empowers sub-national actors as well as social partners.

The history of the EU structural funds points towards a continuous capacity for reform and thereby does not confirm the 'joint decision trap' hypothesis (Scharpf 1988) that is so often associated with policy-making in the EU multi-level system. How can this capacity for reform be explained, taking into account the specific conditions of redistributive policies (Heinelt 1996: 18–19; Scharpf 2001)? The establishment of the structural funds as a redistributive policy has often been explained by reference to the logic of package deals and side-payments in the context of major steps of European integration. But is this sufficient? Furthermore, what is the explanation for the continued development of the structural funds and their relatively high stability or acceptance over time?

In some of the previous literature (Marks 1993; Heinelt and Smith 1996; Hooghe 1996a; Staeck 1997), the main hypothesis has been that specific policy networks (or actor structures and actor relations) matter. According to this hypothesis, the structural funds and their development can be characterized as follows (Heinelt 1996: 16-18):

1. Close actor relations are not only situatively present on the European level at particular points in time when decisions are made pertaining to programme structures and budgeting. Due to the specific requirements of the policy which demand that concrete funding measures must be dealt with according to programme targets and that the flow of EU subsidies must be coordinated with national funds and individual national funding programmes, permanent policy networks had to be created on the implementation level. These implementation networks now form a permanent structure. Moreover, the actors involved have established a 'policy community' (Heclo and Wildasky 1974: 389) held together—across the EU, the national and the sub-national level—by common interpretations of situations, problem definitions as well as perspectives of a 'good policy' over the course of the years.
2. The decision network in which decisions are made about funding objectives and resources after individual programme periods have expired consists of an institutionalized structure made up of member states and the Commission. However, this decision network does not exist in isolation from the implementation networks, which were formed and stabilized while the programme was being implemented. This is the case because both the Commission and the departments of national governments as well as the actors directly involved in the implementation processes are continuously integrated into them (e.g. in the so-called monitoring committees).
3. Due to the high stability and continuity of the policy networks of the structural funds, redistribution and funding objectives, funding resources and the implementation of funding objectives remain a constant theme among the actors involved. Thus, these networks represent 'organized feedback loops' in a multi-level policy arena (Marks 1993: 403). This allows policy reactions to be continually taken up and tackled in political processes which not only relate to problems of implementation, but also to those of policy formation. This in turn may result in learning processes, which alter policies concerning the EU structural funds.

This seems to be a nice and theoretically convincing hypothesis. However, our own empirical research on the historical development of the structural funds from the 1950s to the end of the 1990s as well as their implementation in selected member states (Heinelt et al. 2001; Lang 2003; Malek 2002) raises some doubt on the validity of this hypothesis. According to our findings, there is little evidence for a highly integrated policy network, which might create 'organized feedback loops' between policy implementation and policy reform. On the contrary, in the policy field under consideration there is considerable evidence for a high degree of fragmentation within the policy network. Fragmentation can be observed at least along four different lines:

1. Vertical fragmentation between implementation and policy reform networks in the member states: European decision-making on the revision of structural fund regulations as well as on funding objectives and the allocation of resources at the EU level is prepared by top-level representatives of the member states (together with the Commission) who lack close contact with actors involved in the implementation of the structural funds. The key players in reform processes build a decision arena of their own without close links to the implementation of the funds.
2. Horizontal fragmentation of policy-specific implementation networks in the member states: Within the member states (though to varying degrees), administrative structures (as well as their surrounding societal networks) are fragmented along the lines of the different funds and policy areas. Implementation networks in the field of regional policy (i.e. the European Regional Development Fund, ERDF), for example, hardly ever interact with implementation networks in the field of labour market policy (i.e. the ESF). This fragmentation is encouraged by the variation of implementation rules and routines between different policies concerned.
3. Horizontal fragmentation of fund-specific actor structures within the European Commission: In much the same way as it is the case in the member states, administrative structures within the Commission are fragmented into different directorates-general (DGs), each of which is responsible for a separate fund.
4. Vertical fragmentation between implementation and policy reform networks in the Commission: Within each DG, the so-called geographical units, which are responsible for implementation in the different member states, are clearly separated from the so-called horizontal units, which are responsible for coordination and more general 'political' tasks, including policy reform.

These fragmentations are not only formal organizational features. They shape formal and informal interactions and influence communication and, thus, the transfer of experience and knowledge. In the light of these fragmentations, policy reforms in the field of the EU structural funds cannot be explained by the existence of a single closely knit policy network that encompasses both policy implementation and policy reform and by direct, permanent personal interactions between actors in such a single policy community. What are the implications of this? How can the original hypothesis on the decisive importance of policy networks for the development of the EU structural funds be modified in the light of these findings?

7.2 The relevance of differentiation and loose coupling

Our longitudinal analysis of decision-making processes pertaining to the structural funds as well as the analysis of relations or linkages between the implementation in the member states and the decision-making at the EU level do not question the relevance of such linkages *per se* but instead critically examine their nature. Contrary to our initial considerations and hypothesis, linkages between the different actors and levels do not exist as tightly coupled horizontal and vertical links, but occur at most as loosely coupled structures. On the basis of this finding, our modified hypothesis maintains that governability as well as policy reforms in the field of the structural funds are the result of loose coupling between relatively autonomous actors.

The expression 'loose coupling' has its origin in older approaches developed in connection with organization studies. These approaches emphasized that a coupled part within an organization as well as an organization coupled with other organizations can secure 'its own identity and some evidence of its physical or logical separateness' (Weick 1976: 3), although each unit is dependent on the others as well as exerting influence on them. Based on the observation that the notion of 'loose coupling' had become increasingly used—and thereby more and more blurred—Orton and Weick (1990) clarified relevant meanings of the concept in a way which is instructive for our considerations, too. Orton and Weick (1990: 204-5) draw a distinction between an 'unidimensional' and a 'dialectical interpretation' of loose coupling. The first interpretation considers tight and loose coupling as extremes and, therefore, puts systems characterized by closeness and openness or by 'independent' and 'responsive components' in opposite categories. In contrast, the 'dialectical interpretation' of loose coupling (we adopt in this article) emphasizes the simultaneity of closeness and openness as well as of 'distinctiveness' and 'responsiveness'. This interpretation highlights the fact that units separated by processes of differentiation are able to secure autonomy and to develop and to stabilize specific logics of and orientations for action, although they are still depending on and interacting with each other (Orton and Weick 1990: 205). This increases the opportunities to act more adequately with respect to specific problems and situations, while at the same time being orientated towards common objectives and linked by predominant rules. Thus, it is just the simultaneity of coordination and autonomy or, in other words, the ambiguity of overarching objectives and rules and case- and actor-related selectivity that creates the conditions under which developments can occur quite quickly and, therefore, adaptability can be secured (Weick 1985: 164–5).

This applies not least to changes which can be related to the term 'organizational learning'. This is especially the case with regard to approaches concerned with 'unconventional forms' of organizational learning (Wiesenthal 1995)[1] which can be connected to the concept of loose coupling. Since approaches of 'unconventional forms' of organizational learning question the ability of organizations to control the boundaries separating them from their environments, they emphasize the sensitiveness of organizations to external influences and thereby draw attention to organizational learning by 'intrusion', that is, by 'invasion' of new members with other 'ideas' and new knowledge, tolerable 'dissidence' of members, and 'intersection' of organizations with different rules, cognitive maps, etc. (Wiesenthal 1995: 145–7). Therefore, they are orientated towards options of policy development and organizational change which are related to the simultaneity of closeness and openness as well as to 'connectedness' and 'autonomy'.

With regard to our research findings, the concept of loose coupling suggests on the one hand that we should take the observed phenomena of differentiation seriously—that is,

(1) the internal organizational differentiation of collective actors;[2]
(2) the problem-related and functional differentiation (sequentialization) of decisions on the different levels of policy-making as well as the

---

[1] The expression 'unconventional forms' of organizational learning is used in contrast to 'conventional forms' of organizational learning developed by Argyris (1976) as well as Argyris and Schön (1978).

[2] See, for such phenomena, the analysis of Renate Mayntz. According to her research findings a 'strong internal differentiation of the politico-administrative system' is related to the

sequentialization of decisions on the different levels involved in terms of a break-up of the entire reform project into manageable issues that are repeatedly processed on various levels of the decision system;

(3) the functional differentiation between a decision-making arena on the EU level and implementation arenas in the member states/regions.[3]

On the other hand, we have to consider coherence mechanisms, which can bring about loose coupling of the differentiated 'phenomena'. Such coherence mechanisms comprise accepted rules and norms for the exchange of information and the coordination of actions. They can be subdivided into:

(1) shared values relevant in negotiations;
(2) informal and formal norms for procedures (procedural norms);
(3) coupling institutions where interactions are bound within a specific organizational context;
(4) 'ideas' or paradigms which suggest specific objectives for actions as well as problem definitions and measures through which problems can be solved and objectives can be reached;
(5) the anticipation of a possible authoritative final decision of a not directly involved authority, that is, the 'shadow of hierarchy' within an organization or the option of a political decision on a higher level in negotiation systems.

While the mentioned phenomena of differentiation reflect the autonomy of the units of a system, the coherence mechanisms bring to the forefront various options of their coupling. This addresses the core of the 'dialectical interpretation' of loose coupling, that is, the capacity 'to combine the contradictory concepts of connection and autonomy' (Orton and Weick 1990: 216). How the three dimensions of differentiation can be affected by the coherence mechanisms is briefly described in

---

'observed change of fulfilling political tasks which can be described by a tendency to govern partial tasks through and in bargaining systems' (Mayntz 1996: 157; translation by the authors). The internal differentiation of the politico-administrative system can be seen as a basic requirement for bargaining in it by which 'the societal problems of interdependencies can get on the agenda of governmental actions' (Mayntz 1996). At the same time, 'intra-governmental bargains' are crucial to avoid 'the shift of political decisions into sectoral policy networks [that] only leads to fragmentation' (Mayntz 1996).

[3] We would like to note that these are probably not the only phenomena of differentiation within the policy area of the structural funds—not to mention EU policies in general. But according to our research findings, they are the relevant ones with regard to our case.

Section 7.3. Here, the following has to be mentioned. The coherence mechanisms are in principle functional equivalencies, that is, each of them is able to loosely couple different units within a differentiated organization as well as different organizations. They can also appear together and mutually enhance their (individual) effects.

Loose coupling can be a result of the coherence mechanisms, but there is no automatism in the emergence and effectiveness of these mechanisms. However, without them functional differentiation and organizational fragmentation may result in governance failure. The effectiveness of the coherence mechanisms depends on the corresponding alignment of orientations and routines of the—individual as well as corporate—actors. This applies to 'ideas' or paradigms as well as to the different dimensions of rules and norms for the exchange of information and the coordination of actions. And the anticipation of a possible final authoritative decision of a not directly involved authority—especially of hierarchical interventions—may shape the incentive structure of actors, but may also lead to evasive manoeuvres of the (formally) subordinated actors. This is reflected in the 'dialectical interpretation' of loose coupling 'with its recognition of numerous structural dimensions, its emphasis on simultaneous coupling and decoupling, and its portrayal of structures as malleable through managerial intervention' in that it forces researchers 'to move more deeply into the human workings which underlie organizational structure' (Orton and Weick 1990: 218). Thus, the actions of actors matter; they are a key variable to the understanding of the capabilities for both organizational and policy change.

The emphasis on 'simultaneous coupling and decoupling' is particularly relevant with respect to hierarchical, one-sided and power-based options and competencies of making and enforcing decisions. Especially in a multi-level system of joint decision-making, the employment of such options and competencies can provoke vetoes and blockages. Furthermore, it can reduce the open access and the variety of actors (or units) involved. Nonetheless, such options and competencies remain indispensable steering mechanisms. Even in loosely coupled systems, the binding nature of the results of interactions has to be controlled and enforced in order to avoid individual units becoming (too) independent and a real 'decoupling' of collective actors taking place.[4]

Based on our empirical findings we will present some instructive examples in order to highlight how governability and reform capacity can be

---

[4] Within internally differentiated corporate actors this can be achieved by the 'shadow of hierarchy'.

achieved in the multi-level system of EU structural funds' interventions characterized by a multitude of differentiations as well as coherence mechanisms.

7.3 Functional differentiation and coherence mechanisms: Some examples

The way in which governability and wide-ranging reforms in the EU can be reached by differentiation and appropriate coherence mechanisms will be demonstrated in the following three sections. In our first example, we will demonstrate the positive impact of administrative differentiation on the reform of the structural funds in 1988 (and its history since the late 1970s) in combination with certain coherence mechanisms. How successful decisions in the Council can be reached by sequencing the negotiations (i.e. the differentiation of decision-making processes over time) will be shown by referring to the reform of the structural funds in 1999. Finally, we will highlight the fact that it is the functional differentiation of the following two arenas which can repeatedly provide 'locally' adaptable as well as enforceable general rules: (a) a decision-making arena which is formed temporarily (at the EU level) on the eve and at the time of the periodical reprogramming and budgeting of the funds and (b) implementation arenas which are located at the regional, national, and EU level assembling participants from one level or more.

7.3.1 Administrative differentiation within the European Commission

Examples of administrative differentiation and the effectiveness of different coherence mechanisms within the European Commission have come about in the course of the various reforms of the structural funds. One example in this respect can be seen in the work and status of the Commission's task force on the coordination of the structural funds. This task force worked as a special kind of coupling mechanism in particular between the members of the different DGs which are responsible for the structural funds interventions (DG XVI 'Regional Policy', DG V 'Employment and Social Affairs', DG VI 'Agriculture'). This task force developed substantial principles of the structural funds intervention (such as the integration principle or the promotion of endogenous regional development) some time before they were eventually introduced by the

1988 major reform (Hooghe 1996b: 98, 103–11). The task force consisted of representatives from the European Investment Bank, the DG for competition, DG XVI, DG V as well as DG VI and was headed by the commissioner responsible for the Community's regional policy, Antonio Giolitti. The establishment of the task force and its composition was a reaction to the inefficiencies of coordination. Therefore, its main task was to improve the dialogue between the different DGs by providing a forum in which the representatives of the DGs could meet on a (regular) basis and in doing so could strengthen the coordination of the different financial instruments of the Community.

Additionally, the relevance of the task force was enhanced by the fact that it substantially contributed to the 'reframing' of the basic ideas of the structural funds interventions. This was initially carried out with relative independence from the developments within the DGs responsible for the individual funds as well as from the decisions made in the Council in the context of the periodically recurring structural fund's reforms (Malek 2002). On the one hand the organizational structure of the Commission contributed to this policy-related innovation by securing the aforementioned independence of the subunits. This, in turn, opened opportunities for discursive processes within the task force conducive to the development of alternative and issue-related problem solutions due to the fact that the work of the task force was more or less disentangled from competitive interests prevailing in the other subunits. On the other hand, since the task force was able to develop an alternative way of perceiving and constructing reality based on specific normative premises and assumptions about the reality as well as about causal relationships, the sensitivity to changes in the organizational environment and the readiness to seize chances of innovation grew. This is due to the fact that new information that questions existing beliefs does not necessarily have to make sense within the whole knowledge base of an organization (Wiesenthal 1995). Rather, cognitive innovation which is inconsistent with 'old' normative and cognitive orientations (or frames) may be taken up and implemented within the partially autonomous units of the organization and may be transforming the frame of reference of intra- and inter-organizational decision-making processes. Under these circumstances, collective learning processes may be facilitated, especially since the probability of reaching a reasoned consensus—as a precondition for learning—increases with a smaller number of members in a (sub-)system.

Although the work of the task force resulted in a substantial reframing of the policy field in so far as most of the innovative aspects of the 1988 reform were gradually developed by the task force and implemented through a series of pilot projects (Tömmel 1994), the overall result of these efforts prior to the 1988 reform merely introduced changes at the margin: The three funds continued to be revised in separated institutional arenas, the pilot projects were still implemented on a more or less segmented basis according to the dominant procedures, and routines in the single DGs and on the national level which aimed at an integration of the funds were only realized on paper (Malek 2002: 107–25). It was not until the replacement of sponsorship, extensive personnel shifts, and the direct involvement of members of the task force in the decision-making process had taken place in the run up to the 1988 major reform, that the intended innovations did have a clearly perceptible impact on the development of the structural funds as a whole. In other words, 'frame sponsorship' (Rein and Schön 1993) was taken over by the President of the European Commission, who had a decisive impact on the way the structural policy was (re-)named and hence presented in the negotiations of the Council. In addition, he substantially supported the spreading of the new idea within the Commission not only by communicating it to and discussing it with the responsible DGs (e.g. in the context of some Commission–internal reform–preparatory discussion seminars), but also by concentrating the responsibility for the drafting and negotiation of the new 1988 regulation proposals, which contained the innovative aspects, in one single DG. This was done by transforming the task force into an autonomous DG (DG XXII), which acted more or less isolated from the other DGs. The decision to concentrate relevant competencies in one DG was mainly due to the fact that in the hitherto responsible DGs 'old orientation died hard'. As a result of these structural changes within the Commission, the members of the former task force mainly changed into the newly established DG XXII and were now responsible for the presentation and negotiation of the new regulation proposals within the decision-making processes of the Council.

After the new regulations had been passed, however, extensive personnel shifts took place within the Commission. This was of great importance, since it helped to convince reluctant actors of the advantages of the new approach. Thus, our findings support the conclusion of Rein and Schön (1993: 154) that although some actors are adjusting to a 'new situation rather than deliberately choosing to modify its frames [. . .], the new rules of doing business, adopted in the spirit of adjustment, may have laid the grounds for a substantial frame change downwards'.

7.3.2 Sequencing the decision-making process in the case of the reform negotiations of 1999

The sequencing of decisions makes the decision-making system loosely coupled by, first, generating differentiation and, second, by supporting coherence mechanisms. In the following, the negotiations on the reform of 1999 will be used to illustrate this: The overall, complex subject of the new structural funds regulations was (a) divided into manageable single articles or issues that (b) were discussed on various hierarchical levels of the Council. This made negotiations actually possible and it helped to generate outcomes that were agreeable for the European Council in the end.

The structural funds regulations were formally passed by the General Affairs Council because there is no specific Council of Ministers responsible for the structural funds. At the beginning of negotiations in spring 1998, the British presidency set up the 'structural actions working group' that acted as the lowest, working-level body of the Council. From that point on, the reform negotiations could in principle progress in the regular way through the EC decision-making system (Westlake 1995; Wessels 1996; Hayes-Renshaw and Wallace 1997; Sherrington 2000). This process can be summarized as follows:

1. Each article of the Commission's draft regulations was first read by the working group, which comprised working-level staff of the member states' ministries or permanent representations and met one to three times a week. After the delegations had expressed their views, the presidency formulated a 'compromise text', which aimed at being agreeable to as many delegations as possible.
2. Articles or single issues the working group could not agree upon were handed over to the 'friends of the presidency'. This informal body met about once a month, was staffed by heads of DGs of member state ministries, and was installed in order to relieve the Comité des Représentants Permanents (COREPER) of some of its workload. The 'friends' then either handed back open questions to the working group or asked COREPER to discuss them.
3. When the ambassadors in COREPER discussed the structural funds about every second month, they in effect tested the waters for political compromises on problems not yet resolved by the lower level bodies.
4. The General Affairs Council was confronted with the structural funds regulations only when it started preparing the meetings of the European Council. Based on the outcomes of the COREPER, the foreign ministers pre-formulated possible compromises for the European Council.

5. Eventually, the heads of state and government in the European Council decided on the new structural funds regulations as one part of the Agenda 2000 package at the Berlin summit in March 1999. Before the agreement was reached, they assessed the state of affairs and gave rather general orientations for the lower-level bodies.

Each issue was processed by the different hierarchical levels of Council bodies until a compromise between all national delegations and the Commission was finally worked out. Depending on the specific subject, the interests at stake and the negotiation strategies applied by the delegations, some issues could be settled by the working group and were only formally agreed upon at higher levels, while other topics required further rounds of negotiation going through the entire system and demanding a final decision of the European Council.

This sequencing of decisions helped to substantially reduce the complexity of the subject and thereby facilitated constructive negotiations, which ultimately led to outcomes in accordance with the common interest (Scharpf 1988). The sequencing became effective in interaction with three coherence mechanisms that loosely coupled the differentiated decision-making system: the evolving socialization of the member states' representatives in the Brussels negotiation system, the incentive to agree on the lowest possible hierarchical level, and the increasing importance of reaching compromises. First, the member states' representatives became more and more socialized into a community of practice (Gheradi, Nicolini, and Odella 1998) in the 'structural actions working group'. Since no regular Council working group existed in the field of EU structural funds policy, most of the working-level negotiators were to come directly from the member state ministries. The longer they interacted in the working group in Brussels, the more they formed a social group with a common professional identity and a common experience of the progress of negotiation that was all the more noticeable as the negotiators had started work from scratch rather than integrating it into the regular flow of Council work. As a result of this, the member states' representatives developed common values, rules, and practices as well as a notion of generalized reciprocity. Although the social interactions took place within a time frame which was only slightly longer than one year, they became so dense that for the members of the working group the joint finding of feasible compromises turned out to be a value in its own right.

Second, all the actors involved had a strong incentive to find compromises on the lowest possible hierarchical level of the decision-making system. The fewer the number of open questions the members of one negotiation body handed over to the next above them, the more they were able to demonstrate their negotiating skills, that is their ability to come to compromises that could be eventually agreed on by their own member state, the other delegations, the Commission, and the Parliament. After all, this was exactly the very reason why they were sent to Brussels in the first place. However, the structural funds are no regular Council subject. Due to this fact, for the lower hierarchical levels it was harder than usual to find a compromise.

Third, the importance of reaching compromises increased during the course of negotiations. The longer a particular issue was discussed, the more likely it was that higher levels of the Council were to process it. In general, the inclination to agree to a compromise increases with the hierarchical level because (a) finding a consensus is the core function of administrative and political leaders in each political system and (b) the latter are farther away from implementing the decisions. Therefore, the higher the level of negotiators the less willing and able they are to anticipate possible negative consequences of the compromises they are working out. The less they are able to coordinate with the experts that provide the necessary technocratic knowledge, the less they can assess the possible impacts of their decisions. However, the capabilities of the member state delegations to coordinate their positions with the ministries at home substantially decreased during the course of negotiations. This basically resulted from a multiplication of time pressure and the number of issues that had to be processed simultaneously: At the beginning of the negotiations thorough discussions of all issues were possible, while shortly before the final summit as many open questions as possible had to be resolved quickly.

These mechanisms were not exclusively employed for structural funds reforms, but can also be observed in other areas of EC decision-making and in other decision systems. However, the specificities of the structural funds amplified their potential. Since no regular Council working group exists in this policy field, the negotiators had to be recruited directly from the capitals, and meet a fixed and comparatively short deadline during which meetings would take place almost on a daily basis. The socialization effect was, therefore, stronger than in other cases.

The three observed coherence mechanisms were less effective in the case of those issues that were considered to be politically explosive such as the distribution of resources between the member states. These issues were only treated on higher levels. However, the effectiveness of the coherence mechanisms is evident from an analysis of the negotiations on the so-called 'technical' issues in terms of the institutional design of the implementation system (Lang 2001). This system consists of the procedural rules for implementing the structural funds programmes and the allocation of influence between the actors involved in the implementation. Together, they form the structural funds' policy model that has been developed by exactly such cumulative policy processes and has shaped at least large parts of the EC as it is today.

7.3.3 Functional differentiation of arenas

Functional differentiation of arenas (Benz 2000: 111) allows us to differentiate between two processes: the decision-making processes on the parameters of the structural funds for the entire EU on the one hand, and the implementation processes in the member states and their regions on the other. It is expressed in the formation of different organizations and corporate actors according to different functions which have to be fulfilled in the two arenas.

At the EU level, the differentiation is apparent in the internal division of the DGs, both regarding the formal organizational structures and the daily communication processes. The geographical units within the DGs are responsible for implementation in the different member states, whereas the horizontal units are responsible for decisions at the EU level, that is, the revision of regulations. This differentiation reflects the need to adapt the implementation of the structural funds to the specific circumstances of the member states, since the substantive and institutional preconditions for the implementation of the structural funds as well as the preferences of the relevant actors vary between the member states. Similarly, the differentiation is apparent within the member states, where implementation and policy-making functions are often allocated to different organizational units.

Such specializations are likely to emerge responding to the specific demands of implementation and decision-making processes. In addition, they are necessary because efficient implementation has to pay tribute to diverse regional environments and, therefore, demands an open and flexible administration. Finally, reducing complexity is a prerequisite to enhance the capacity of the European decision-making system to act. The periodical European decision-making processes on the revision of the structural funds regulations would be quickly congested if the implementation experiences of all actors involved would get access to the negotiation table. Consequently, the sequencing of decisions mentioned above becomes crucial. In the different sequences, the involved actors 'filter' the information relevant for the revision of the regulations. The outcomes of the decision-making system, that is, the revised regulations, then leave the necessary room to manoeuvre for the actors involved in the implementation process. Besides setting general policy objectives and budgets, the regulations define the procedures for programming and project selection that have to be applied in order to attain the policy objectives by spending the budget.

This points to particular coherence mechanisms: substantive and procedural norms such as the principles of programming or partnership introduced in 1988 loosely couple the entire structural funds system. This becomes possible despite the fact that the decentral actors involved in implementation do not lose their autonomy, which still enables them to adapt the structural funds to their specific socio-economic and institutional context. Additionally, the paradigms connected to the structural funds comprise problem perceptions and possible solutions that can influence the actors' behaviour when they make decentral decisions about how to implement the programmes—and, in the end, make these decisions coherent with what is done elsewhere. The paradigms of regional 'cohesion' and of mobilizing the 'endogenous potential' of regions, but also the 'European Employment Strategy' and the 'Luxembourg process' which have shaped both the implementation and the reform of the structural funds provide illustrative examples in this field.

Seen against this background, the Commission has a particular function in supporting coherence, too (even though it was characterized above as being quite segmented internally): oriented towards implementation, it has the power to sanction member states and regions during implementation if they appear not to act in compliance with the regulations. The scope of these sanctions ranges from the use of evaluations and financial control instruments to declining the approval of programmes and the denial of payments. Oriented towards European decision-making, the Commission holds the right of initiative, thus controls the agenda and substantially influences the decision-making process and its outcomes.

Coherence mechanisms between the arenas are also apparent within the Commission: although the internal differentiation of the DGs into geographical and horizontal units has led to the emergence of partially autonomous units, which pursue and carry through their own interests, the danger of organizational fragmentation and the isolation of subunits is reduced by internal organizational rules related to the exchange of information and the coordination of actions. In other words: The subunits are dependent on the resources (such as knowledge, money, etc.) of the other subunits as well as on their approval of proposals, etc. Many of these interdependencies did not evolve 'naturally', but rather are the result of rules set intentionally. After all, individual units still operate 'under the shadow of hierarchy'. Besides, as regards the way in which linkages between differentiated organizational subunits function, codified—that is consciously and explicitly set—organizational goals also play a central role. They are again accomplished by implicit action-guiding principles, which apply to the whole organization. Together, they provide a frame of reference for the intra-organizational relations, which facilitates processes of 'positive coordination' (through bargaining) as well as processes of 'negative coordination' (through mutual self-adjustment; Scharpf 1993). Such processes are especially relevant for organizations—such as the European Commission—which are involved in various networks due to functional requirements (Mayntz 1996).

7.4 Conclusions

As we have highlighted in the previous sections, (1) the internal organizational differentiation of collective actors, (2) the differentiation (sequentialization) of decisions on the different levels of European policy-making, and (3) the functional differentiation between a decision-making arena on the EU level and implementation arenas in the member states/regions represent specific intra- and inter-organizational capabilities in a system of EU multi-level governance which proved to be conducive for the development of innovative and environmentally open policies. They provide the actors involved in this multi-level system with room for decisions and they offer area-related opportunities for institutional evolution and organizational learning. However, these forms of differentiation need to be loosely coupled by certain coherence mechanisms. Otherwise, they would run the risk of fragmenting the organizations and isolating single subunits within certain policy areas which in turn could lead to implementation deficits and to the encapsulation of newly gained insights and normative orientations.

Accepted rules and norms for the exchange of information and the coordination of actions (e.g. informal and formal norms for procedures), 'ideas' or paradigms which suggest specific objectives for actions, problem definitions and solutions, and the threat of a commanding decision by a not directly involved authority (i.e. either at the top of an organization or at a higher level of the bargaining system) together illustrate the functioning of coherence mechanisms both with respect to the development and the operation of the EU structural funds. If coherence is guaranteed by such forms of loose coupling ensuring that actors are still related to each other, then inter- and intra-organizational differentiation is likely to promote adaptation and learning processes of the units involved and thus to strengthen governability with regard to the purposeful alteration of policies.

The fragmented structure as well as the operating coherence mechanisms which can be observed in the EU structural funds policy have not been developed and linked in a systematic and consistent way.[5] They have emerged incrementally from pragmatic decisions in response to the specific structures of the governance system at the European level and the different path-dependencies of policy-making in the member states. In other words, the multitude of options available to actors in EU decision-making and the divergence of organizational structures in the member states which shape the implementation of the structural funds make it difficult to collectively pursue a successful, systematic, and consistent design.

Nonetheless, some important elements of the mechanisms observed are the result of strategic political attempts to structure the multi-level system of the EU cohesion policy. This is demonstrated, for example, by the introduction of the principles for programming and implementation (and not least, the partnership principle) through the reform of 1988 as well as the partial withdrawal of the geographical units of the Commission from the implementation arenas after the reform of 1999. Although there is some evidence that these policy reforms had been inspired by scholarly debates (Hooghe 1996*b*; Heinelt and Malek 2002), they were mainly based on the 'intelligence of the practice'. In other words, they result from processes of policy or organizational learning (be it 'conventional' or 'unconventional'

---

[5] These findings may be a prolific basis for the attempt to draw some lessons from our research and to develop design principles for European governance arrangements reflecting the observed potentials for successful policy-making and reform. However, this was not the intention of the article. For an attempt to develop 'generic design principles for European governance arrangements' focusing on the achievement of effectiveness and legitimacy, see Schmitter (2002).

in the sense sketched out in Section 7.2 of this chapter) as well as from the ability of actors to use favourable (historical and/or organizational) conditions to put through their specific perception of the 'right' problem definition and a corresponding 'adequate' perspective of action in a hegemonic position during their involvement in EU decision-making.

References

Argyris, Chris (1976). 'Single-Loop and Douple-Loop Models in Research on Decision Making', *Administrative Science Quarterly*, 21: 363-75.

—— and Schön, Donald A. (1978). *Organizational Learning. A Theory of Action Perspective*. Reading, Mass.: Addison-Wesley.

Benz, Arthur (2000). 'Politische Steuerung in lose gekoppelten Mehrebenensystemen', in Raymund Werle and Uwe Schimank (eds.), *Gesellschaftliche Komplexität und kollektive Handlungsfähigkeit*. Frankfurt: Campus, 97-124.

Gheradi, Silvia, Nicolini, Davide, and Odella, Francesca (1998). 'Toward a Social Understanding of How People Learn in Organizations. The Notion of Situated Curriculum', *Management Learning*, 29/3: 273-97.

Hayes-Renshaw, Fiona and Wallace, Helen (1997). *The Council of Ministers*. Houndmills: Macmillan.

Heclo, Hugh and Wildavsky, Aron (1974). *The Private Government of Public Money*. London: Macmillan.

Heinelt, Hubert (1996). 'Multilevel Governance in the European Union and the Structural Funds', in Hubert Heinelt and Randall Smith (eds.), *Policy Networks and European Structural Funds*. Aldershot: Avebury, 9-25.

—— and Malek, Tanja (2002). 'Neuere Steuerungsformen im europäischen Mehrebenensystem', in Michèle Knodt and Thomas Conzelmann (eds.), *Regionales Europa, europäische Regionen* (Mannheimer Jahrbuch für Europäische Sozialforschung, Vol. 6). Frankfurt a. M.: Campus, 69-86.

—— and Smith, Randall (eds.) (1996), *Policy Networks and European Structural Funds*. Aldershot: Avebury.

——, Lang, Jochen, Malek, Tanja, and Reissert, Bernd (2001). *Die Entwicklung der europäischen Stukturfonds als kumulativer Politikprozeß. Zur Institutionalisierung und Veränderung von Politikinhalten im Mehrebenensystem der EU* (Report on a research project funded by the German Research Council (DFG) under the programme 'Governance in the European Union'). Darmstadt and Berlin.

Hooghe, Liesbeth (ed.) (1996a). *Cohesion Policy and European Integration. Building Multi-level Governance*. Oxford: Oxford University Press.

—— (1996b). 'Building a Europe with the Regions: The Changing Role of the Commission', in Liesbeth Hooghe (ed.), *Cohesion Policy and European Integration. Building Multi-level Governance*. Oxford: Oxford University Press, 89-126.

Lang, Jochen (2001). 'Dezentralisierung à la Kommission. Prozeß und Ergebnisse der Reform 1999', in Hubert Heinelt, Jochen Lang, Tanja Malek, and Bernd Reissert, *Die Entwicklung der europäischen Stukturfonds als kumulativer Politikprozeß. Zur*

Institutionalisierung und Veränderung von Politikinhalten im Mehrebenensystem der EU (Report on a research project funded by the German Research Council (DFG) under the programme 'Governance in the European Union'). Darmstadt and Berlin, 114–54.

—— (2003). Symbolische Implementation als Flexitilitäts-reserve in der Europäischen Union (Ph.D. thesis).

Malek, Tanja (2002). *Politikgestaltung auf europäischer Ebene*. Baden-Baden: Nomos.

Marks, Gary (1993). 'Structural policy and multilevel governance in the EC', in Alan W. Cafruny and Glenda G. Rosenthal (eds.), *The State of the European Community* (The Maastricht Debate and Beyond, Vol. 2). Longman: Lynne Rienner Publishers, 391–410.

Mayntz, Renate (1996). 'Politische Steuerung: Aufstieg, Niedergang und Transformation einer Theorie', in Klaus von Beyme and Claus Offe (eds.), *Politische Theorien in der Ära der Transformation*. Opladen: Westdeutscher Verlag, 148–68.

Orton, J. Douglas and Weick, Karl E. (1990). 'Loosely Coupled Systems. A Reconceptualization', *Academy of Management Review*, 15/2: 203–23.

Rein, Martin and Schön, Donald (1993). 'Reframing Policy Discourse', in Frank Fischer and John Forester (eds.), *The Argumentative Turn in Policy-Analysis and Planning*. Durham and London: Duke University Press, 145–66.

Scharpf, Fritz W. (1988). 'The Joint-Decision Trap. Lessons from German Federalism and European Integration', *Public Administration*, 66: 239–78.

—— (1993). 'Positive und negative Koordination in Verhandlungssystemen', in Adrienne Héritier (ed.), *Policy-Analyse. Kritik und Neuorientierung*. Opladen: Westdeutscher Verlag, 57–83.

—— (2001). *What Have We Learned? Problem-Solving Capacity of the Multilevel European Polity* (MPIfG Working Papers, 01/4). Köln: MPIfG.

Sherrington, Philippa (2000). *The Council of Ministers. Political Authority in the European Union*. London and New York: Pinter.

Schmitter, Philippe (2002). 'Participation in Governance Arrangements: Is there any reason to expect it will achieve "Sustainable and Innovative Policies in a Multi-Level Context"?', in Jürgen R. Grote and Bernard Gbikpi (eds.), *Participatory Governance. Political and Societal Implications*. Opladen: Leske + Budrich, 51–69.

Staeck, Nicola (1997). *Politikprozesse in der Europäischen Union. Eine Policy-Netzwerkanalyse der europäischen Strukturfondspolitik*. Baden-Baden: Nomos.

Tömmel, Ingeborg (1994). *Staatliche Regulierung und europäische Integration: Die Regionalpolitik der EG und ihre Implementation*. Baden-Baden: Nomos.

Weick, Karl E. (1976). 'Educational Organizations as Loosely Coupled Systems', *Administrative Science Quarterly*, 21/1: 1–19.

—— (1985). *Der Prozeß des Organisierens*. Frankfurt: Suhrkamp.

Wessels, Wolfgang (1996). 'Verwaltung im EG-Mehrebenensystem: Auf dem Weg zur Megabürokratie?', in Markus Jachtenfuchs and Beate Kohler-Koch (eds.), *Europäische Integration*. Opladen: Leske + Budrich, 165–92.

Westlake, Martin (1995). *The Council of the European Union*. London: Cartermill.

Wiesenthal, Helmut (1995). 'Konventionelles und unkonventionelles Organisationslernen. Literaturreport und Ergänzungsvorschlag', *Zeitschrift für Soziologie*, 24/2: 137–55.

8

Policy Implementation in a Multi-Level System: The Dynamics of Domestic Response

Jochen Lang

8.1 Introduction

The European Community (EC) structural policy has inspired political science to theorize about the nature of the emerging political system of the EC, and particularly about the concept of multi-level governance (Marks 1996; Marks, Hooghe, and Blank 1996; Hooghe 1996a,b; Benz 2000). The EC structural funds policy presents more than one puzzle: While in the preceding article our research team tries to explain the ongoing success of EC policy shaping and reform in the field, this chapter will explore the differences and inconsistencies in the patterns of implementation in the member states. Many European, national, regional, and local authorities as well as societal actors such as interest groups are involved in the daily implementation of EC structural policy. They cooperate in the formulation of multi-annual programmes, the selection of projects, and the assessment of the results of the programmes. This cooperation involves multiple interactions across different levels of government.

<small>Earlier drafts of this contribution were presented at two workshops organized by Beate Kohler-Koch. It is based on my dissertation supervised by Arthur Benz and would not have been possible without the discussions with and guidance from my academic teacher and mentor Frieder Naschold who died in November 1999. The empirical data was collected in two research projects coordinated by Hubert Heinelt and Bernd Reissert and financed by the German research council (*Deutsche Forschungsgemeinschaft*) and the Hans-Böckler-Stiftung. Many helpful comments and suggestions on earlier drafts came from Katrin Auel, Arthur Benz, Silke Bothfeld, Thomas Conzelmann, Hubert Heinelt, Kristine Kern, Brigid Laffan, Maria Oppen, Bernd Reissert, Oliver Schwab, Holger Strassheim, and Nathalie Strohm and are gratefully acknowledged. Particularly Liesbet Hooghe's and Beate Kohler-Koch's comments and suggestions were instructive and, not least, most motivating.</small>

Overall, the policy model of the structural funds—which is codified in EC regulations—is more elaborate and more demanding than those of most domestic regional policies. It requires the cooperation of more actors and, as a result, demands more efforts in terms of time and resources of the participants in implementation. Therefore, it would be plausible to assume that implementation takes place within narrow confines. This conventional wisdom will be queried in this chapter, which is trying to give answers to the following questions: what actually is the meaning of the European policy on the ground? Do European decision-makers have the capacity to control the actions of decentral actors by defining detailed requirements for the implementation of structural funds regulations? Or do decentral actors, in the end, decide on the meaning of EC decisions?

These questions were not the point of departure of my research. They rather arose during the empirical fieldwork. Here, the impression was gained that in many regions, some components of the structural funds policy model were implemented in a quite ritualized and symbolic way, failing to exert sustainable influence on implementation results. Starting from this initial evidence, I investigated in a systematic way the scope of action available to decentral actors in the process of implementing the structural funds regulations.

In the following section, hypotheses are developed that may help answer the questions formulated above. The political science concepts for the analysis of interactions in the EU multi-level system (Jachtenfuchs and Kohler-Koch 1996) can be supplemented by findings from implementation research and organization studies. Based on these approaches, I first define the notion 'effective implementation'. Second, I describe the institutional context of structural funds implementation and stress the coexistence of European and domestic instruments within the policy field. Third, the main hypothesis will be presented which stipulates that effective implementation largely is at the discretion of member state actors. They do have the choice to implement the structural funds regulations effectively, that is to transform the change of regulations into changed actions, organizational routines, and policy outcomes—or to abstain from it. The responses of member state actors depend on the compatibility between the structural funds policy model and the domestic policy paths. In addition, actors in a stable domestic environment will choose other reactions than actors in a domestic constellation which is experiencing paradigmatic policy change or even constitutional polity change.

In the third section, I present the results of an empirical analysis of the structural funds implementation in Germany, Ireland, and Sweden.[1] Based on a detailed reconstruction of the implementation processes, I identify how the decentral actors react to changes in the European regulations. In order to get a more detailed picture, I compare different dimensions of the structural funds implementation policy, that is, the requirements for programming, for evaluation, for the involvement of sub-national, and for the involvement of non-state actors, with the implementation practice in the three member states.

8.2 Domestic responses depend on domestic change or stability

In this Section I develop a simple model of the implementation of EC structural funds. How the EC regulations are implemented essentially depends on the context conditions of the respective member state. In order to be able to analyse an assumed interdependence of the implementation of the structural funds on the one hand and domestic policy instruments on the other, a detailed reconstruction of the specific implementation processes in the regions is necessary.

8.2.1 Policy formulation, implementation, and policy change

European Union (EU) policy decision-making such as the revisions of the structural funds regulations produces policy change in the member states only if the respective regulations are implemented effectively. Besides defining a budget and rules how to distribute it, the structural funds regulations contain the codification of a specific policy model, which is placed in a set of formal institutions. In neo-institutionalist terms (see the overviews in Hall and Taylor 1996; Immergut 1997), the implementation of the regulation is

---

[1] These member states have been chosen in order to attain a 'most different systems design': They differ as regards centralization of the political system, length of EC membership, and domestic paths of regional structural policies. Within Germany (Berlin and North-Rhine Westfalia) and Sweden (Jämtland and Fyrstad), two regions were selected for in-depth analyses of the implementation processes. They were chosen according to three criteria: (a) the structural funds support categories '1' and '2' should be covered, (b) they should differ as much as possible in their economic development problems and other structural factors, and (c) they should be assessed as being 'innovative' in their way of implementing the structural funds by Commission officials, national government officials and, not least, independent academic experts from the member state. Due to the last criterion, none of the regions studied are supposed to be particularly reluctant or even opposed to the structural funds policy model.

seen to be the transformation of formal ('European') institutions into actions, routines, and informal as well as formal ('domestic') institutions. When a change in regulations is implemented effectively, it will result in changed actions, routines, and institutions as well as in changed actor roles, constellations, and distribution of resources.

Three decades of implementation research have generated plenty of evidence that effective implementation is everything but automatic (Pressman and Wildavsky 1973; O'Toole 1986; Sabatier 1986; Goggin et al. 1990; Palumbo and Calista 1990; Crosby 1996). At the same time, the studies also show that it is not easy to actually assess to what extent political decisions are implemented. In the case of European structural policy, the methodological situation is a bit easier than in other cases of EU policies: one and the same EC policy model is implemented by fifteen member states with different sets of policy instruments and polities. Starting from this observation, one can use the occurrence of changed routines across different policy instruments as an indicator for the degree of effective implementation as will be shown in the next sub-section.

8.2.2 Interpenetrated polity and coexisting policy instruments

The EC and its member states have become interpenetrated polities. This notion emphasizes the perception that there are no longer separate 'layers' in a multi-level system that can be clearly distinguished. Rather, 'European' actors participate directly in 'national' policy areas and vice versa (Kohler-Koch 1999; Conzelmann 2000*a*). In the field of structural policy, this interpenetration is reflected in the coexistence of policy instruments which comprise roughly two sets: European (the structural funds) and domestic (basically national and regional) instruments. On the one hand, these two sets are separated from each other because they operate on different legal bases and are funded from different budgets that originate from different decision-making processes. On the other hand, they are closely interconnected because, in principle, they aim at the same general objectives, address the same target groups, and involve the same implementation agencies. In addition, in most member states the structural funds are substantively coupled, in terms of budget and/or procedures, to domestic instruments (Fig. 8.1).

It is plausible to assume that the closer the two sets of instruments are interrelated with each other in terms of joint implementation systems and, particularly, in terms of joint implementation agencies, the less it is possible to restrict a change in routines to one instrument alone. In

European instrument	Domestic instrument
Legal base budget	Legal base budget
Objectives Clients Implementing agencies	
Partial coupling	

Fig. 8.1 Coupling of structural funds and national policies

principle, some regions can have a project selection process for the structural funds that is separate from those for the domestic instruments, while other regions can have joint processes. In most EU member states, however, one and the same organization is responsible for the back-office work of programming, cash flow, reporting, etc. It is hard to imagine that they use different routines and procedures and that both are taken seriously at the same time. Organizations have limited sets of standard operating procedures that constitute their reservoirs of possible action programmes (Allison 1969, 1971: 68–89). A change in such standard operating procedures that form the core of an organization's 'production function' will affect all actions of the organization and can, thus, hardly be restricted to parts of its tasks, that is, to one instrument that it implements. To sum up, changed regulations will effectively be implemented if, first, the actions and routines have also changed, and, second, if these changed routines can also be found in the implementation of other instruments that are implemented by the same agencies.

8.2.3 *Domestic responses to European decisions*

8.2.3.1 Situation of implementing actors

The decentral actors which are involved in the implementation of the structural funds in the member states have very limited influence on the revision of the structural funds regulations at the European level (Heinelt et al., this volume; Benz and Eberlein 1999: 336). The changes concerning the codification of the European policy instrument are negotiated by senior and operational staff from the Commission and the national ministries that are different from those in charge of implementing them. Moreover, the two groups of actors lack systematic and effective links for communication and coordination. As a result, changes to the structural funds regulations can be conceived of as an external demand on the decentral actors who implement them. The way in which these actors conceptualize their situation and in which they react is influenced by a twofold framework of reference: On the one hand, the European regulations stipulate requirements on how to implement the structural funds. On the other, the legal framework of the domestic policies comprises own (and possibly different) requirements for the implementation of structural policy, not to mention the constraints imposed by the overall institutional context of member state policies and polity.

In the following, two possible options for immediate responses to new demands from the structural funds policy model are introduced. How these short-term responses will develop further is discussed below.

8.2.3.2 Short-term options for response

To implement a new requirement means to change actions, routines, and even formal institutions. According to the path dependence theorem of neo-institutionalism (North 1990: 93–4, 97–8, 112), change is always costly. Actors will, therefore, try to avoid it or at least minimize the costs it causes (Bulmer and Burch 1998: 5–6; Schmidt 2001: 7). Which costs the actors expect and how high they estimate them to be, is a question of their assessment of the compatibility between the new requirement of the structural funds regulation and domestic policy: the less the contradiction between the European set of institutions and the ideas, interests, power constellations, and resource distributions that are linked to them on the one hand and the respective national set of institutions on the other, the lower are the costs of implementation.

In a short-term perspective, the decentral actors can choose between two options (Fig. 8.2): If there is already a functional equivalent in domestic policy which can be used to comply with the new requirement of the structural funds regulations, then there is no need for change because the new requirement can simply be absorbed. The necessary routines can easily be taken from the organization's repertoire of standard operating procedures. Whether the response 'absorption' is possible depends therefore on the 'goodness of fit' (Knill and Lenschow 1998; Börzel 1999) between the new requirement and the purpose and performance of the domestic institutions and operational routines.

The second option, which is to isolate the change, is chosen in cases of mismatch between the demands of the structural funds policy model and those of domestic policy. Absence of fit creates the need for a change in actions and routines in order to be able to comply with EU requirements. Such a mismatch results either from the non-existence of any respective domestic institutions or from contradictions between the ideas, norms,

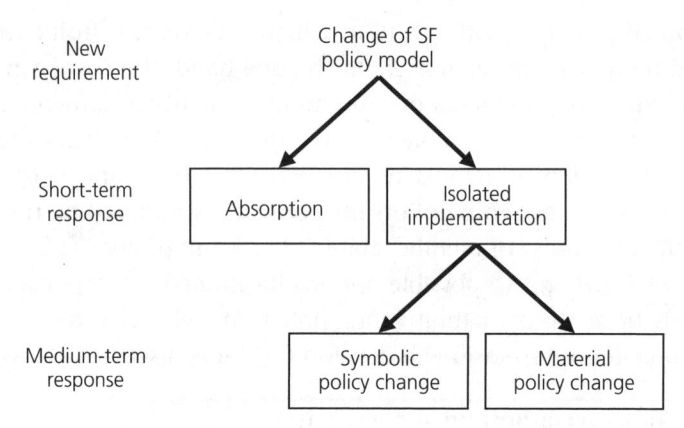

Fig. 8.2 Domestic responses to change of the structural funds regulations

values, interests, and power constellations linked with domestic institutions and those perceived from the implementation of the new structural funds regulations. If the actors feel an obligation to implement them, nonetheless, they will tend to minimize the costs resulting from it. In order to pursue that end, they can try to delimit the change in actions to the realm of the structural funds where there is the legal obligation to do so. At the same time, in domestic policies, even in those parts that are closely attached to the structural funds, for example, in terms of cofinancing, the pre-existing practice is continued without any change.

The strategy to isolate change like an alien element by developing a parallel system can be explained by a concept developed by Nils Brunsson and Johan P. Olsen (1993) for the analysis of organizational reform: An organization will develop parallel structures if it receives from its social environment a strong demand that it is not willing or able to fulfil. Such demands—in the perception of the members of the organization—either make no sense, produce too high costs or undermine the effectiveness of the organization's processes. An organization may develop a parallel structure by formally changing its structures in order to meet the demand, but at the same time it is still keeping its established procedures in the informal processing of the subject matter, thereby using the traditional structures for the actual coordination of its actions. As a result, there are parallel processes: the informal processes are necessary to produce outcomes, while the formal or even ritualized processes are necessary to demonstrate that the demand is fulfilled. The latter processes do not have impacts on the key processes of the organization, leave alone their results (Brunsson and Olsen 1993: 9–11). The transfer of this concept from the analysis of single organizations to the institutional structure and process of multi-organizational programme implementation needs to take into account that both structures are formal: one is used in a ritualized way to produce outcomes for the Commission and the structural funds regulations, the other is used to follow the domestic government's aims and objectives. The 'domestic' structure, however, is the one that is taken seriously by the domestic actors. Based on his comparative analysis of the content of European, British, and German regional policy, Thomas Conzelmann identifies a similar kind of parallel structures: with the structural funds, an alternative supply of regional policy has developed. For the regional actors, it has become a point of reference, which is alternative to the previously dominant domestic policy instruments. This resulted neither in a replacement nor in an adaptation pressure for domestic policies (Conzelmann 2000b).

8.2.3.3 Medium-term responses

If decentral actors do have the short-term option to comply with legally binding requirements by developing parallel systems, it is still open what exactly happens in the long run. Considering the fact that some actors (such as the European Commission) will demand more effective implementation, the crucial question arises how such parallel systems can be sustained. While the case of absorption remains the same, of course, there are again two options for isolated implementation to develop further. Depending on whether or not a diffusion of the new practice becomes attractive for the decentral actors, the isolated implementation of revised structural funds regulations will result in symbolic or material change.

In the case of a continued mismatch between the structural funds policy model and domestic institutions, a consolidation of isolation leading to symbolic change becomes likely: the parallel systems are maintained, because the need to implement the structural funds regulation remains just as persistent as the differing domestic needs. It is important to point out the difference between such symbolic change and Murray Edelman's concept of symbolic politics. He stresses the symbolic function of political actions as an integrative ritual (Edelman 1964, 1971). The concept used here emphasizes the occurrence of ritualized behaviour embodied in setting up parallel structures. Such a procrastination instead of real change can be pursued because at face value implementation actors can symbolically demonstrate compliance: if organizations are dealing with such parallel systems, they will stress the formal processes all the more, as they themselves are questioned and challenged by external actors.

As a result, the decoupling from the informal and policy-relevant structures and processes are increased even further (Brunsson 1989: 200–3).

An alternative option is the breakthrough to material change. Here, the parallel systems are merged into one by changing actions and routines in the realm of domestic policy. Such a spillover of requirements from the structural funds falls on fertile ground when the domestic setting is dynamic rather than stable. A change in actions, routines, and institutions in both European and domestic policy implementation is likely when actors involved perceive the new European requirement as an opportunity to invest in policy change. Such an opportunity emerges, if the underlying domestic change is following the same line as the development of the structural funds policy model—in general terms (Héritier and Knill 2000: 32) as well as in terms of the operational routines required to implement it. Domestic change that aims at other directions does not enable spill-over but rather reinforces isolation because the contradiction between the structural funds policy model and the domestic institutions further increases. In addition, it has to have the necessary potential and importance for the domestic actors. Examples are evolutionary shifts of the polity that are far-reaching enough to affect constitutional questions or paradigmatic policy shifts like what Peter Hall calls 'third order change', that is revisions of 'instrument settings, the instruments themselves, and the goals behind policy' at the same time (Hall 1993: 279).

However, what I model as a simplified two-stage flow chart here for analytical purposes is an iterative process empirically. European and domestic policies can change or remain stable independently from each other, but a change in one policy may cause or trigger a subsequent change in other policies. Therefore, the empirical analysis in the following section has to take into account the temporal order of events carefully.

The possibility that both European and domestic policies can change independently of each other is the most visible difference between the analysis presented here, and the analysis others have put forward in the debate on European policies and politics and domestic change (see, in particular, Risse, Cowles, and Haverland 1999; Börzel 2000; Héritier and Knill 2000; Radaelli 2000; Caporaso 2001; Schmidt 2001). Domestic policies and politics are more than just passive sounding boards that need to be stimulated by top-down EU politics in order to make a sound. Therefore, this contribution takes the perspective that to analyse European and domestic policies each has to be taken in its own right in order to be able to identify sources of change in both domains. This contribution is less concerned with the question whether European policies simply cause domestic change. The focus of my analysis is on the effectiveness of the implementation of a European policy instrument within a penetrated system and among coexisting domestic policy instruments. Whereas the other studies look for mechanisms of pressure and adaptation, I conceive of the possibility for decentral actors to change their actions within a delimited area and a possible, but not automatic diffusion of new practice later on. As regards outcomes, the symbolic change analysed here cannot be part of the approaches cited above, because it sits uneasily with their categories like pressure and coercion.

8.3 Empirical patterns of effective implementation

The hypotheses concerning reactions of the decentral actors to changes in the structural funds regulations are in the following tested by an empirical analysis of the implementation processes in Germany, Ireland, and Sweden. In order to be able to analyse responses in depth, I first divide the structural funds policy model into four characteristic components, each of them representing a set of specific routines. Second, regarding each of these components I compare the demand stipulated in the regulations with the implementation practice in the three member states. Finally, I summarize the analysis by drawing an encompassing picture of cross-sectional and cross-country patterns of implementation.

The development of the European structural funds is well documented in the relevant literature (see among others, Armstrong 1995; Hooghe 1996*b*; Wishlade 1996; Bache 1998). The policy model was developed by experimentation during the 1980s (Smyrl 1998; Heinelt et al., this volume) and formally introduced in 1988. Since then, the structural funds are implemented jointly by the European Commission, national ministries, and regional or local authorities. Each of them remains formally autonomous. However, they share responsibilities for the set-up and implementation of programmes. In addition, societal and private organizations such as labour market organizations, social policy, or environmental organizations are partially involved in the implementation system.

Each programming document comprises an analysis of the development problems of the respective region, a set of objectives, a strategy how to attain them by spending a given budget, and an operationalization into specific measures. Each project is funded from the structural funds as well as from national or regional budgets. In practice, the national or regional match funding can either be acquired for every single project (like in the

UK) or the EC resources can be attached to national or regional support schemes including their budget lines (like in Germany). Since the beginning of 2000, new regulations are in force. They define a more decentralized model: The Commission's competencies shall be concentrated on the strategic issues, while the regional actors shall have more responsibility and more flexibility in implementing the programmes. Complementary to that, the feedback instruments of monitoring, evaluation, and financial control were to be strengthened

From this brief sketch of the policy model, four elements can be identified that (a) represent the basic features of the structural funds' implementation system and that (b) respectively refer to a specific set oforganizational routines. These are:

- formulation of programmes
- evaluation
- involvement of sub-national state actors and
- involvement of non-state actors.

For each of them, first, the requirements stipulated in the regulations are briefly described, and then the responses across member states are compared. For reasons of simplification, I will not differentiate between the regions that have been studied. This is justified by the empirical observation that the variance between two regions within one member state is far less than the variation between member states and, particularly, the variance between the four different elements within one and the same region.

8.3.1 *Programming*

Programming is the core element of the structural funds' policy model. Since 1988, the regulations[2] demand the formulation of multi-annual programmes for the eligible regions or sectors of the member states. Since its introduction, the element in principle remained the same. But the revisions in 1993 and 1999 brought about more detailed rules and an increase in the substantive and procedural requirements. Basically, the regulations demand an analysis of the socio-economic situation at the outset of the

---

[2] The following is based on Recitals and Articles 5, 8, and 9 of Council Regulation (EEC) No. 2052/88; Articles 5 and 8 of Council Regulation (EEC) No. 4253/88; Article 2 of Council Regulation (EEC) No. 4254/88; Articles 8 and 9 of Council Regulation (EEC) No. 2081/93; Recitals and Articles 5 and 8 of Council Regulation (EEC) No. 2082/93; Recital 34 and Articles 9, 16–19 and 35 of Council Regulation (EC) No. 1260/99.

programme. Based on this, the objectives for development and a strategy how to attain them shall be formulated. In the operational parts of the programmes, concrete instruments for the implementation of the strategy have to be defined and the programme budget comprising European and national funds has to be allocated to these instruments. The decentral actors, thus, have to organize processes of problem analysis and the formulation of objectives and strategies. These processes must result in a programme that is negotiated with the Commission.

The German authorities successfully isolated this element of the structural funds' policy model from domestic policies as the programming approach is in conflict with the implementation mode of most domestic regional policy instruments. The latter are defined by framework plans or directives that lay down eligible areas and expenditure as well as the distribution of the budgets, but not regional analyses or strategy developments. This results from the fact that the dominant policy paradigm has remained stable for the last couple of decades. The strategy it prescribes is not adapted to specific needs, but applied in the same fashion in all eligible areas. Thus, programmes are just formulated for the structural funds and do not comprise national policies. The isolated implementation has been consolidated during the 1990s and became symbolic change.

In Ireland, the introduction of the structural funds policy model in 1988 matched with the establishment of 'national agreements' in 1987. These neo-corporatist instruments emanated in a macroeconomic crisis and define the basic lines of public policies, including commitments on government spending. Their initial purpose was to help consolidate the national budget and to prevent wage rises by finding a national consensus. However, for the purpose of the structural funds, a separate programme was formulated at first. With each programming round, the scope of the structural funds programme was widened to comprise more parts of domestic policy. Therefore, though the element was isolated at first, the general development of domestic policies, however, aimed at the same direction as the structural funds. This way, the European policy model could spill over to domestic policies and, finally, induce material change in the structural funds implementation.

Before Sweden joined the EU in 1995, the domestic regional policy followed a logic of compensation for peripheral areas. Subsidies were handed out by the central government's regional governors without a preceding formulation of programmes. From 1995 on, the requirements from the structural funds' policy model were implemented deliberately in isolation from domestic policy. The government decided to set up an entirely separate implementation system. During the implementation of the first Swedish programmes, the parliament passed a regional policy act in 1998 that codified a paradigmatic shift in the domestic regional policy. Since then, in each county 'regional growth agreements' have been formulated that comprise similar elements as the structural funds programmes including concrete policy instruments and an own budget. After an isolated implementation in the first round, the element has been effectively implemented since 1999, and therefore, indicates material change.

8.3.2 Evaluation

The structural funds' element of evaluation refers to the systematic assessment of a programme, its implementation and/or its socio-economic effects against a normative yardstick. Evaluation was introduced as part of the policy model in 1988. The regulations[3] stipulated just a general demand until the revision in 1999. Since then, substantially higher requirements have been part of the regulation. However, largely this is the codification of standards that were developed during the implementation process in the years before. The demands on the implementing actors stem from the requirement to systematically evaluate the programmes. The responsible administration has to scrutinize the effectiveness of its own actions, and it has to do this in cooperation with external actors such as the Commission as well as other 'stakeholders' like the so-called economic and social partners (see below).

In Germany, evaluation was implemented in isolation from domestic policies. The systematic and comprehensive approach, the involvement of external actors, and the methodological endeavour demanded by the Commission mismatched with the national practice. If domestic regional policy was evaluated at all, econometric model calculations or analyses of funding statistics predominated. As a result, the obligatory evaluation of the structural funds was restricted to the European funds. Although, meanwhile, some progress in the evaluation of domestic regional policy is observable, basically the isolated implementation of the element is continued and became a symbolic change.

Besides some niches, Ireland had no tradition of evaluation with regard to public policies. Consequently, this element of the structural funds' policy

---

[3] Article 6 of Council Regulation (EEC) 2052/88 and Article 26 of Council Regulation (EEC) 4253/88; Recitals of Council Regulation (EEC) 2081/93 and Article 26 of Council Regulation (EEC) 2082/93; Recitals 54 and 55 and Articles 14, 16-18, 34-5, 40-3 of Council Regulation (EC) 1260/99.

model mismatched with the practice of domestic regional policy. Occasionally, the government commissioned studies that discussed possible strategies of industrial or regional development, but refrained from studies on the results of the existing policy instruments. Despite the lack of an evaluation tradition, Ireland was quicker than Germany and even Sweden in developing a high evaluation quality. However, the institutional structures as well as the concrete studies are still restricted to the structural funds programmes, and therefore, work isolated from domestic policies. As long as this isolation persisting since the late 1980s remains, evaluation in Ireland will stay a case of symbolic change, too.

Similarly to the Irish case, Swedish regional policy was rarely subject to evaluation. Because systematic and external assessments mismatched with the tradition of a compensation policy, the structural funds were implemented entirely separated from domestic policy instruments. As a result, the element evaluation was implemented in isolation. The recent paradigmatic change in domestic regional policy brought about a new implementation mode that also includes evaluation. The first round of evaluation of the new regional programmes seems to indicate a transformation from isolation to material change, because now, at least in principle, all regional policy activities shall become subject to evaluation.

8.3.3 *Involvement of sub-national state actors*

The demand to involve sub-national actors became obligatory with the last structural funds reform in 1999. The new regulation[4] stipulates that they have to be consulted in the programming process, that they shall be members of the monitoring committees where the involved administrations meet in order to coordinate the implementation and that their approval of the detailed programming documents is required. During the 1990s, the regulations just asked the member state to coordinate the implementation with the regional and local actors it chose. However, even by naming the regional and local actors and requesting their involvement, the regulations have been containing a demand since 1988. The member state governments, thus, had to deal with this demand to share the tasks of implementation with sub-national actors, to coordinate with them or at least to argue about their involvement when the latter and the Commission pressed for it. Since 1999, the obligatory minimum

---

[4] Recitals and Article 4 of Council Regulation (EEC) 2052/88; Article 5 of Council Regulation (EEC) 4253/88; Article 9 of Council Regulation (EEC) 4254/88; Recitals of Council Regulation (EEC) 2082/93; Articles 8–9, 15–16, and 35 of Council Regulation (EC) 1260/99.

requirement has been raised: it now demands the member states to organize a consultation procedure in the programming process and to change the routines of the programming committees in order to enable an involvement of sub-national actors.

Taking a look at the implementation of this element, the German case provides a clear example of absorption: the German *Länder* are traditionally responsible for domestic regional policy, hence they also received the competence to implement the structural funds.

In Ireland, the element of the involvement of sub-national actors was deliberately isolated. It is in conflict with the stable territorial structure of a strong centralized national government and traditionally weak municipalities. In order to fulfil the requirement to involve regional actors in the implementation process, small regional authorities were established. They are staffed with two to three people each and their sole competence is to comment on monitoring data from the structural funds. During the 1990s, this isolation was stabilized and effected symbolic change, even more since the country established a regional structure in order to remain partly eligible for objective 1 status after 1999. Only marginally have some minor alterations in the local government structure been observable since the end of the 1990s. However, their range is far too limited to speak of material change.

In Sweden, the element of the involvement of sub-national actors was isolated at first, but effected material change later on. The structural funds' requirement was taken up by elected local and regional politicians who pressed for their share of the new policy instrument. The central government involved them in the formulation of the programmes and handed over the competence to select projects to them. It isolated this element by deliberately separating the implementation of the structural funds from that of domestic policy instruments that remained the responsibility of central government's regional offices. In the 1999 round of programming, the regional actors were given a larger role than before. This followed the change from compensational domestic budget transfers to a regional competitiveness policy in 1998.

8.3.4 Involvement of non-state actors

The element of non-state actor involvement, just like the involvement of sub-national actors, concerns the distribution of competencies and power in the implementation system. Differently from the involvement of sub-national actors, the involvement of non-state actors has become an element of the structural funds' policy model since the revision of the regulations[5] in 1993. Then the 'economic and social partners' were introduced and the member states were obliged to coordinate the implementation with them as well as with the sub-national actors. Since the new regulation of 1999 has come into force, those responsible for implementing the programmes are faced with the demand to organize the consultation of societal and private actors in the programming process and to open the monitoring committee meetings to them.

The implementation of German domestic regional policy is the task of the respective federal and regional ministries without any participation requirements. The structural funds' element, therefore, mismatched with the existing routines. This led to heavy political conflicts between the Commission and the *Länder* ministries when the revised regulation was implemented after 1993. Eventually, a compromise was found on the political level that opened the monitoring committees to the 'economic and social partners'. They also became involved in the programming processes that started in 1998/99. However, their access is still clearly restricted to the structural funds programmes. The isolated implementation of the element, therefore, was consolidated and became a symbolic change.

The Irish authorities isolated the element at first because they lacked the routines to involve non-state actors in the implementation systems of the domestic programmes. However, the neo-corporatist 'national agreements', started in 1987, indicate a major change in national policy formulation. As described above, these arrangements initially were a means of macroeconomic crisis management. They changed the relationship between state and interest groups and enabled the involvement of the latter on the level of programmes. On the local level, societal and private actors are even more involved in policy formulation and implementation. The local economic development policy is part of an anti-poverty policy that was enabled by the national agreements in the late 1980s. Following this change in domestic policy, the briefly isolated implementation became material change on the national as well as on the local level.

Swedish domestic regional policy was the task of the central government and its regional representatives. When the structural funds were implemented for the first time in 1995, the involvement of non-state actors mismatched with the national tradition. The government consulted non-state actors by public presentations and discussions of the programme

---

[5] Recitals and Article 4 of Council Regulation (EEC) 2081/93; Recitals of Council Regulation (EEC) 2083/93; Articles 8 and 9 of Council Regulation (EEC) 1260/99.

drafts and opened the monitoring committees to them. Because of the strict separation of the structural funds and national policy instruments, the element was implemented in isolation. This mode of operation changed partly after the paradigmatic change of domestic regional policy in 1998. The new 'regional growth agreements' shall be formulated by all relevant actors in the regions including societal and private actors. Up to now, it is, however, difficult to assess whether this will lead to material change. The non-state actors are in a considerably weaker position than the sub-national state actors, and therefore, symbolic change seems to be more likely.

8.3.5 Pattern of policy change

The analysis of the four elements of the policy model in three member states reveals a differentiated pattern of policy change. Six out of the twelve cases investigated indicate effective implementation of the European policy model. This is due to autonomous domestic change: paradigmatic revisions of domestic policy such as the introduction of neo-corporatist macroeconomic agreements in Ireland in 1987 or constitutional change in the polity such as the regionalization experiment in Sweden enabled the diffusion of new actions and routines from the European structural funds to domestic instruments. As the cases have clearly shown, these complementary domestic changes were not caused by the structural funds implementation. Only one out of the twelve cases represents absorption. The new requirement to involve sub-national state actors in regional policy met a functional equivalent in the domestic German regional policy institutions and routines and did not provide any challenge to them. In the remaining five cases, the particular elements of the European policy model did not match national traditions or were even in open conflict with them. Consequently, the national actors tried to implement the element in isolation from domestic policies. The isolation was consolidated over the years and became symbolic change. While the five cases are concentrated on Germany and Ireland, they spread across all four elements (Table 8.1).

As regards effective implementation in terms of material change in routines on the ground, one can identify a variance across member states as well as across elements of the policy model: no case of material change is found in Germany. This can be explained by the absence of any complementary domestic change in this member state. Thus, either adaptation or isolation of structural funds requirements is possible. However, this kind of response can be found in Ireland and Sweden as well. It results from durable contradictions between the element of the structural funds

Table 8.1 The pattern of policy change

	D	IR	S
Programming	S	M	M
Evaluation	S	S	M
Involvement of sub-national state actors	A	S	M
Involvement of non-state actors	S	M	S

A: absorption; S: symbolic change; M: material change.

policy model in question and the respective domestic policies and polity. For example, Irish centralism has not seriously been challenged during the last decades, while at the same time the way of formulating public policies has been paradigmatically revised. As a result, the European policy model's requirement to involve sub-national state actors is implemented symbolically, whereas the requirement to involve non-state actors is implemented effectively. Overall, in each case of effective implementation, the complementary domestic change that enabled it had started well in advance of the change in the structural funds' policy model. Therefore, the domestic change is obviously independent from the structural funds and was not caused by them either, although the latter may have helped it along.

8.4 Summary and conclusions

The pattern of policy change essentially confirms the main hypothesis: Whether the structural funds regulations are implemented effectively or not, lies within the discretion of the member state actors. All four types of responses presented above can be observed in the three member states. However, it is striking that there is only one case of 'absorption'. This occurs only if an element of the structural funds policy model matches a static member state equivalent. Therefore, the rare occurrence of absorption indicates the high degree of difference between EC and member state institutions.

Half of the remaining cases represent merely symbolic change, the other half represent a material change. Nevertheless, it is important to point out that we do not observe that an impact of the structural funds on domestic policies directly 'hits home' (Börzel and Risse 2000), as other studies have suggested. Rather, effects of interaction between EC and domestic policies are materializing over a longer period of time, which can only be identified by procedurally oriented analysis. By tracing back the origins of the domestic change and the temporal order of events, one can point out that domestic change that was caused independently of the structural funds enables the effective implementation of the latter. This result confirms once more that the decentral actors are embedded first of all in the domestic institutional context and only to a much lesser extent in the EC structural funds' institutional context.

The latter argument also helps to explain the striking finding on the variance of responses. Regarding the effectiveness of implementation, there is far more cross-sectional variance in the implementation of different elements of the policy model within one and the same region than there is cross-country variance in the implementation of the same element in different member states. One can almost neglect the variance between regions within one member state because for the choices of action of the decentral actors, the general institutional structures of the polity, the national paths of implementing public policies, and the national structural policy instruments are far more important than the structural funds' policy model.

Finally, the results of the analysis presented here point to a considerably limited capacity of EC decision-makers to control structural policy implementation by defining EC regulations. However, the option of isolated implementation and symbolic change in the end substantially increases the opportunities for policy development. It opens the possibility to buffer outcomes of EC decision-making that are in conflict with domestic policies and polities. If they are implemented in parallel to domestic policy, such uneasy policy innovations can be tested, adapted to emerging changes in the member state's paths, and possibly diffuse later as the Swedish example of new programming arrangements for domestic regional policy shows. However, if the member state institutions remain stable, the isolation will be consolidated and lead to symbolic change: the member state submits to an unwelcome demand and refuses to do so effectively at the same time.

References

Allison, Graham T. (1969). 'Conceptual Models and the Cuban Missile Crisis', *The American Political Science Review*, 63/3: 689–718.

—— (1971). *Essence of Decision. Explaining the Cuban Missile Crisis*. Boston: Little, Brown and Company.

Armstrong, Harvey (1995). 'The Role of European Community Regional Policy', in Barry Jones and Michael Keating (eds.), *The European Union and the Regions*. Oxford: Clarendon Press, 23–64.

Bache, Ian (1998). *The Politics of European Union Regional Policy. Multi-level Governance or Flexible Gatekeeping*. Sheffield: Sheffield Academic Press.

Benz, Arthur (2000). 'Two Types of Multi-Level Governance: Intergovernmental Relations in German and EU Regional Policy', *Regional & Federal Studies*, 10/3: 21–44.
—— and Eberlein, Burkhard (1999). 'The Europeanization of Regional Policies: Patterns of Multi-Level Governance', *Journal of European Public Policy*, 6/2: 329–48.
Börzel, Tanja (1999). 'Institutional Adaptation to Europeanization in Germany and Spain', *Journal of Common Market Studies*, 37/4: 573–96.
—— (2000). 'Europäisierung und innerstaatlicher Wandel. Zentralisierung und Entparlamentarisierung?', *Politische Vierteljahresschrift*, 41/2: 225–50.
—— and Risse, Thomas (2000). *When Europe hits home. Europeanization and domestic change* (EUI Working Papers, RSC 00/56). San Domenico: European University Institute.
Brunsson, Nils (1989). *The Organization of Hypocrisy. Talk, Decision and Action in Organisations*. New York: Wiley.
—— and Olsen, Johan P. (1993). *The Reforming Organization*. London: Routledge.
Bulmer, Simon and Burch, Martin (1998). *The 'Europeanisation' of Central Government: The UK and Germany in Historical Institutionalist Perspective* (EPRU Working Papers, 6/98). Manchester: University of Manchester, Department of Government.
Conzelmann, Thomas (2000a). 'Große Räume, kleine Räume: Die Europäisierung der Regionalpolitik in Deutschland', in Beate Kohler-Koch and Michèle Knodt (eds.), *Deutschland in Europa*. Frankfurt a. M. and New York: Campus, 357–80.
—— (2000b). *Große Räume, kleine Räume. Parallele Institutionalisierung und die Europäisierung der Regionalpolitik in Deutschland und Großbritannien* (dissertation). Mannheim: Universität Mannheim.
Crosby, Benjamin (1996). 'Policy Implementation: the Organizational Challenge', *World Development*, 24/9: 1403–15.
Edelman, Murray (1964). *The Symbolic Uses of Politics*. Urbana: The University of Illinois Press.
—— (1971). *Politics as Symbolic Action. Mass Arousal and Quiescence*. New York: Academic Press.
Goggin, Malcolm L., Bowman, Ann O. M., Lester, James P., and O'Toole, Laurence J. (1990). *Implementation Theory and Practice. Toward a Third Generation*. Glenview: Scott, Foresman and Company.
Hall, Peter A. (1993). 'Policy Paradigms, Social Learning, and the State. The Case of Economic Policymaking in Britain', *Comparative Politics*, 25/3: 275–96.
—— and Taylor, Rosemary C. R. (1996). 'Political Science and the Three New Institutionalisms', *Political Studies*, 44/5: 939–57.
Haverland, Markus (1999). *National Adaptation to European Integration: The Importance of Institutional Veto Points* (EUI Working Papers, RSC 99/17). San Domenico: European University Institute.
Héritier, Adrienne and Knill, Christoph (2000). *Differential Responses to European Integration: A Comparison* (Preprints of the Max Planck Project Group on Common Goods: Law, Politics and Economics, 2000/7). Bonn: Max Planck Project Group.
Hooghe, Liesbet (1996a) (ed.). *Cohesion Policy and European Integration. Building Multi-level Governance*. Oxford: Oxford University Press.
—— (1996b). 'Building a Europe with the Regions: The Changing Role of the European Commission', in Liesbet Hooghe (ed.), *Cohesion Policy and European Integration. Building Multi-level Governance*. Oxford: Oxford University Press, 89–126.

Immergut, Ellen (1997). 'The Normative Roots of the New Institutionalism. Historical Institutionalism and Comparative Policy Studies', in Arthur Benz and Wolfgang Seibel (eds.), *Theorieentwicklung in der Politikwissenschaft—eine Zwischenbilanz*. Baden-Baden: Nomos, 325-56.

Jachtenfuchs, Markus and Kohler-Koch, Beate (1996). 'Einleitung: Regieren im dynamischen Mehrebenensystem', in Markus Jachtenfuchs and Beate Kohler-Koch (eds.), *Europäische Integration*. Opladen: Leske + Budrich, 15-44.

Knill, Christoph and Lenschow, Andrea (1998). 'Change as "Appropriate Adaptation": Administrative Adjustment to European Environmental Policy in Britain and Germany', *European Integration online Papers*, 2/1.

Kohler-Koch, Beate (1999). 'The Evolution and Transformation of European Governance', in Beate Kohler-Koch and Rainer Eising (eds.), *The Transformation of Governance in the European Union*. London and New York: Routledge, 14-35.

Marks, Gary (1996). 'Exploring and Explaining Variation of EU Cohesion Policy', in Liesbet Hooghe (ed.), *Cohesion Policy and European Integration. Building Multi-level Governance*. Oxford: Oxford University Press, 388-422.

——, Hooghe, Liesbet, and Blank, Kermit (1996). 'European Integration from the 1980s', *Journal of Common Market Studies*, 34/1: 343-77.

North, Douglass C. (1990). *Institutions, Institutional Change and Economic Performance*. Cambridge: Cambridge University Press.

O'Toole, Laurence J. (1986). 'Policy Recommendations for Multi-Actor Implementation. An Assessment of the Field', *Journal of Public Policy*, 6/2: 181-210.

Palumbo, Dennis J. and Calista, Donald J. (1990). 'Opening Up the Black Box', in Dennis J. Palumbo and Donald J. Calista (eds.), *Implementation and the Policy Process. Opening up the Black Box*. New York: Greenwood Press, 3-17.

Pressman, Jeffrey L. and Wildavsky, Aaron (1973). *Implementation. How Great Expectations in Washington are Dashed in Oakland, or Why it's Amazing That Federal Programs Work at All*. Berkeley: University of California Press.

Radaelli, Claude (2000). 'Whither Europeanization? Concept Stretching and Substantive Change', *European Integration online Papers*, 4/8.

Risse, Thomas, Cowles, Maria Green, and Caporaso, James (2001). 'Europeanization and Domestic Change: Introduction', in Maria Green Cowles, James Caporaso, and Thomas Risse (eds.), *Transforming Europe. Europeanization and Domestic Change*. Ithaca and London: Cornell University Press, 1-20.

Sabatier, Paul A. (1986). 'Top-Down and Bottom-Up Approaches to Implementation Research. A Critical Analysis and Suggested Synthesis', *Journal of Public Policy*, 6/1: 21-48.

Schmidt, Vivien A. (2001). 'Europeanization and the Mechanisms of Economic Policy Adjustment', *European Integration online Papers*, 5/6.

Smyrl, Marc E. (1998). 'When (and how) do the Commission's Preferences Matter?', *Journal of Common Market Studies*, 36/1: 79-99.

Wishlade, Fiona (1996). 'EU Cohesion Policy: Facts, Figures, and Issues', in Liesbet Hooghe (ed.), *Cohesion Policy and European Integration: Building Multi-Level Governance*. Oxford: Oxford University Press, 27-58.

9

Structuring the State—The Case of European Employment Policy

Frank Deppe, Michael Felder, and Stefan Tidow

9.1 Introduction

Following intensive debates, the Amsterdam Treaty (1997) laid down the legal basis for a European employment policy. Its centrepiece is the coordination of national policies at the European level, to which 'management by objectives' and benchmarking strategies are central. The European forms of governance aim at opening up domestic labour market regimes to new practices and at generalizing specific labour market strategies. These forms of policy transfer seem to differ from the traditional policy method, the so-called 'Community method'. They represent new modes of linking the European and national levels (Héritier 2000: 186–7). The new quality of this linkage is however determined by a transformation of the state which is characterized by new modes of articulating the political sphere and the economic sphere. It is our contention that European employment policy, its effects and mechanisms, are based upon partially common structures of statehood. The single market project has initiated a changed quality of integration. The European and the national levels can no longer be understood as complementary spheres. European integration itself structures statehood.

Our analysis draws on approaches within political economy and crisis theory (Section 9.2). It focuses on the question of how the contradiction between internationalization and the nation state is dealt with in a historically specific form. European employment policy must be understood against the background of this contradiction; traditional instruments of

We thank first of all Beate Kohler-Koch for her comments to improve and clarify our argument as well as Friedrich Heinemann and Bob Jessop who criticized an earlier draft of the paper.

employment policy are eroded as a consequence of globalization and Europeanization. The options available for a European solution are limited by the dominance of a hegemonic project of integration, whilst simultaneously new forms of mediation between the political and the economic are being developed.

Section 9.3 is dedicated to the analysis of the policy itself. How is the relationship between politics and economics changing in this field? By analysing the central documents and programmes we try to reconstruct the targets and the rationales of European employment policy. Shifts are identified on three levels: the reduced range of politics (Section 9.3.1), the dominance of criteria of economic rationality (Section 9.3.2), and a new demarcation between the public and the private spheres (Section 9.3.3). We aim to demonstrate that the significance of European employment policy cannot be reduced to the development of new methods of policy coordination within the European Union (EU). Rather, it induces a fundamental structural change of modern capitalist societies, which eventually leads to a new topography of the social sphere.

Section 9.4 delineates the new forms of governance and the new division of labour between the national and the European levels. This section focuses on the formulation of the national action plans (NAP) as well as their effects, along with methods of benchmarking and the role of the structural funds. Although employment policy is based on a soft mode of governance avoiding hierarchy and binding legislation, it should not be rated as symbolic politics. Soft modes of governance may hit hard and enforce the transformation of the state.

In Section 9.5, the findings of our research will be reflected in the context of the present theoretical debate on integration. In our opinion, the new quality of the linkage between the European and the national levels is responsible for both the dynamic and the crisis-prone character of European integration.

9.2 A new reality of integration—theoretical remarks

Our theoretical approach draws on the assumptions developed in political economy and crisis theory according to which European integration has to be understood as a relative form of resolving the secular contradiction between internationalization and the nation state (Deppe 2000). The history of integration can be read as a permanent reorganization of the relationship between the economic sphere and the political sphere within a given territory (Statz 1979: 224). The formal separation of politics from the economy is a central element of capitalist societies, which is combined with historical concrete and complex mediations between political and economic rationales in a topology of the social sphere (Felder 2001). In a historical perspective different modes of regulation can be analysed, which establish a compatibility of the political and economic order that is not restricted to the boundaries between the state and the market, but also focuses on the social and behavioural preconditions of a market society. It includes several levels: a macro-level, which refers to relations between social systems, a meso-level, which refers to the interorganizational relations, and a micro-level, which refers to the manifestation of actor orientations in their everyday routines. 'Reproducing and regularizing capitalism involves a "social fix" that partially compensates for the incompleteness of the pure capital relation and gives it a specific dynamic through the articulation of its economic and extra-economic elements. This helps to secure a relatively durable pattern of structural coherence in the handling of the contradictions and dilemmas inherent in the capital relation. One necessary aspect of this social fix is the imposition of "spatio-temporal fix" on these economic and extra-economic elements. It achieves this by establishing spatial and temporal boundaries within which the relative structural coherence is secured and by externalizing certain costs of securing this coherence beyond these boundaries' (Jessop 2000: 334–5). Particular phases of European integration are characterized by such a 'spatio-temporal fix', which demands a new alignment of the relationships between different spatial levels, following on from processes of de- and re-territorialization.

The history of integration was accompanied by continuous crises in its development. These crises initiated processes of adaptation, which restructured the basic relationships between the political and the economic sphere as well as the division of labour between the European and the national levels. The failure of the Economic and Monetary Union (EMU) in the early 1970s intensified intergovernmental methods and stimulated the transition to supply-side politics as the dominant paradigm of economic policies. At the same time intergovernmentalism meant re-nationalization, which prevented ambitious projects of integration. The strategy to follow the traditional path of integration led to a crisis of the economy as well as to a crisis of the structures, the institutions, and the patterns of solidarity within the European Community (EC) (Ambrosius 1996: 145). It was not until co-operation within the frame of the European Monetary System (EMS 1979) was enforced that this crisis was overcome.

Intergovernmental methods of integration—strengthened by the introduction of the European Council and first steps of foreign policy cooperation—ensured that national and European structures were complementary. Integration was again a reaction to the experience of the inadequacy of national spaces and resources to meet economic as well as political challenges and aimed at the modernization of national societies. The European level did not weaken but strengthened the nation state as a 'level complementing national statehood' (Ziltener 1999: 124).

Nevertheless, the conditions for 'embedded liberalism' (Ruggie 1982) were already eroding. The EMS, with the strong German DM, enforced pressure upon national governments to follow a policy of monetary and fiscal discipline. The EC crisis of the late 1970s did not threaten the basic elements of market integration and common interests; it did, however, require a new orientation of integration policies. The strengthening of intergovernmentalism and at the same time the limitation of the scope of action of national governments in economic policies opened the door to a structural change in European integration, which was eventually driven forward by the single market initiative. After the failure of the 'French experiment' (Ross 1998), an alignment between the economic policies of the major member states became possible (Moravcsik 1991)—in reaction to the decline of Europe in the triadic competition with the USA and Japan and to the victories of liberal and conservative parties.

The single market—which, in a second step, was linked to the monetary union—constituted a new, hegemonic project of integration policy. Its implementation enlarged the scope of European politics and deeply transformed the relationship between the European and the national levels. The post-Maastricht crisis (Deppe and Felder 1993), however, indicated new problems with respect to the legitimacy of the project. It was less a crisis between European governments and their national political ambitions than the manifestation of a deep cleavage between those who rule—be it in politics or the economy—and those who are ruled. Despite a joint effort to stem the tide of public scepticism, it turned into a crisis of both European and national politics. Since the failure of the referendum in Denmark in June 1992, the erosion of the permissive consensus (Reif 1993) is evident both in public opinion polls and in the low participation in the European elections and again in the Irish referendum in 2001 rejecting the ratification of the Treaty of Nice. The increasing opposition within national societies to the social consequences of domestic policies of competitive adaptability has exerted massive pressure upon governments (Youngs 1999: 301–6). The degree of economic and political interdependence which had already been achieved, particularly in the course of the transition to monetary union, prevented any independent reorganization of national political projects. A further deepening of integration could have presented a solution, but it failed precisely as a result of the political weakening of the nation states which—under the pressure of legitimacy problems—became increasingly introspective. National governments and the EU system were drawn further into the vortex of a mutual deficit of legitimacy. This dilemma articulated by the post-Maastricht crisis stresses the necessity of a renewed orientation of the integration process. Recent political initiatives like the launching of a European constitutional convention and the presentation of a White Paper on European Governance (European Commission 2001b) testifies the awareness and the willingness to find an escape route in institutional reforms. At the same time, it has created favourable conditions for placing the idea of an employment policy on the European agenda. The deficiencies of European and national politics create a demand for an intensified Europeanization as well as for a demarcation of the scope of this Europeanization. Widening the range of economic and political action, which produces the necessity of market-oriented regulations at the European level, goes hand in hand with the call for the protection of national structures which are a reaction to precisely these transformations.

Since the beginning of the 1990s, European integration has faced a new development prone to lead to more crises ahead. In order to react politically to the contradiction between internationalization and the nation state in the age of globalization, the new quality of European integration now has to be taken into account. Until the introduction of the single market project, it was still possible to understand the relationship between the national and European level in terms of complementarity. The erosion of this constellation was ultimately based on the increasing globalization of capital markets and the internationalization of commodity markets. Now, the 'dis-embedded world market' has a strong effect on the scope of action of national policies. This, however, is not simply a result of the adaptation to globalized markets, but is ultimately brought about by a transformation of the state. It is a process that is at the core of European integration and is determined by new forms of mediation between the spheres of the economic and the political. This process poses a theoretical challenge. Thus, Cerny (1999) calls for new links between state theory and a theory of International Political Economy in order not just to capture the interactive processes between attempts of national restructuring, internationalization, and transnationalization, but also to re-politicize the understanding of globalization.

Our main assumption is that Europeanization represents the specific form through which globalization occurs in Europe. The two levels of national and European governance are becoming blurred, and processes of mutual structuration take place between the member states and the European Union. According to Jessop (1990, 1993), the internationalization of the state pushes the transition from the Keynesian welfare state to the Schumpeterian workfare regime. Different central dimensions of the state are affected: modes of representation, internal organization, forms of intervention, social bases of state power, state projects (the state in its internal unity), and hegemonic projects (the conduct of state policy in a wider societal context). In all these aspects, it will be interesting to analyse the emergence of new mediations between economic and political rationales. Changes are not only relevant in the individual dimensions, but also with regard to the relations between the different dimensions which produce a new strategic selectivity. It is mainly the state projects and their discursive reproduction which link the individual dimensions of the state and provide the necessary unity which permits us to refer to the state as a societal relation (Poulantzas 1977) and an 'illusory community' (Marx and Engels 1956: 33).

For the member states within the EU, the internationalization occurs as an uneven Europeanization of particular dimensions of statehood. Europeanization is not synonymous with 'competitive state building' (Banting 1995) or with the emergence of a European federal state. It is based upon partially common structures of statehood (Felder 2001: 193–210). Not all dimensions of statehood become Europeanized. While the forms of representation and the social basis of the state remain national, there is a dynamic process of building new forms of European governance. The European and the national levels can no longer be conceived as separate spheres. This is the end of the former complementarity between the European and the national levels: European integration does not strengthen the state anymore, but, instead, pushes its transformation. Beyond territorial borders, new mediations between the political and the economic sphere are forced by aiming at increased productivity and competitiveness.

The contradiction between internationalization and the nation state finds a new, provisional solution in this uneven and partial Europeanization of statehood. Common axes of intervention characterize—as new forms of governance—the dynamic aspects of the integration process. They are detached from the relationship of social forces in the nation states. European governance works well in the field of policy transfer but is less efficient in interest-mediation. Because of the missing social embeddedness, the dynamic of integration is limited to an intergovernmentally shaped political process which installed a hegemonic integration project with the EMU at its core. This European project was constituted by a synthesis of the interests of member states and their respective concrete state projects (Dyson and Featherstone 1999). It fixed the dominance of economic integration legally. Since this project has lost much of its public support, the disciplinary elements are becoming more obvious (Gill 1998). The dynamics of the multi-level system with respect to the transformation of the state correspond with barriers to the reform of European politics. Modifications are only possible within the hegemonic integration project.

European employment policy is a prominent case by which one can understand both the structural change of a European policy and the structuring of the state by European integration. Our analysis concentrates on two decisive aspects. First, we will study the new boundaries which are drawn between the economic and the political spheres by European employment policy, in particular, the reduced range of politics, the expanded effects of certain criteria of economic rationality and the new demarcations between the public and the private sphere. Second, we will describe the transformation of the state by European integration utilizing new modes of governance. With the method of open coordination and the employment programmes of the European Social Fund (ESF) new techniques of integration have been added to established supranational and intergovernmental instruments. Exploring these new modes of governance provides us with a more precise understanding of the limits of European politics. They do not result primarily from differences between national interests or from the inherent dynamics of the process of bargaining, but from the insufficient social embedding of European politics.

9.3 New articulations of the political and the economic sphere in European employment policy

From its beginnings, European employment policy was confronted with two critical arguments. The first stressed national responsibility, the second saw a conflict between the concept of market liberalization and deregulation on the one hand and European employment policy—as some kind of a re-regulation policy—on the other (Tidow 2000). However, it was possible to institutionalize employment policy in the course of the 1990s, because both arguments were revised under the aegis of an 'advanced liberalism' (Dean 1999: 149–75). Employment policy was no longer conceived as an instrument for limiting and controlling markets, but as a means of increasing and improving their dynamics. The emphasis upon a plurality of national paths was transformed into efforts to optimize combinations of national policies by permanent comparison and the adoption of best practices. The debates and conflicts concerning European employment policy were themselves part of the institutionalization of new techniques and new rationales of governance.

9.3.1 *Limited scope of politics*

At the beginning of the 1990s, the increase of unemployment in Western Europe was perceived as a dramatic challenge. With the White Paper on Growth, Competitiveness, and Employment, the European Commission (1993) drafted its first strategic response to these problems. The analytical point of reference was the lack of employment-intensive growth. The former single market optimism of the Cecchini report (Cecchini 1985), which had predicted that deregulation, privatization, and flexibilization would lead to economic growth and hence to more employment, had vanished. The Commission did not want radical change, but rather a modification of the economic policy. It raised the question of insufficient demand (as a cause of low growth rates) and pleaded for stronger national fiscal engagement. Simultaneously, it demanded structural change and modernization co-managed at the European level. Its proposals contained some elements of Keynesian politics, but were mainly oriented towards Schumpeterian innovation politics, which transcend mere supply-side politics.

At its meeting in Essen (1994), the European Council emphasized the 'paramount task' of solving the employment crisis. But the heads of state and government immediately discarded all the sparse-Keynesian elements. What remained was the recommendation of structural reform with a supply-side orientated approach focusing in particular on the flexibility of labour markets and workforce (European Council 1994). In addition, the strategy was reduced to an intergovernmental exchange of information—a procedure for coordinating national policies whereby the European Council called upon the member states to undertake specific measures. This procedure, however, was not linked to any sanction mechanisms, political instructions, or quantitative objectives.

In the course of the Intergovernmental Conference of 1996/7, the employment issue again became politicized. It was felt that a strictly monetarist stability pact at the European level might further reduce the range of national politics with respect to labour markets. Therefore, the French Socialists demanded that employment should be considered as an integral part of a European economic policy. After the electoral victories of New Labour in Britain and of the French socialists, the political balance of power within the Council had changed. A new title on employment was incorporated into the Treaty of Amsterdam (Goetschy 1999; Tidow 1998). On the one hand, European employment policy was strengthened and the procedure laid down in Essen was slightly modified; on the other hand, however, the provisions of the treaty barely deviated from the course which had been followed up to this point. The stability and growth pact remained unchanged. The new employment title was not tied to any genuinely European competencies; annual employment guidelines were to be taken into account by the member states in national action plans. The Council was to control progress and could direct specific recommendations to national governments. The political profile of European employment policy was significantly limited to 'promoting a skilled, trained and adaptable workforce and labour markets responsive to economic change' (Article 125 TEU). At the same time, a foundation for adopting incentive measures 'aimed at developing exchanges of information and best practices' was laid. At the Luxembourg job summit in the autumn of 1997, the new procedure was applied for the first time. To improve the efficiency of national labour markets the EU was given the authority to spell out objectives—based on the 'pillars' of employability, entrepreneurship, adaptability of businesses and their employees, and equal opportunities for men and women in finding gainful employment—which were to be taken into account by national policy-makers.

As a result of this so-called Luxembourg process, a procedure of coordination and benchmarking was created for the modernization of national labour markets without any change in the dominant orientation of European economic and monetary policy. Labour market policy remained subordinate to the policy of stability and consolidation, as defined by the convergence criteria of the Maastricht Treaty. Structural problems of the labour markets were predominantly interpreted as a consequence of institutional paralysis. The guidelines mainly referred to the individual level of professional qualification and to inadequate incentives in the systems of social protection (Council 1997). The new European instruments were directed towards screening the efficiency of national systems and instruments. The recommendations accepted a kind of pre-political measure for solving the problems which reduced the complexity of social problems to seemingly objective indicators. As a consequence of these measures, the potential scope of politics did not only become limited, but also a new perspective on the economic problems of governance was adopted. The logic of the market and the logic of the state were no longer regarded as diametrically opposed. Modernized state institutions were seen rather as a precondition for improving the dynamics and the innovative capacities of the markets.

In spite of this rather clear-cut supply-side profile of the new policy, conservative governments opposed the institutionalization of the policy as a gateway for a new European re-regulation policy. At the European summit in Cardiff, they tried to reinforce the Cecchini logic. The summit set out the agenda for further progress in structural economic reform and sound public finances as the central basis for job creation, without linking it explicitly to the European employment policy (European Council 1998).

Only one year later, the Cologne summit of 1999 demonstrated that the worries of conservative forces had not been groundless. In Germany, the conservative–liberal government had been replaced. The new social–democratic hegemony in Europe was reflected by the 'European employment pact', which for the first time represented a comprehensive approach, bringing together all the Union's employment policy measures. It called for the further development and better implementation of the Luxembourg process and for the improvement of the innovative capacity and efficiency of the markets in goods, services, and capital (Cardiff process). As a third pillar, the pact endorsed a new 'Cologne process': The 'co-ordination of economic policy and improvement of mutually supportive interaction between wage developments and monetary, budget and fiscal policy through macroeconomic dialogue (between representatives of the Council, the Commission, the European Central Bank and the social partners) aimed at preserving a non-inflationary growth dynamic' (European Council 1999a).

Linking an employment-oriented approach to macroeconomic politics had been a fundamental concern of the European left (Aust 2001). The French socialists, in particular, had championed the cause of a European 'economic government' for years. When they came to power, however, they had to agree upon an agenda with completely shifted parameters: monetary and exchange rate policies had been removed from national control, and henceforth served the purpose of fighting inflation. Under the pressure of fiscal policy consolidation, expansive growth and demand strategies were out of the question. Redistribution was only possible in so far as it did not threaten international competitiveness. As a central variable of employment policies, wage issues had assumed a strategic status. In the course of the transition from fordism to post-fordism, there is a paradigm shift and a change in the significance of the role of wages. Being no longer a source of national demand, they become a cost factor in terms of international competitiveness. The Cologne employment pact reflects precisely this 'new Keynesian consensus' (Teague 1999). While there is a general acceptance of the need to coordinate individual policies, monetary and fiscal policy as crucial points of reference remain untouched by the 'co-operative macro-economic policy mix'. The agreement rather calls on both sides of industry to adjust their wage bargaining positions to accommodate the European Central Bank objective of price stability.

The third pillar, that is, the 'Cologne process', has had no practical consequences so far. Decisive progress was made in combining policies from the second and the third pillar, from the 'Luxembourg process' and the 'Cardiff process'. This progress was due to an initiative by the British and the Spanish governments, which shared a concern about the integration of the macroeconomic dimension, and therefore wished to push forward structural reforms in the markets for labour, capital, and goods (European Council 1999b). This initiative was picked up by the Portuguese presidency, which combined it with its own priorities. From now on, within the framework of a generally accepted limitation of the scope of politics, even full employment could be proclaimed as a goal. The European employment policy was now connected to new strategic purposes: The EU was to become the most competitive and dynamic knowledge-based economy in the world, capable of sustainable economic growth with more and better jobs and greater social cohesion (Council 2000a,b). The existing European politics and competencies should be realigned in support of these objectives. Obviously, the Lisbon summit strengthened the importance of employment policy. Yet the new employment policy has lost its critical impetus as an instrument for eliminating social inequality. It has become a prime example for reflexive government. 'Rather than seeking to "pull the levers" of macroeconomic policy, governance is increasingly concerned to reform the conduct of individuals and institutions in all sectors to make them more competitive and efficient. In this sphere, at least, a government of economic processes is being displaced by a government of governmental mechanisms' (Dean 1999: 195). New demarcation lines between the political and the economic within the context of European integration drive forward the transformation of the state.

9.3.2 New orientation within the policy

The new concept of governance accentuates the self-restraint of politics and the expanding constraints resulting from economic calculations and criteria. This is expressed by the recent shift in labour market policies from 'welfare' to 'workfare'. This approach—originally developed in the USA—has met with increasing acceptance throughout Europe, first of all in Britain: 'Labour's emerging approach is distinctively "workfarist" in the sense that welfare stands for the principles of needs-based entitlement and universality, workfare stands for market-based compulsion and selectivity. Under workfarism, welfare and work become the dominant modalities of reform discourse, rather than unemployment and poverty per se' (Peck 1999: 367). This market-based approach also marks the European employment policy guidelines. Although they address different problem groups and issues (youth, long-term unemployment, older employees, gender equality, and social inclusion), the specific strategies are not significantly differentiated. Individual defects with respect to employability and inadequate structures of incentives to work are regarded as the main causes of unemployment and exclusion.

This new orientation has also influenced policies connected to the European structural funds, especially the ESF. In previous periods, the distribution of grants tended to be attached to a traditional labour market policy. There were, however, two aspects that pointed beyond the model of an active, traditional labour market policy. Firstly, particular emphasis was placed on the support of target groups (long-term unemployed people, women, the young, and the marginalized). However, their reintegration into the labour market was defined as a policy of human resources support reflecting the conditions of actual demand. The policy instruments had been designed to open up new fields of employment and were, thus, closely tied to the requirements of economic and competition policies. The second point stressed by the ESF policy referred to the inclusion of those who are still employed, with the intention of strengthening preventive labour market policy. 'Objective 2' of the structural policy and the community's initiative ADAPT were the most important instruments. The orientation to socio-economic structural change and support for regional competitiveness had been the central objective of the programme (European Commission 1994). Both aspects had become dominant in the new period of regional and structural policy. Now the development of human resources has become an independent goal; at the same time labour market policy in all 'objectives' of the ESF has shifted from a reactive to a preventive policy. The orientation towards special problem groups is now less important, whereas the importance of the adaptability of the systems of education, training and employment has been increased (Regulation 1999).

However, the new rationales are not only characteristic of the general guidelines for employment policy and the directives concerning the ESF. They have also been inscribed into the strategies, techniques, and instruments of employment policy. Via the programmes and the national action plans, they have permeated national contexts, based upon extensive statistical information, which is increasingly standardized. By these means, the issues and objects of the new employment policy become comparable and a new field for intervention is mapped out. The construction of indicators and the method of benchmarking obviously favour the dominance of economic over political rationales. In recent years, the 'Luxembourg process' has undergone a systematic change from a coordinating procedure to labour market (policy)-oriented benchmarking (Tidow 1999). For the first time the 1998 report presented a genuine comparison of key characteristics in which the individual countries are assessed in relation to the 'European champion'. It contained a detailed evaluation of national labour market policies and an as yet tentative recommendation of innovative (workfarist) reference practices (European Commission 1998*a*). A comprehensive set of indicators was used to disclose labour market performances. The EU also drew on a set of methodological instruments recommended by an international network of experts (Employment Observatory RESEARCH Network 1998) working on behalf of the Commission. The problems of labour market policies and innovation are no longer at the centre of political interest and are regarded instead as instruments that apparently promise a professional solution. They have acquired economic legitimacy and no longer require normative justification; state decisions are reached through the mechanisms of benchmarking and competition.

In the meantime, this technique of governance has been employed more generally at the European level; in Lisbon it was transferred to other policy areas. Education policy, welfare systems, research, and technology policy are examples of areas in which the 'method of open co-ordination' is preferred. This method involves the 'establishing, where appropriate, (of) quantitative and qualitative indicators and benchmarks against the best in the world and tailored to the needs of different Member States and sectors as a means of comparing best practice' (European Council 2000: paragraph 37). The Lisbon strategy is reduced to 35 indicators which measure Europe's progress towards its objective of developing the most dynamic and competitive economic space (European Commission 2001a) and which provide the basis for further actions and decisions. Access to the Internet, pricing systems in economic branches connected to the net, and the amount of capital in the financial markets are considered to be as important as employment rates. Microeconomic reasoning pervades the political field in increasingly complex ramifications.

9.3.3 A new relationship between the public and the private

Workfarist strategies may be classified according to the relationship between constraint and innovation. In the US and in Australia, the obligation to work determines strategies of employment policy (Dean 1995; Peck 1999). European employment policy, however, stresses the element of innovation. Active labour market policy does not only aim at the creation of additional jobs, but also concentrates on the issue of qualification. This approach to the transformation of the national labour market and employment policies was already laid down in the Luxembourg guidelines. In accordance with the programme of laying the foundation for a knowledge-based economy, education policy became more important. The rather modest objectives of the Luxembourg process were now supplemented by the project of systematically evaluating national systems of education and professional training and by a detailed working programme aimed at the national implementation of 'lifelong learning' (European Council 2001).

Two premises guide the 'workfarist' orientation. The first premise concentrates on the insufficient employability of the individual, which prevents him or her from finding a job (Employment Observatory RESEARCH Network 1999). The general cause of this is a deficient investment in human capital. Lifelong learning and investment in human resources, therefore, become individual imperatives. Accordingly, the second premise concerns the relationship between the claims and duties (of the unemployed), which is formulated in a new way. Cuts in passive transfer payments are not merely the result of deficit pressure within welfare systems. They rather result from a new definition of the contractual relationship between the state and employers on the one hand and employees on the other: continuous modernization no longer guarantees 'vested interests'.

The individual's duty to look for work and to improve his or her adaptability to the demands of labour markets is reinforced.

It is for this reason that the European Council proposed that the reform of social welfare systems should include a revision of the systems of transfer, incentive, and social security. 'Benefit, tax and training systems must be reviewed and adapted to ensure that they actively support the employability of unemployed persons. Moreover, these systems should interact appropriately to encourage the return to the labour market of those inactive persons willing and able to take up a job. Particular attention should be given to promoting incentives for unemployed or inactive people to seek and take up work' (Council 2001). Obviously, innovation remains the central point of reference; yet the duty to work is intensified by the reorganization of the social welfare systems. Differences between the national welfare systems within the EU are still significant. The European initiatives to strengthen cooperation between public labour market administration and local administrative bodies tend towards transnational alignments, such as local employment pacts (European Commission 1998b) or the financing of ESF programmes. In Germany, for instance, projects to improve cooperation between different administrative institutions responsible for the labour market (*Arbeitsamt*) and for social security (local *Sozialamt*) (Bundesrepublik Deutschland 2000: 169). The boundaries between different levels of government and between social and employment policy become blurred. At the same time European education policies are redefined in order to improve employment rates within the EU (Maurer 1999: 148-9).

The tension between 'citoyen' and 'bourgeois' is inscribed from the outset into capitalist societies as a consequence of the separation of politics and the economy. It has now become the object of new strategies of socialization which reorganize the relationship between the public and the private spheres, between the state and the individual. 'Welfare interventions aimed at guarantees of social and economic basic conditions for social participation and integration of the Citoyen. They constituted a field of permanent social and political struggle. State intervention in the Schumpeterian Workfare Regime, however, addresses the homo oeconomicus. It aims at state-managed technocratic perfection through governmental techniques and the proclamation of a new public virtue' (Felder 2001: 124). The latter is based on a new combination of sociability and innovation. Via the programmatic discourses of the 'third way', it is deeply inscribed into the basic normative structure of European societies. The concept of social justice is reconstructed according to the imperatives of a highly economized education policy, which remains within the conceptual limits of an 'entrepreneurial self' (Wagner 1995). The new demarcations between politics and economy, which are motivated by European integration, go beyond the modification of single policies: they aim at a new topography of the social sphere.

9.4 Streamlining of national employment policies by new forms of governance

After this survey of the new content of European employment policy, which focuses on the shifting boundaries in the articulation of the political and the economic, we would like to examine the division of labour between European and national governance more closely. Traditional ideas of statehood as well as classic models of European integration impede an understanding of Europeanization as a 'multitude of co-evolving, parallel and not necessarily tightly coupled processes' which 'signify a new constellation of change processes' (Olsen 1996: 271). While the mechanisms establishing the new modes of governance are ultimately based on 'imposition', their evolution and new characteristics rely mainly on 'involvement' and 'attraction' (Kohler-Koch 1999: 26–30). Hence the proponents of a multi-level approach tend to emphasize the 'soft policies' when describing the new quality of European integration.

The whole concept of European employment policy relies upon such 'soft policies'. Originally, it did not go beyond a rather vague procedure of intergovernmental coordination. Today, the European employment strategy is much more than a symbolic policy, primarily due to its incremental expansion. The Commission, in particular, made extensive use of the new opportunities offered by the Treaty of Amsterdam and successfully maintained its role as manager of the whole process and as political entrepreneur (Tidow 1998). In the historical process of the formation of the new strategy—with regard to the new forms of interplay between the European and the national levels—the following points seem most significant: (1) In its proposal for the Luxembourg strategy, the Commission issued 19 concrete guidelines (as opposed to the very general priority areas of the heads of state and government) and put qualitative concepts of reform into concrete terms by means of quantitative objectives, (2) the Commission then extended this 'management by objectives' to include the development of a benchmarking process, and (3) created a link to European structural policy.

All three forms of intervention aim at opening national labour market regimes to new practices. They represent examples of policy transfer (Dolowitz and Marsh 1996) within a multi-organizational setting. From a micro-perspective they can be described as network learning, leading to specific forms of integration (March 1999). Their structuring effect is achieved to the extent that the forms of intervention convey specific contents, which, however, do not go beyond the scope of the hegemonic project. Nevertheless, they clearly aim at bringing about changes in the regulation of labour market policy. Thanks to the encouragement of competitive elements and the diffusion of common problem-solving philosophies, they require no harsh regulative measures but aim at a harmonization from below. The crucial strategic points of reference are processed within national institutional frameworks, which in turn are modified and given a new objective.

Initially, it seemed that the Luxembourg guidelines meant little more than an additional workload for the labour market administrations of the member states. The ongoing and planned measures (programmes and legislation) now had to be brought together in the national action plans. As soon as the first cycle was completed, however, the Commission expressed unusually harsh criticism of the varying quality of the individual plans and amended the non-committal nature of the procedure by exercising public pressure (Tömmel 2000). Since then, the Commission has gone even further, instructing the Council to issue political recommendations for the member states (European Commission 2000). This implies closer ties between the European and the national levels as national authorities have to respond to criticism and are forced to address the rationales of the proposed European solutions. This will not lead to a hierarchical supervision of the policies of member states or to a reorientation of the national action plans. It does, however, initiate a communicative process between the national and the European level, in the course of which individual measures have to be presented and justified.

European politics, thus, not only provoke an evaluation of national programmes but also, due to the broad political range of the guidelines, discussions concerning the varying orientations of their contents. The ultimate effect will not be the immediate revision of previous national labour market policies, but the initiation of a revised division of labour and cooperation between the national ministries.

Common problem-solving philosophies are generated in particular by the labour market policy of benchmarking. While the coordination procedure is largely restricted to the convergence of broad objectives, benchmarking is already a step towards the convergence of means and, consequently, of policy formulation and implementation. The emphasis on best practices and benchmarking has become a conceptual centrepiece of European employment policy. Best practices are not only 'self-justifying', but also appeal to various players in the labour market. With neoclassical recipes for success being gradually replaced as points of reference by the real experience and policies of the member states, even trade unions are beginning to look to 'best practices' as a pragmatic and professional solution (Tidow 1999). This approach was additionally strengthened by a Commission programme aimed at encouraging the identification and the exchange of best practices in active labour market policy (AAmpol). Since 1999, peer reviews have been carried out in the member states. National and European executives and experts meet within this network to discuss the data for exemplary practices in the member states (Peer Review 2000).

Sceptics merely emphasize the appeal-oriented nature of the new employment strategy (Keller 1999). However, when the strategy is considered from our preferred perspective of the emergence of partially common structures of European statehood, a different picture emerges: 'The new benchmarking procedure seeks to build fairly close and meaningful connections between national labour regimes without requiring much institutional harmonization. Balancing policy convergence and institutional diversity is the centrepiece of the new employment strategy' (Teague 1999: 54). Here, convergence is not prescribed from above, but is rather the aim pursued by means of processing problem-solving strategies. In this context it is not so much the subversive activity of the Commission which safeguards the prospect of success of this form of governance, but rather the new modes of articulating the political and the economic which are inherent in these instruments.

This explains the attractiveness of the 'open method of co-ordination', which has been applied since Lisbon to more and more policy fields. Initially, it was the Commission that discovered and conceived 'benchmarking' (Tidow 1999; Bomberg and Peterson 2000) in order to strengthen its position in the European employment policy. Meanwhile, the European Council and the national executives have adopted the instrument. 'The open method of coordination is to be combined with other available methods depending on the problem to be addressed. These methods can range from integration and harmonization to cooperation. The open method of coordination itself takes an intermediate position in this range of different methods' (Council 2000b: 6). As a concrete way of developing modern governance using the principle of subsidiary the method has become attractive to national executives who employ it in order to prevent 'hard' regulations.

The programmes of structural policy provide another example of the transmission of specific contents which drive forward the national reorganization of the regulation of labour market policy, particularly at the regional level. This emphasis on specific contents is coupled with financial concerns; it is linked to the pressure to accommodate national programmes to new practices (Knodt 1998). With reference to employment policies, the ESF assumes an especially important role. In Section 9.3.2 we demonstrated that a workfarist orientation has recently characterized the programmes of the ESF. National and sub-national players continue to occupy a strong position in the programming process and decide which focal points are selected from the European support menu. But they are no longer able to control the process entirely. A further diffusion of the specific profile of European policies was also strengthened by the latest reform (1999) of the structural funds, which stressed a decentralized approach. The Commission is pushing its views on labour market regulation by emphasizing relating institutional structures. One instrument is to ask the relevant actors to get engaged in territorial employment pacts and to agree upon a common problem definition and strategy (European Commission 1998*b*).

Against this background, we would now like to look at the new procedural aspects within the recent programming period (Lang and Reissert 1999). The following aspects of the revised procedure deserve particular attention: First, the evaluation instruments were enhanced; in addition, the member states were required to name the quantitative and qualitative objectives of the measures they adopted. Second, in the middle of the planning period, a 4 per cent efficiency reserve (per member state) was allocated to the most effective measures. As a result of the new efficiency reserve, there is increased pressure to administer programmes efficiently. The more extensive evaluation now provides an instrument to measure efficiency (with respect to both the actors' own goals and competing programmes or measures). Altogether the role of the Commission has been strengthened, it has an enhanced say in strategic programming, and ideas generated by the Commission have a greater impact. In the words of Monika Wulf-Mathies, the former commissioner: 'In this way we create at the very least the basic conditions for a genuine "best practice" competition, in which the European Commission will assume a much more significant function as a "turn table" for innovative concepts' (Wulf-Mathies 1999: 371).

Last but not least, one has to realize that another aspect of structural policy regulation goes even further in suspending the boundaries in the division of labour between the European and the national levels: The new 'objective 3' of the structural support scheme, which has replaced the former emphasis on target groups with an endorsement of the modernization of educational systems, also serves as a 'policy frame of reference for all measures to promote human resources in a national territory' (Council 1999). This includes the NAPs for employment. Thus, on the one hand the structural support policy is intended to supplement the European employment policy, while on the other it steps up the pressure for NAP and the 'policy frame of reference' to become coherent. This in turn increases the pressure on national policy-makers in different departments to reach common interpretations of the situation and to formulate common problem-solving strategies. Meanwhile, NAP, employment policy guidelines, ESF regulation, and structural policy are all political points of reference and accordingly constitute diverse European channels of influence (European Commission 1999), which further blur the boundaries between EU and member state responsibilities.

To sum up, we can verify a rearrangement of the division of labour between the European and the national levels and a parallel process of de- and re-territorialization of the relevant responsibilities. In future, labour market policy will be Europeanized without necessarily implying a harmonization of structures. Nevertheless, the individual nation states are subject to a certain pressure to adapt to this process, both institutionally and in terms of content. They are part of a hegemonic integration project which curbs the potential for reform within European employment policy and frustrates hopes of being able to reassess the relation of economic and social integration via employment policy. The political point of reference is not social integration, but competition-oriented structural change.

9.5 New modes of integration: Between dynamism and crisis

The new modes of integrating European and national politics, analysed through the lens of employment policy, point to the limits of current patterns of integration theory debates. Neither of the contending concepts of supranationality (Sandholtz and Stone Sweet 1998) and intergovernmentality (Moravcsik 1998) gives an explanation of the processes of European employment policy described here (see, for example, Moravcsik and Nicolaïdis 1999; Johansson 1999). The combined effects of domestic politics and European cooperation rather call for an expansion of theoretical perspectives to attain a multi-level approach which encompasses comparative approaches and policy analysis (Hix 1994). However, an informed perspective and a new analytical tool-kit are only of theoretical use, if the micro- and meso-perspectives can be combined with the macro-state level. The study of the processes of policy transfer as a model for policy change must link different levels of analysis (Evans and Davies 1999) and examine new forms of strategic selectivity. Otherwise, one captures only part of the picture.

The post-Maastricht crisis demonstrated that relations between European and national politics could no longer be characterized by the concept of complementarity. Subsequently, the state-oriented nature of European integration was increasingly emphasized (Caporaso 1996; Armstrong and Bulmer 1998: 49). The descriptions of European governance in this context focus primarily on the dynamic aspects of the emergence of European bargaining systems, a European form of intervention which—contrary to the conclusions of the joint-decision trap thesis (Scharpf 1988)—pushes ahead the process of the transformation of the state. The much-deplored disregard for the resulting legitimation deficits (Kohler-Koch 1999) as well as for the technocratic and top-down nature of European integration are not only the result of an analysis focused on problem-solving and performance; the material substance of the governance perspective lies in the uneven Europeanization of statehood.

A theoretical approach with a stronger emphasis on state theory is able to embrace the aspects of dynamism as well as of crisis. The divergence of territory and territoriality (Sassen 1998) resulting from a new quality of globalization processes proceeds in the context of regional integration within Europe in the form of the emergence of partially common structures of European statehood. While the forms of state intervention are based on a deterritorialized European policy cycle, the mechanisms of the mediation of interests remain tied to the nation state context. This uneven Europeanization is the cause of dynamism and stagnation, stability, and crisis in equal measure.

European governance promotes new forms of articulation of the political and the economic, and accelerates the process of the transformation of the state. The related instances of radical social change, however, must be processed within the individual nation states. Yet, a balance of interests within society cannot be achieved through European state structures. The European balance of interests remains dependent on intergovernmental mediation between state projects, which accumulate in the hegemonic integration projects. Policy-specific integration projects like the

European employment policy can, thus, be enriched and concretized, but are not capable of achieving a reorientation of the hegemonic integration project. The dynamism of the multi-level system in the context of the transformation of the state is confronted with the institutionally established intergovernmental constraint of the EU—the result of a lack of civil society buffers. Dynamism and the blockade of the political are in equal measure the product of European integration in the wake of the post-Maastricht crisis.

European employment policy, thus, remains tied to the orientation of liberal productivism. Efforts with regard to a productivist reconstruction of solidarity (Streeck 1999: 12), by contrast, can be considered to represent qualitatively new elements. This orientation is the common denominator of the individual employment policy measures and reveals the outline of the social model behind it. The question of the marketability of individuals, which neoliberalism has until now tacitly assumed, is becoming a topic of politics, albeit with the societal dimension left out of the equation. The exclusion of redistributive policies points to a continuation of neoliberal politics, but at the same time new forms of a supply-side egalitarianism emerge, which no longer aim at the de-commodification of individuals, but at equal opportunities for commodification (Streeck 1999: 8). The recent debate about the 'third way' reveals the instability of these new strategies of socialization. In spite of all tendencies towards canonization, the future of the European model of society and the further process of European integration have not yet been decided (Felder, Tidow, and Wolfswinkler 1999). The debate on these issues will continue to shape the development of a European employment policy.

References

Ambrosius, Gerold (1996). *Wirtschaftsraum Europa*. Frankfurt a. M.: Fischer.
Armstrong, Kenneth and Bulmer, Simon J. (1998). *The Governance of the Single European Market*. Manchester and New York: Manchester University Press.
Aust, Andreas (2001). *The Party of European Socialists (PES) and European employment policies: From 'Eurokeynesianism' to 'Third Way policies'* (paper prepared for the ECPR—Joint Sessions, 6–11 April, Grenoble). www.essex.ac.uk/ecpr/jointsessions/grenoble/papers/ws11/aust.pdf.
Banting, Keith G. (1995). 'The Welfare State as Statecraft', in Stephan Leibfried and Paul Pierson (eds.), *European Social Policy*. Washington, DC: Brookings Institution, 269–300.
Bomberg, Elizabeth and Peterson, John (2000). *Policy Transfer and Europeanization* (Queen's Papers on Europeanization, 2/2000). Belfast: Queen's University, Institute of European Studies.

Bundesrepublik Deutschland (2000). Einheitliches Programmplanungsdokument zur Entwicklung des Arbeitsmarktes und der Humanressourcen für die Intervention des Ziels 3 in Deutschland. Struturfondsperiode 2000–2006. Berlin.

Caporaso, James A. (1996). 'The European Union and Forms of State', *Journal of Common Market Studies*, 34/1: 29–52.

Cerny, Philip G. (1999). *Reconstructuring the Political in a Globalizing World* (paper presented at the ECPR-Workshop 'National Models and Transnational Structures: Globalisation and Public Policy', 26–31 March, Mannheim).

Cecchini, Paolo (1985). *Europa '92—Der Vorteil des Binnenmarktes*. Baden-Baden: Nomos.

Council (1997). 'Council Resolution of 15 December 1997 on the 1998 Employment Guidelines', *Official Journal of the European Communities*, C 30, 28.1.1998: 1–5.

—— (1999). 'Council Regulation (EC) No 1260/1999 of 21 June 1999 laying down general provisions on the Structural Funds', *Official Journal of the European Communities*, L 161, 26.6.1999: 1–42.

—— (2000a). Document from the Presidency: Employment, Economic Reforms and Social Cohesion—towards a Europe based on innovation and knowledge. 5256/00. Council of the European Union.

—— (2000b). Presidency Note: Follow-up of the Lisbon Council—the ongoing experience of the open method of coordination. 9088/00. Council of the European Union.

—— (2001). 'Council Decision of 19 January 2001 on Guidelines for Member states' employment policies for the year 2001', *Official Journal of the European Communities*, L 22, 24.1.2001: 18–26.

Dean, Mitchell (1995). 'Governing the Unemployed Self in an Active Society', *Economy and Society*, 4: 559–83.

—— (1999). *Governmentality*. London, Thousand Oaks and New Delhi: Sage.

Deppe, Frank (2000). 'Zum Wandel kritischer Integrationstheorien', in Hans-Jürgen Bieling and Jochen Steinhilber (eds.), *Die Konfiguration Europas*. Münster: Westfälisches Dampfboot, 331–49.

—— and Felder, Michael (1993). *Zur Post-Maastricht-Krise der Europäischen Gemeinschaft (EG)*. Marburg: Forschungsgruppe Europäische Gemeinschaft.

Dolowitz, David and Marsh, David (1996). 'Who Learns What from Whom', *Political Studies*, 44/2: 343–57.

Dyson, Kenneth H. and Featherstone, Kevin (1999). *The Road to Maastricht: Negotiating Economic and Monetary Union*. Oxford: Oxford University Press.

Employment Observatory RESEARCH Network (1998). *Benchmarking Employment Performance and Labour Market Policies—Final Report 1997*. Berlin: Institute for Applied Socio-Economics.

—— (1999). *Employability: Concepts and Policies—Report 1998*. Berlin: Institute for Applied Socio-Economics.

European Commission (1993). *White Paper on Growth, Competititveness, and Employment*. COM (93) 700 final. Luxembourg: Office for Official Publications of the European Communities.

—— (1994). 'Leitlinien für ADAPT-Programme oder Globalzuschüsse', *Official Journal of the European Communities*, C 180, 1.7.1994: 30–5.

European Commission (1998a). *Employment Policies in the EU and in the Member States. Joint Report*. Luxembourg: Office for Official Publications of the European Communities.

—— (1998b). *Second Report on Local Development and Employment Initiatives*. SEC (98) 25. Luxembourg: Office for Official Publications of the European Communities.

—— (1999). *Vademecum*. www.inforegio.cec.eu.int/wbdoc/docoffic/vm20002006/vademecum_en.htm.

—— (2000). *Recommendation for a Council Recommendation on the implementation of Member States' employment policies*. COM (2000) 549 final. Luxembourg: Office for Official Publications of the European Communities.

—— (2001a). *Realizing the European Union's potential (Annex 2)*. COM (2001) 79 final/2. Luxembourg: Office for Official Publications of the European Communities.

—— (2001b). *European Governance*. COM (2001) 428. Luxembourg: Office for Official Publications of the European Communities.

European Council (1994). *Presidency Conclusions*. Essen 9 and 10 December. http://ue.eu.int/en/info/eurocouncil/.

—— (1998) *Presidency Conclusions*. Cardiff 15 and 16 June. http://ue.eu.int/en/info/eurocouncil/.

—— (1999a). *Presidency Conclusions*. Cologne 3 and 4 June. http://ue.eu.int/en/info/eurocouncil/.

—— (1999b). 'British–Spanish Declaration on Employment and Economic Reform', in European Council, *European Employment Pact—Member States contributions*, 8906/99. Luxembourg: European Council.

—— (2000). *Presidency Conclusions*. Lissabon 23 and 24 March. http://ue.eu.int/en/info/eurocouncil/.

—— (2001). *Presidency Conclusions*. Stockholm 23 and 24 March http://ue.eu.int/en/info/eurocouncil/.

Evans, Mark and Davies, Jonathan (1999). 'Understanding Policy Transfer', *Public Administration*, 77/2: 361–85.

Felder, Michael (2001). *Die Transformation von Staatlichkeit*. Opladen: Westdeutscher Verlag.

——, Tidow, Stefan, and Wolfswinkler, Günther (1999). *Jenseits von Eurooptimismus und-pessimismus* (EU-Krit Discussion Paper, No. 4). http://politik.uni-duisburg.de/publikationen/eukritend.rtf.

Goetschy, Janine (1999). 'The European Employment Strategy: Genesis and Development', *European Journal of Industrial Relations*, 5/2: 117–37.

Gill, Stephen (1998). 'European Governance and New Constitutionalism', *New Political Economy*, 1: 5–26.

Héritier, Adrienne (2002). 'New Modes of Governance in Europe: Policy-Making without Legislating?', in Adrienne Héritier (ed.), *Common Goods. Reinventing European and International Governance*. Lanham: Rowan & Littlefield, 185–206.

Hix, Simon (1994). 'The Study of the European Community', *West European Politics*, 17/1: 1–30.

Jessop, Bob (1990). *State Theory*. Cambridge: Polity Press.

—— (1993). 'Towards a Schumpeterian Workfare State?', *Studies in Political Economy*, 1: 7–39.

—— (2000). 'The Crisis of the National Spatio-Temporal Fix and the Tendential Ecological Dominance of Globalizing Capitalism', *International Journal of Urban and Regional Research*, 24/2: 323–60.

Johansson, Karl Magnus (1999). 'Tracing the Employment Title in the Amsterdam Treaty: Uncovering Transnational Coalitions', *Journal of European Public Policy*, 6/1: 85-101.

Keller, Berndt (1999). 'Aktuelle Entwicklungen "europäischer" Beschäftigungspolitik', *Sozialer Fortschritt*, 48/6: 141-50.

Knodt, Michèle (1998). *Tiefenwirkung europäischer Politik*. Baden-Baden: Nomos.

Kohler-Koch, Beate (1999). 'The Evolution and Transformation of European Governance', in Beate Kohler-Koch and Rainer Eising (eds.), *The Transformation of Governance in the European Union*. London and New York: Routledge, 14-35.

Lang, Jochen and Reissert, Bernd (1999). 'Reform des Implementationssystems der Strukturfonds', *WSI-Mitteilungen*, 52/6: 380-9.

March, James G. (1999). 'A Learning Perspective on the Network Dynamics of Institutional Integration', in Morten Egeberg and Per Laegreid (eds.), *Organizing Political Institutions*. Oslo, Stockholm, and Copenhagen: Scandinavian University Press, 129-55.

Marx, Karl and Engels, Friedrich (1956), 'Die deutsche Ideologie', in Karl Marx and Friedrich Engels (eds.), *Werke* (Vol. 3). Berlin: Dietz, 13-530.

Maurer, Andreas (1999). 'Bildungspolitik', in Werner Weidenfeld and Wolfgang Wessels (eds.), *Jahrbuch der Europäischen Integration 1998/99*. Bonn: Europa Union, 147-52.

Moravcsik, Andrew (1991). 'Negotiating the Single European Act', in Robert O. Keohane and Stanley Hoffmann (eds.), *The New European Community*. Boulder: Westview Press, 41-84.

—— (1998). *The Choice for Europe*. Ithaca and New York: Cornell University Press.

—— and Nicolaïdis, Kalypso (1999). 'Explaining the Treaty of Amsterdam: Interests, Influence, Institutions', *Journal of Common Market Studies*, 37/1: 59-85.

Olsen, Johan P. (1996). 'Europeanization and Nation-State Dynamics', in Sverker Gustavsson and Leif Lewin (eds.), *The Future of the Nation State*. London: Routledge, 245-85.

Peck, Jamie (1999). 'New Labours?', *Environment and Planning C: Government and Policy*, 3: 345-72.

Peer Review (2000). *Peer Review Programm 2000*. http://peerreview.almp.org/en/.

Poulantzas, Nicos (1977). *Staatstheorie*. Hamburg: VSA-Verlag.

Regulation (1999). 'Regulation No. 1262 of the European Parliament and of the Council of 21 June 1999 on the European Social Fund', *Official Journal of the European Union*, L 161, 26.6.1999: 48-53.

Reif, Karlheinz (1993). 'Ein Ende des "Permissiv Consensus"?', in Rudolf Hrbek (ed.), *Der Vertrag von Maastricht in der wissenschaftlichen Kontroverse*. Baden-Baden: Nomos, 23-40.

Ross, George (1998). *French Social Democracy and the EMU* (ARENA Working Papers, 98/19). Oslo: ARENA.

Ruggie, John G. (1982). 'International Regimes, Transactions, and Change', *International Organization*, 36/2: 379-415.

Sandholtz, Wayne and Stone Sweet, Alec (1998). 'Integration, Supranational Governance, and the Institutionalization of the European Polity', in Wayne Sandholtz and Alec Stone Sweet (eds.), *European Integration and Supranational Governance*. Oxford: Oxford University Press, 1-26.

Sassen, Saskia (1998). *Globalization and its Discontents*. New York: New Press.

Scharpf, Fritz W. (1988). 'The Joint-Decision Trap. Lessons from German Federalism and European Integration', *Public Administration*, 66: 239-78.

Statz, Albert (1979). *Grundelemente einer politökonomischen Theorie der west-europäischen Integration*. Frankfurt a. M.: Haag & Herchen.

Streeck, Wolfgang (1999). *Competitive Solidarity* (MPIfG Working Papers, 99/8). Köln: MPIfG.

Teague, Paul (1999). 'Reshaping Employment Regimes in Europe', *Journal of Public Policy*, 6/1: 33-62.

Tidow, Stefan (1998). *Europäische Beschäftigungspolitik*. Marburg: Forschungsgruppe Europäische Gemeinschaft.

—— (1999). 'Benchmarking als Leitidee', *Blätter für deutsche und internationale Politik*, 44/3: 301-9.

—— (2000). 'Europäische Beschäftigungspolitik im Wandel der Integrationsprojekte', in Hans-Wolfgang Platzer (ed.), *Arbeitsmarkt- und Beschäftigungspolitik in der EU*. Baden-Baden: Nomos, 145-65.

Tömmel, Ingeborg (2000). 'Jenseits von regulativ und distributiv', in Edgar Grande and Markus Jachtenfuchs (eds.), *Wie problemlösungsfähig ist die EU?* Baden-Baden: Nomos, 165-87.

Wagner, Peter (1995). *Soziologie der Moderne*. Frankfurt a. M. and New York: Campus.

Wulf-Mathies, Monika (1999). 'Agenda 2000 und die Reform der Europäischen Struktur- und Regionalpolitik', *WSI-Mitteilungen*, 52/6: 362-71.

Youngs, Richard (1999). 'The Politics of the Single Currency', *Journal of Common Market Studies*, 37/2: 295-316.

Ziltener, Patrick (1999). *Strukturwandel der europäischen Integration*. Münster: Westfälisches Dampfboot.

10

Horizontal Enforcement in the EU: The BSE Case and the Case of State Aid Control

Jürgen Neyer and Dieter Wolf

With the completion of the single market in 1992, the question of the effectiveness of European law has achieved primary importance for integration research.[1] In the view of the European Commission, deficiencies in compliance on the part of member governments are one of the greatest challenges to the proper functioning of the single market. This problem has been on the Commission's agenda since 1985.[2] It indicates the Commission's concern that member states react to the intensifying integration process with a strategy of selective and recalcitrant compliance with European regulations. Snyder (1993: 22) terms this process a 'new challenge of compliance', which threatens to undermine the normative foundations of the European Community (EC) as a legal community as well as the credibility of the European Court of Justice (ECJ). Deficient compliance is directly linked to questions of constitutional practice regarding the relationship between member state and supranational competencies, that is, the task of the Community to legislate and the duty of member states to administrate and enforce. It, therefore, can be analysed in the context of the vagueness of Article 10 EC Treaty and must be sensitive to institutional provisions which aim at overcoming deficient compliance. Compliance, however, is not only a constitutional issue, but also

---

[1] This chapter presents some results of a research project funded by the German research council (*Deutsche Forschungsgemeinschaft*) and chaired by Christian Joerges (Florence) and Michael Zürn (Bremen) on 'Compliance in Modern Political Systems'. Although the chapter has heavily benefited from discussions with the two chairs, any shortcomings of this chapter are the sole responsibility of the authors. We are grateful for the comments by Beate Kohler-Koch and Helen Wallace.

[2] In its current fifteenth annual report on the monitoring of the application of Community law the Commission reports—similar to previous years—a 'substantial increase in appeals and treaty violation procedures' (COM (1998) 317 final, XI).

a matter of domestic public discourse: For both analytical and normative reasons, democratic governments need to take domestic concerns and the interests of affected parties seriously. Analysing compliance, therefore, is intimately connected to assessing the degree to which these concerns and interests are reflected in supra-national law.

Thus, answering the question of whether and how European law is able to elicit the compliance of member state governments, contributes an essential aspect to the task of disclosing the central mechanisms of the linkage between European Union (EU) and national governance. Without understanding the way European law is able to change the behaviour of the 'masters of the treaties', it is impossible to correctly assess the effectiveness of European multi-level governance.

With respect to compliance with European regulations, supra-national bodies, especially the European Commission, and member state governments tend to show different interest structures. The Commission promotes a high degree of compliance, not only because it is its task to supervise the national implementation of common policies and to deal with infringements or because well-implemented European regulations usually strengthen the position and political influence of the Commission. Brussels also needs a high degree of compliance because a continuously low compliance level would destroy any trust in the efficacy of common policies and, hence, invite other addressees to freeriding. This freeriding perspective offers the member governments an incentive to accept common regulations and to hope that all other addressees will comply with the rules, while at the same time they will attempt to freeride in order to avoid the compliance costs.

Without the hierarchical power of a centralized enforcement mechanism, such an incentive structure tends to lead to low degrees of compliance. Accordingly, the EU historically was, and in certain areas still is, plagued by such compliance problems. However, although the EC lacks any capacity to coerce recalcitrant member states, it has managed to achieve very high compliance records in various important single market areas. This leaves the political scientist with the puzzle of why and how it was possible for the Community to overcome these cooperation problems and to change the behaviour of the member governments. How is the EC able to do so? What are the means by which the EC enforces its law and how does it cope with cases in which the interests of member governments are incongruent with the obligations imposed by European law?

It is not the aim of this contribution to draw up a systematic inventory of the extent and reasons of compliance deficiencies on the part of the member states. Instead, the chapter will confine itself to pointing out the specific strengths and weaknesses of the EC in promoting compliance in specific areas. In order to tell an interesting story, we will investigate two cases of diverging interests with a lot of opportunities for freeriding during the implementation. In our research, it is necessary to hold constant the addressees of the regulation, hence, the focus will be primarily on governmental actors. The examples chosen in this chapter, the EU's struggle with Bovine spongiform encephalitis (BSE) and the control of member states' subsidies to their industries, are most interesting for elaborating on these questions. The case of BSE was not only a technical matter, but also a highly politicized issue in which the involved member governments and the Commission were forced by their constituencies not to accept any easy compromise. The same applies to the issue of state aids, since the EC imposes strict limitations on the freedom of member governments to support their businesses. Such restrictions, however, are rather often confronted with strong domestic constituencies, which demand public spending to rescue scarce employment opportunities. Thus, both examples can be analysed as hard cases for the enforcement capacity of the EC.

The chapter is divided into five sections. Section 1 briefly reviews the literature on the administrative process of the EC and introduces the term 'horizontal enforcement'. It offers the theoretically based argument on why and how the Community is able to enforce its regulations without hierarchical, centralized power. Sections 2 and 3 elaborate on the two cases, identify institutional means of horizontal enforcement, and point to some of their limitations. Finally, Sections 4 and 5 discuss the two cases in tandem and draw some conclusions for the analysis of compliance in the multi-level governance system of the EC.

10.1 Compliance and horizontal enforcement

Generally speaking, the term compliance refers to the extent to which addressees 'in fact adhere to the provision of the accord and to the implementing measures that they have instituted' (Jacobson and Weiss 1998: 4). Although there may be some empirical overlap, the analysis of compliance needs to be distinguished from both implementation research and the question of effectiveness. The focus of implementation research is on the analysis of the difference between legislative requirements on the one hand and how they are actually put into practice on the other (Victor, Raustiala, and Skolnikoff 1998: 4), that is, on the policy and its development. In contrast, the focus of effectiveness research is on the capacity of a political regulation to solve commonly perceived problems (Young 1999), that is the question of political instruments and their effective use. Compliance research, however, deals with the question of whether and to what extent any policy or regulation is able to change the behaviour of its addressees. Researchers are less interested in the development of the policy over time or the effective problem-solving capacity of any political or administrative instrument, but rather in its success or failure to induce the intended (or non-intended) behavioural change (which even in the case of success not necessarily corresponds to the effective solution of the underlying political problem).

The issue of non-compliance with European regulations is by no means irrelevant in the EU. Table 10.1 shows the total number of cases in which the Commission has instituted infringement proceedings against a member state in the past few years.

Deficient compliance in European politics is evidently not a marginal problem. In each of the years monitored, the Commission had sent more than 1,000 letters of formal notice regarding supposed violations of regulations (first stage of the infringement procedure) to the member states. What is equally striking, however, is that most of these cases could be settled through consultations and negotiations between the Commission and the respective member government. It needs to be mentioned, however, that the ratio between formal notices and legal action has significantly deteriorated. Whilst in 1995 only 7.1 per cent of all alleged violations were dealt with by the Court, this ratio has increased over the years to 16.6 per cent. One reason for this deterioration could be an increasing reluctance of the member states to shoulder the domestic costs of adapting to intensified economic interpenetration. Another reason might be

Table 10.1 Infringement procedures in the EU, 1995–99

	1995	1996	1997	1998	1999
(1) Formal notice	1,016	1,142	1,461	1,101	1,075
(2) Reasoned opinion	192	435	334	675	460
(3) Legal action at the ECJ	72	92	121	123	178
(3)/(1) × 100	7.1	8.0	8.3	11.2	16.6

Source: COM (2001) 92 final: 72

that the Commission is becoming more and more tired of conducting time-consuming negotiations with reluctant member states and, therefore, is increasingly relying on means of legal enforcement. Even legal enforcement, however, is far from automatic. At the end of 1999, about 80 decisions of the ECJ had not been implemented by the member states. In two instances member state implementation has been overdue since 1990 (with appellate proceedings or a procedure as according to Article 228 currently in progress), in one instance even since 1988 (present status: the Commission has applied for the imposition of an administrative fine).[3] Thus, regulatory compliance in the EU can by no means be taken for granted. Often it is only achieved after lengthy, time-consuming negotiations, with both sides applying legal and political pressure and fighting with no holds barred.

Not least due to the limited capacity of the EU's institutions to enforce compliance vertically, a number of recent contributions emphasize the horizontal nature of compliance enforcement. In contrast to the traditional understanding which views compliance as a function of centralized enforcement (Fearon 1998; Tallberg 1999), its extent in the EU must be understood as the product of a 'recursive and circular' political process (Snyder 1993: 26). Because the EU does not command any centralized coercive capacities, the member states accept European law only 'as an autonomous voluntary act, endlessly renewed on each occasion, of subordination' (Weiler 2000: 13). Particularly in the multi-level system of the EU with its division of political competencies between supra-national, governmental, and sub-national levels, recurring bargaining processes about the specific implications of a legal norm and its adaptation to specific circumstances must be considered to be structural elements of the political process. Contrary to the technocratic assumption that administration merely means the application of a legal norm on the basis of such criteria as appropriateness or justifiability, administration in the EC is an intrinsically political business: its main objective is the reconciliation of divergent interests, perceptions of problems, and problem-solving philosophies (Héritier et al. 1994) against the background of—often coexisting—majoritarian and deliberative procedures (Joerges and Neyer 1997). The Commission's central function in promoting compliance, therefore, is to create an institutional framework for the continuous discourse on questions of compliance and enforcement, through informal structural reforms (Snyder 1993), the promotion of inter-administrative

---

[3] COM (2000) 92 final: 185-91.

networks (Wessels 1997) and an intensive exchange of information with member state administrations (Mendrinou 1996).

10.2 Horizontal enforcement at work I: The implementation of the action plan to eradicate BSE

In many respects, the BSE crisis is an excellent example for the investigation of the EC's capacity to deal with explicitly antagonistic interests and to ensure compliance with its regulations. Such an approach to the BSE crisis starts with the ban on British beef in 1996, focuses on the negotiations between the Commission and the British government about how to eradicate BSE, highlights the struggle between the two for adequate measures and the Commission's acknowledgement of their successful implementation in July 1999, proceeds with the rejection of the partial lifting of the embargo by France and Germany in Winter 1999/2000[4] and ends with the lifting of the embargo in March 2000.

10.2.1 The BSE saga, part I

On 25 March 1996, the Standing Veterinary Committee of the EU adopted the Commission's proposal to impose a ban on British beef with a 14 to 1 majority. After fierce protests by the British government, the Committee convened again to repeat the vote on 27 March, with exactly the same result as before. Backed by this clear decision of the member state delegates and by a resolution of the European Parliament to the same effect (but also in the face of increasing unilateral member state action against the import of British beef), the Commission imposed a ban on British beef and beef products for an indefinite period of time.[5] Moreover, the British government was placed under obligation to submit to the Commission a fortnightly report on the implementation of the measures it was taking to fight BSE.

Only two days later, the Turin European Council meeting discussed the first British proposals for a programme to slaughter British cattle. In a meeting of the Agrarian Council on 1 April 1996, these negotiations were continued by the ministers of agriculture. Even a forty-hour marathon

---

[4] For a more detailed account see Neyer (2000). Detailed chronologies of the BSE crisis can be found on the website on the BSE Inquiry (www.bse.org.uk).

[5] Decision 96/239/EC prohibited the export from Great Britain of live cattle, beef and beef products, tallow, gelatine, meat meal, and bone meal deriving from mammals.

meeting, however, produced no agreement between the Community and the British government. The next day John Major, speaking before the House of Commons, criticized the conclusions as totally inadequate and threatened to bring the case before the ECJ (*Agence Europe*, 4 April 1996). When the Commission, backed by expert opinions of the World Health Organization and the Scientific Veterinary Committee proposed a partial lifting of the ban by exempting at least certain beef derivatives, which had been classified as harmless, this did nothing to ease the tension. On the contrary, the rejection of the proposal by the member states in the Standing Veterinary Committee (9 to 6 votes; for the partial lifting of the ban a qualified majority would have been necessary) produced an angry response by the British government. The following day, it announced that as long as the EC did not take a more accommodating stance in the BSE affair, Britain would veto all legislative Community acts.

The fierceness of the British reaction did not only reflect the concern that the agreed Community measures would result in estimated costs of £500 million per year; it must also be seen against the background of the then upcoming general election in Britain, of the disunity within the ruling Tory party, and of the hope to be able to use the conflict with the EU as a means to strengthen party unity and to increase the chances for re-election. The government was extremely susceptible to these pressures because, at the time of the decision against a partial lifting of the ban, its majority in the House of Commons was reduced to one vote, and a number of back-benchers seemed ready to bring down the Major government if it failed to take a hard stand against the Community. Furthermore, in its attempt to use the EU conflict for its domestic purposes, the government was pushed forward by conservative tabloids. Newspapers such as the *Sun*, the *Telegraph*, the *Daily Express* or the *Daily Mirror* gave the impression that the conduct of the other member states was only partly induced by public health concerns and that they were at least equally motivated by the intention to rid themselves of an unwanted competitor. Headlines of the *Daily Mail* and other conservative mass-circulation papers portrayed the conflict with the EU as a question of national pride, not as the search for adequate measures to reduce public health risks, and they were not above using military terminology to describe the conflict.[6]

The British government's lack of willingness to acknowledge the potential danger of BSE-infected cattle for consumers was reinforced by the

---

[6] Headlines in the *Telegraph* of 20 June 1996 read: 'How Britain capitulated on BSE' and 'Surrender by Britain over beef ban'; in the *Daily Express* of 22 May 1996: 'Major goes to war at last'; in the *Observer* of 23 June 1996: 'How the beef war was lost'.

statements and behaviour of the British government between 1990 and early 1996. With recurrent statements about the safety of beef, the British government had manoeuvred itself into a position that it could not back down from without risking a major loss of face and a subsequent setback in popularity with the electorate. Furthermore, a more conciliatory stance of the British government would have met with broad public opposition in the UK. As late as November 1998, government inspectors were faced with strong resentment in the slaughterhouses they had to inspect: 75 per cent of all inspectors reported attempts of intimidation or even physical assault by slaughterhouse operators, and 10 per cent had been threatened with weapons (*The Independent*, 30 November 1998).

Meanwhile, administrative efforts to solve the crisis through compromise were continued, and both sides moved towards each other. While Britain had already shown its goodwill by submitting a catalogue of intended measures on 14 June 1996, it was now up to the member states to refrain from their demand to eradicate the BSE disease in Great Britain and settle for a procedural solution. Thus, on 22 June 1996 the European Council in Florence 'gave favourable consideration' to the Commission paper based on the British proposals, refrained from the demand for total eradication and declared that the measures proposed as well as the procedure for progress assessment met with broad member state consent. After the summit, statements of the British prime minister and other European heads of government reflected the general acceptance of the compromise. When the final conclusions drawn by the Council were put to the vote, Britain was the only member state that did not explicitly agree to them, but abstained from voting. At the same time, however, the British foreign minister Rifkind declared the end of the policy of obstruction and announced that the agreed measures would be implemented.

10.2.2 The BSE saga, part II

After the competent scientific committee had certified in May 1999 that the protective measures in Britain were adequate and that a consumer risk could be ruled out, the Commission decided in July 1999 to lift the ban on the export of beef from Great Britain. France, Austria, and Germany objected to the Commission's decision, but were unable to reverse it. The Commission acknowledged that BSE had indeed not yet been eradicated, but argued that this was in fact not the benchmark for its decision. Instead the decisive criteria were the full implementation by the British government of the measures agreed in Florence and the confirmation of the relevant scientific bodies that beef from Great Britain represented no health risk.

In spite of the Commission's decision, the French government declared on 1 October 1999 that it would not lift the ban on British beef, justifying its measure with a report by the national *Agence Française de Sécurité Sanitaire des Aliments* (AFSSA), which gave reason to seriously doubt the appropriateness of the Commission decision. On 30 September 1999 the AFSSA had published a statement, based on the findings of a government-appointed expert group, in which it set down a number of reasons why the import embargo for British beef ought not to be lifted.[7] According to the statement, the test methods available to identify infected meat were much better now than they had been at the time when the Commission decided on the criteria to be applied; the number of new BSE cases was declining at a remarkably slow pace, thus giving rise to new concern, and the findings of the on-the-spot checks by Commission inspectors gave reason to doubt the proper implementation of the measures agreed in Florence.

On 29 October 1999, after two days of deliberation, the Scientific Steering Committee (SSC) unanimously rejected the French arguments in favour of maintaining the import ban on British beef. According to the committee, the examination of all relevant data had clearly shown that there was no reason to alter the conclusions drawn in the committee statements, which had served as the basis for the Council decision. The safety conditions were met and the British safety standard of beef and beef products was comparable to that of foodstuff produced in the rest of the EU.[8] Unimpressed by the SSC's decision, France refused to lift its import ban for the time being.

Similarly, the German minister for health, Andrea Fischer, declared in direct reaction to the Commission's decision that she would not allow the import of British beef without additional guarantees regarding its safety.[9] In both these instances, the interests of the respective governments reflected closely the concerns of domestic consumers. Particularly in Germany, due to adverse press coverage on BSE a dramatic decline in beef sales of approximately up to 50 per cent was to be noted in 1996 (*Die Welt*, 11 April 1996). A spokesman for the Federal Association of Central Abattoirs in Bonn described the beef market situation as 'utterly desolate': abattoirs

---

[7] Summarized in http://europa.eu.int/comm/dg24/health/sc/ssc/out62_en.pdf.

[8] *Agence Europe*, 30 October 1999. The SSC report can be found at http://europa.eu.int/comm/dg24/health/sc/ssc/out62_en.pdf.

[9] Press release by federal minister of health, Andrea Fischer, on 29 October 1999.

had drastically reduced their output, had filed applications for short-time work and sent their personnel on vacation. According to the guild of the *Land* Thuringia, many of the *Land*'s 1,000 cattle breeding farms would face ruin if the situation prevailed. Similarly, the Federal Association of Food Retailers noted that in the self-service sections with pre-packed beef the market had 'collapsed completely'. An important reason for the collapse was that German media coverage was completely out of proportion.

Thus, between March and June 1996, public opinion in Germany was dominated by the self-interest of farmers and the fears of consumers, rather than by scientific evidence, and the same situation occurred again in 1999. Nothing had been forgotten. Once again emotions were running high on all sides. At the end of October 1999, the headline of the British newspaper the *Sun* read 'We don't want War but France is Wrong', while *l'Humanité* took up an image from the previous day's *Daily Mirror* which had compared the BSE controversy with the Battle of Waterloo. But what was probably more significant than the wild exaggerations of the yellow press was the fact that even respected observers in France and Germany regarded the Commission's decision to lift the ban with extreme scepticism. German and French scientists declared in the major papers that the lifting came too early and that it ought to be postponed until more reliable testing methods were available. In an interview, the French scientist Jeanne Brugère-Picoux pointed out that BSE was by no means eradicated: there were still thousands of new BSE cases each year, inspections in Great Britain were patchy, and therefore, consumers had no guarantee that British beef was safe for consumption (*l'Humanité*, 4 November 1999). In Germany, Hans Kretzschmar, head of the Institute for Neuropathology at the University of Göttingen and member of the SSC, argued in a couple of interviews that the ban should, under no circumstances, be lifted before the year 2001, that is, before the end of the estimated incubation time of 5 years, since it would be impossible to evaluate earlier whether the protective measures in force since 1996 had actually been effective. These expert opinions were widely reviewed in the respective national media, and both governments found them hard to ignore, the more so, since they had always stressed that their prime criterion for any admission of foodstuff was that it was absolutely free from health risks. Accordingly, now that the respective national experts were publicly declaring that the emphasis on health protection required the continuation of the ban, the governments could hardly argue for the re-admission of products which constituted a health risk.

Only after the Commission had succumbed to political pressure by France and Germany, and developed the new legal position that it was quite permissible to label British beef with 'British XEL Beef', a diplomatic compromise could be found which was acceptable to all parties involved. As opposed to the label 'Made in Britain', so the Commission argued, this new label could be viewed as informing the consumer that this product was fit for export and in conformity with the health requirements of the pertaining European provisions (*Agence Europe*, 19 November 1999). Although this solution was no doubt a cheap compromise, it formed the basis for the decision of the German Federal Council (*Bundesrat*) in March 2000 to agree to lift the ban on British beef. *De facto* this meant that the Commission had yielded to German pressures by agreeing to a regulation which was in clear violation of the former EU practice of rejecting any discriminatory rules for labelling a product. Compliance with European law was re-established. However, it came at the price of making the vulnerability of the EU to political pressure obvious.

10.3 Horizontal enforcement at work II: The control of member states subsidies

The central aim of the original Treaty establishing the European Economic Community (EEC)—and now establishing the EC as major part of the Treaty on European Union (TEU)—was to establish a common European market in which goods, services, and capital could be produced and traded without any discrimination or intervention that might distort the operation of market forces. From the early beginnings of this endeavour, the 'masters of the treaty', the member governments, insisted on the necessity to institutionalize a common competition policy and were readily prepared to transfer major policy competencies in this realm to the supranational level (Rosenstock 1995: 79-86). Hence, the European Commission got considerable formal administrative power in the area of subsidies control (Bleckmann 1997: Rz 2071-2). This strong position is best illustrated by

(1) the unconditional requirement for the member states to notify all plans for financial support of businesses to the European Commission;[10]
(2) the broad margins of discretion for the Commission to decide upon the notified cases;

---

[10] See the Transparency Guideline: Guideline 80/723/EEC of the Commission of 25 June 1980 (OJ L 195/80: 195).

(3) the direct applicability of the treaty provisions and the relatively few elements of secondary legislation in this realm of common policy (Slot 1993: 45);[11]
(4) the direct access to the ECJ in disputed cases. This access is not based on Article 226 EC Treaty (violation of the treaty), which is considered to be a very slow and ineffective procedure, but rather on Article 88 paragraph 2 EC Treaty especially created for the judicial review of subsidies control cases (Caspari 1987: 77-8);
(5) the suspensive character of the examination procedure initiated by the Commission after the notification of a subsidy case by a member government. The member state has to await the approval of its case in order to proceed with the actual transfer of funds.

The central provisions of the subsidies control regulation on the European level consist of Article 87 EC Treaty, a set of important case rulings of the ECJ and a number of policy frameworks and guidelines published by the Commission (now consolidated in Council Regulation 656/99). Whereas the first two elements are established parts of European law, the third category is seen as an unofficial instrument to inform the member governments about the intentions of the Commission guiding the decisions on the notified cases (Rawlinson 1993; Bleckmann 1997: Rz 2072). Article 87 paragraph 1 EC Treaty is rather blunt in its prohibition of state aids: Any form of financial state aid to specific companies or business sectors is incompatible with the common market, if this aid distorts competition and imperils trade between the member states. Thus, the European Commission is able to deny any financial support to the member states if they are likely to interfere with the functioning of the market and impede trans-border exchanges of goods, services, or capital.

Paragraph 2 of Article 87 EC Treaty lists the exemptions from this general rule. State subsidies are basically allowed if they are paid as elements of social policies to certain consumers and if they do not discriminate against the origin of the supported goods or services; or applied in case of natural catastrophes or similar unforeseeable events in order to restore the normal functioning of the economy.

Finally, paragraph 3 of Article 87 EC Treaty defines reasons under which the Commission is empowered to allow certain state aids if they do not

---

[11] The Council Regulation 656/99 of 23 March 1999 (OJ L 83/99: 1) replaced the network of Commission decisions and court rulings, which governed the application, and interpretation of these treaty provisions.

unduly interfere with market forces. Under these provisions state subsidies might be compatible with the common market if they are earmarked for the restructuring of regional economies; if the standards of living and employment of these regions are far lower than the European average; also if they are in support of important economic measures of common European interest or in order to restore the proper functioning of the economy of one member state after a massive economic disruption; and if they are used to support cultural activities or to ensure the protection of cultural traditions and culturally valuable goods; or if they are in support of any other measure which is advocated by a qualified majority of the Council on the basis of a recommendation by the European Commission.

The standard procedure of the EU for the examination and eventual permission of subsidies is equally clear-cut and straightforward: Any member state which wishes to subsidize one of its companies or one of its business sectors has to submit a detailed proposal of this measure to the European Commission. On the basis of this examination, the Commission reaches a decision, which—especially in case of refusal—has to be published in the Official Journal. Both the applicant (member state) and third parties are entitled to challenge this decision before the ECJ (Bleckmann 1997: Rz 2082). In the event that the member government does not comply with the decision the Commission is empowered by Article 88 paragraph 2 to bring the case before the ECJ in order to seek a ruling confirming the decision.

What does the compliance record of this European procedure to limit the subsidies race look like? Is there any sign of influence on the amount of state aids given to companies in the member states? (See Table 10.2.)

The figures reveal a clear-cut picture. Even if one considers the overall amount of subsidies recorded in the statistics of the Commission as grossly underestimating the real extent of the financial support by state

Table 10.2 Annual total amount of state aids in the EU (in billion Euro)

	88	89	90	91	92	93	94	95	96	97	98
EU 12	43.9	33.6	44.2	39.8	39.1	44.1	41.2	37.4	35.4	34.4	28.4
EU 15								38.6	36.6	35.8	29.7
% GDP	4.1	3.2	4.0	3.6	3.2	3.8	3.4	2.9	2.7	2.6	2.0

Sources: COM (2000) 205 final; COM (98) 417 final; COM (97) 170 final; COM (95) 365 final; COM (99) 148 final

actors in the Community, the trend nevertheless is obvious: In 1998, the fifteen member states of the expanded community did spend less on financial aid than the twelve members in 1992 before the introduction of the single market and considerably less than the twelve member states in 1993, the year of the official introduction of the single market. The reduction amounts to more than 25 per cent. There are still a lot of cases of open non-compliance of the member governments. But the severity of disputed subsidies is steadily decreasing over the years.

This picture corresponds with the observations of economists and law scholars dealing with the question of European subsidies control. Although the provisions of Article 87 EC Treaty remained basically unchanged since the introduction of the Treaty establishing the EEC in 1958, until the 1980s the member governments only sporadically and inadequately notified the Commission on their subsidy programmes. Furthermore, during the first 15 years the Commission reached a positive decision in virtually all of these few notified cases (Rosenstock 1995: 82–6). In the context of the introduction of the Single European Act (SEA) and the renewed efforts to establish the common market, this behaviour changed drastically (Caspari 1987: 87).

With the formal completion of the single market in 1993, the Commission underlined that it considered the limitation and the subsequent reduction of the subsidies to be one of the most important goals of achieving a truly common market. Although the Commission was harshly criticized for some of its decisions, it nevertheless acquired considerable authority in questions of competition policy during the 1990s. In the absence of centralized hierarchical powers of the Commission, this steep increase in the degree of compliance with EU state aid provisions during the 1990s calls for an explanation.

10.4 Horizontal enforcement

The EC is a non-hierarchical system of governance, which cannot rely on police force to sanction non-compliant behaviour on the part of a member state. It is basically a legal community, which can only function to the degree that its law is accepted by its constituent units, the member states. Furthermore, its competence to sanction non-compliant behaviour has to be seen against the conflicting background of the powers it derives from Article 226 EC Treaty (recourse to the ECJ by the Commission) and Article 228 EC Treaty (effectiveness and enforcement of judgements, administrative fines) on the one hand and the political regard it is required to pay to overriding member state interests on the other hand. Consequently, it is safe to assume that in cases of conflict the formal sanctioning powers held by supra-national institutions do not automatically fully translate into the discharge of these powers. Particularly in politically sensitive matters, the integrity of European legal norms has to be weighed against possible political damage (Garrett 1995).

Over the years, however, the supra-national institutions developed at least three sets of instruments with the help of which they were and are able to strengthen the compliance record of the Community. These sets of instruments are mechanisms of indirect control, judicial review and, finally, financial sanctions. The following paragraph is intended to show how these instruments contribute to the 'horizontal enforcement', which conditions are necessary for a successful employment of these instruments and under which conditions the EC was able to develop these instruments.

10.4.1 *Mechanisms of indirect control*

The classical 'command and control' approach in regulatory politics essentially argues that a high degree of compliance depends on two aspects: clear and easily understandable rules and direct control with the option of heavy sanctions in case of non-compliance (Rahmsdorf and Schäfer 1980). Because of several reasons the supra-national institutions are usually not in the position to exert such direct command and control powers. One problem is the still rather limited legal authority of the Community institutions to do more than to report infringements and to call on the respective member government to change its behaviour. Another one is the rather small amount of resources which the Community is able to invest into control measures. Even if the Commission commands the right to control the national implementation process and to sanction noncompliance, it simply does not have enough administrative and financial resources to be able to exert its powers properly. Nevertheless, the Commission was able to cope with this problem and to introduce two new instruments in order to strengthen its position vis-à-vis the member governments: the control of the controllers and the increased influence of third parties.

10.4.1.1 **Control of the controllers**

One of the Commission's main instruments, which is frequently used especially in the veterinary field, is to carry out on-the-spot checks in order to verify the application of Community measures. In the context of the BSE problem, such checks were carried out by Commission experts and members of the newly founded Food and Veterinary Office in April and July 1996, between September and October 1996, in June 1997 and in June 1998.[12] During these inspections, the Commission experts are to be given access to all persons, information and documentation concerned.[13] If the Commission discovers deficiencies, the respective member state has to thoroughly investigate the general situation in the area concerned and to notify the results of the checks and of the measures taken to remedy the situation to the Commission within the time set by the latter.[14] If the corrective measures are found to be insufficient, the Commission may take all the measures which it deems necessary.[15] This is, however, subject to the comitology procedure (IIIa), that is, it requires a qualified member state majority in the committee or, in the case of recourse to the Council (if the Commission cannot secure a majority for its proposals), the measures must at least not be rejected by the Council.[16]

Such on-the-spot checks on a random choice basis introduce an efficient element of control, which allows the Commission to focus on important and disputed cases and to threaten the member governments with a wholesale ban if the national controllers do not enforce Community standards. Thus, a few cases of national non-compliance, if properly detected by the Commission, could lead to the exclusion of the objected goods or services from the common market or at least to stricter and regular controls by the Commission until the problem is fixed. This preserves the administrative and financial resources of the Community and allows the application of political pressure even if the objected cases are not the rule, but rather the exception in national implementation.

10.4.1.2 Influence of third parties

In the case of the state aid control scheme the EU, quite contrary for example to the German national rules, opened its procedures to interested third parties, especially to competitors of potential beneficiaries and, thus, created a very powerful tool for horizontal enforcement. This tool works in two ways: On the one hand, it responds to the fact that

---

[12] See Final Consolidated Report, 10–11, COM (1998) 598 final.

[13] Commission Decision of 4 February 1998 laying down certain detailed rules concerning on-the-spot checks in the veterinary field by Commission experts in the member states (98/139/EC), OJ L 38 of 12 February 1998, 10–13, Article 6.

[14] 98/139/EC, Article 7 paragraph 3.   [15] 98/139/EC, Article 7 paragraph 4.

[16] In this context, 98/139/EC, Article 7 paragraph 4, refers to the procedure laid down in 89/395/EC, Article 17, which is identical with procedure IIIa of the Comitology Decision (87/373/EC).

third parties are important sources of information (Löw 1992; Reufels 1997). Thus, the Commission does not only accept confidential news about perceived national financial support efforts, but also opens the formal inquiry into a subsidies case to any interested party. Accordingly, competitors or interest groups are allowed to supply their opinions with respect to the case in question and the Commission is able to examine not only the perspectives of the potential beneficiary and the corresponding national government, but also the interests of potentially affected parties. This broadens the case, improves the amount of information, and eventually gives the Commission useful allies in cases in which it does not accept the proposed measures. On the other hand, third parties have their own right to challenge the state aid schemes or the decisions of the Commission in court. Thus, competitors are able to seek the judicial review of a Commission decision allowing subsidies as well as to force the Commission to inquire into a disputed case of state aid (Polley 1996; Sinnaeve 1999).

Although the Commission refrains from publishing details on the influence of third parties in state aid cases, circumstantial evidence points to substantial involvement. Of fifty-two cases dealing with questions of state aids, which in January 1996 were pending either before the Court of First Instance or the ECJ, twenty-four cases were brought to the attention of the courts by competitors of (potential) beneficiaries of the financial support. And the numbers of such cases are rising since 1993 (Mederer 1996). For example, '*Systraval* v. *Commission*' can be seen as a paradigmatic case in this respect. In 1987, the state-owned French postal service created a subsidiary for the transportation of moneys and valuables, advanced some 5 million FF as a loan, converted this loan into capital, transferred its money transport business (worth an estimated 19 million FF) to the new firm, advanced a cash contribution of 9 million FF to the firm and, finally, advanced a second loan about 15 million FF in 1989. Some competitors of the new business considered these measures as cases of state aid and informed the Commission, which in March 1990 sought further information from the French government. After receiving the requested clarification, Brussels rejected the complaints of the competitors. They, in turn, challenged this decision in court, which prompted the Commission to withdraw its decision, to reconsider the action of the French postal service as a case of not-notified state aid, but—in December 1993—to reject the complaint again.

The competitors brought the case before the Court of First Instance, which annulled the decision of the Commission on the grounds that it was not sufficiently reasoned (ECJ 1995, II-2651). The ruling especially called for an elaborate inclusion of third parties into the procedures for the examination of state aid cases. Appealed by the Commission, the ECJ in 1998 finally upheld the ruling (ECJ 1998, I-1719). The Commission was forced to reopen the case and had to strengthen the position of third parties in the process of examining the character of the actions of the French postal service. Thus, third parties are not only a valuable source of information for the Commission. They also function as a very effective instrument of control with respect to member state governments and their state aid policies. And they are able to exert pressure on the controllers (i.e. the Commission), too.

10.4.2 *Judicial review*

The second major element of the European horizontal enforcement mechanisms is the ECJ. It certainly lacks the status of an independent actor since it has to wait for the cases to be brought to its attention. However, it constitutes an important institution, not only for the clarification of the precise meaning of European legal statutes and the systematic subsumption of disputed cases under the respective legal provisions. In its capacity as a European constitutional court the ECJ is also able to develop and expand the treaty law and to establish basic principles and legal doctrines for the application of primary and secondary legislation in the EU. There are different venues to implicate the court: the treaty violation procedure and the special judicial state aid control procedure.

10.4.2.1 Treaty violation procedure

Since the comitology procedure involves the risk of a renewed politicization of the BSE affair (possible involvement of the Council regarding the decision on appropriate measures), it is not the Commission's most favoured option. Fortunately, it has a second option for counteracting non-compliant behaviour of a member state, the initiation of a formal treaty violation procedure according to Article 226 EC Treaty. This is a three-stage procedure: in the first stage the Commission sends a 'letter of formal notice' and demands a statement from the member state, in the second stage a 'reasoned opinion' by the Commission has to be submitted, and only the third and final stage entails reference before the ECJ. Thus the treaty violation procedure is not so much a classic court procedure, primarily concerned with determining the difference between the specific implications of a certain legal norm and the actual behaviour of the respective addressee. Instead its central characteristic is that it provides a formalized framework aimed at solving disputes of interpretation and accomplishing cooperation between Commission and member state.[17] When inspection missions carried out in September/October 1996 and June 1997 brought to light serious deficiencies in the border control system,[18] the Commission initiated the first stage of the treaty violation procedure on 8 July 1997 by demanding a statement from the British government. The British authorities concerned (minister of agriculture, fisheries, and food) reacted by adopting new administrative regulations for a stricter control of the enforcement of the embargo (introduction of border controls for lorries) three weeks after the Commission's letter. This induced the Commission to declare a postponement of the treaty violation procedure and to arrange for a further inspection (September and October 1997) in order to verify the effectiveness of the British measures.

In their report, the inspectors stated that the new border controls, although no doubt an extended, flexible and useful measure, could only be expected to yield limited results, since only a small number of lorries were actually checked on crossing the border.[19] Furthermore, the Commission found inspections of meat-processing factories in Great Britain to be still inadequate. As a result, it initiated on 22 September 1997 a new treaty violation procedure against Great Britain.[20] On 12 November 1997 it sent a reasoned opinion to the British government (stage II of the procedure), declaring that the veterinary checks in British meat cutting and cooling facilities did not meet the standard demanded by EU legislation.[21] Besides, in its reply to the Commission's first letter the British government had declared its intention to cooperate with the Commission. However, the British answer had also revealed that Britain was unable to meet the requirements set by EU legislation regarding the frequency of inspections by public veterinary surgeons because of a distinct shortage of veterinary surgeons. In its reasoned opinion, the Commission pointed out that such shortages did not relieve Great Britain of its responsibilities

---

[17] Only a small percentage of all treaty violation procedures instituted are brought before the ECJ (third stage of the procedure). The vast majority of disputes are settled through negotiations between Commission and member state. In 1997, the Commission instituted a total of 1,422 (1996: 1,142) procedures, submitted 331 reasoned opinions and involved the Court in only 121 cases (1996: 92) (General Report on the Activities of the European Union 1997, Luxembourg 1998, chapter X). For a survey detailing the different stages of the treaty violation procedure see Mendrinou (1996: 3).   [18] Final Consolidated Report, 11.

[19] See Special Report to the European Parliament Concerning Recommendations on BSE (http://europa.eu.int/comm/dg24/health/bse/bse01_en.html).

[20] Final Consolidated Report, 72.

[21] Here, the Commission referred to Directive 64/433/EC.

deriving from the relevant legislation. Hence, the Court's function is not only to settle disputes via rulings. It also offers a formal forum for negotiations and problem solving under the shadow of the European law.

10.4.2.2 Special judicial procedure in state aid cases

In state aid control cases, the ECJ constitutes an important instrument to employ the powers of both the Commission and third parties, since Article 88 EC Treaty offers direct access to the Court. Hence, it has been the Court together with the Commission, which developed the elaborate state aid control law of the EU (Winter 1993). Until 1999, the Commission did not introduce any secondary legislation based on Article 89 EC Treaty because it feared that the Council would use the chance to roll back most of the existing case law by introducing new less demanding state aid control rules. Only after the establishment of a tight legal framework and with the guarantee of the member governments to uphold the Commission proposals, the Commission introduced the initiative for the Council Regulation 659/99 of 22 March 1999, which structured and summarized the existing case law and established coherent rules for the application of Article 88 EC Treaty. Until then, the ECJ with some 300 state aid control cases since the 1960s provided a major source of law for the limitation of state subsidies in the common market. Yet it is to be stressed that the Commission has not been the only actor which brought these cases to the attention of the Court. In 1986, the Court acknowledged the right of affected third parties, especially competitors of potential beneficiaries of state aids, to challenge Commission decisions in court.[22] In this way, the basis for participation was increased and the equal balance of interests was strengthened (Slot 1999).

10.4.3 Financial sanctions

In the BSE case a third option of sanctioning insufficient compliance is offered by the conditional linking of discernible progress in the implementation of the Commission's action plan and the (partial) lifting of the ban. With the drafting of its proposal of 14 January 1998 regarding the lifting of the ban for beef and beef products from Northern Ireland[23]—not, however, from the rest of Britain—the Commission made it clear that

---

[22] See ECJ 1986, I-391, Rs 169/84 'COFAZ'.

[23] Commission proposal for a partial lifting of the export ban for beef from the United Kingdom to authorize the export of beef and beef products under the Export Certified Herds Scheme (ECHS) in Northern Ireland (http://europa.eu.int/en/comm/spc/cp4pleb_de.html).

it was ready to reward compliance by being accommodating, but that it had no qualms about being selective and upholding the embargo for a longer period of time in case of insufficient implementation ('carrot and stick policy'). Thus, the Commission has the power to sanction inadequate compliance if Great Britain should persistently refuse to adhere to the measures laid down in the action plan or even if it should ignore an imposed fine (according to Article 256 EC Treaty, fines imposed on member states cannot be enforced).

The sanctioning power of the Community is further increased by the fact that it may make compensation payments to British farmers subject to discernible progress in the implementation of the action plan even if they have already been consented. As a parallel measure alongside the action plan the Council agreed in the same meeting to make available 650 million ECU (plus a reserve of 200 million ECU) in support of European cattle owners, who were seriously hit by the BSE crisis. Formally, these funds represented compensation payments for individual economic damages incurred in connection with the implementation of Community measures to eradicate BSE and were not territorially specified. It has to be taken into account, however, that at the time when these payments were agreed upon, 99 per cent of all known BSE cases had occurred in British herds.[24] The nexus between the action plan and financial assistance was on the Community agenda from the very beginning of the BSE crisis: as early as 29 March 1996, bilateral talks were held between the Commissioner for Agriculture, Franz Fischler, and the British minister for agriculture, Douglas Hogg, concerning the financial implications of 'Community-wide solidarity'[25] with Great Britain.

10.5 Conclusion: Implications for the analysis and explanation of horizontal enforcement

Both cases point to a number of factors which are theoretically relevant for the description and explanation of compliance: First and foremost,

---

[24] Commissioner for agriculture, Franz Fischler, before the European Parliament in Strasbourg (*Agence Europe*, 20 June 1996).

[25] Afterwards, Hogg said: 'I think I have discerned the willingness to show true solidarity on a certain number of financial consequences' (*Agence Europe*, 30 March 1996). Commissioner of agriculture, Franz Fischler, on 3 April 1996: 'What was needed here was solidarity of the member states in the EU, and we have shown it, and will also try to show it in future. We have never intended to exclude the UK; basically our decisions amount to the EU extending a hand' (*Agence Europe*, 4 April 1996).

they must be seen as a warning against over-simplifying approaches, which restrict the analysis of European integration to the level at which legal acts are created, and which thereby equate these acts with factual cooperation. Instead, what is needed is an understanding which differentiates between the adoption of a legal act at the supra-national level and its adherence by the member states. In the BSE case, intergovernmental cooperation and supra-national adoption was achieved, at the latest, after the Florence summit in June 1996 when the Commission's action plan was agreed. In the meantime, the implementation of this agreement, and thus, its factual realization has progressed considerably, but the present level of implementation is the result of an arduous and time-consuming bargaining process among the Commission and the competent member state authorities. The same can be said with regard to the subsidies control during the late 1980s. Although none of the member state governments was in favour of reducing its budgetary room for manoeuvre in any of the contested cases, the Commission was able to muster the support of all other governments and the overwhelming majority of the European Parliament.

Furthermore, both cases reveal the necessity of analysing the process of the implementation of law with special emphasis on the aspects of co-operation and conflict between the national and the supra-national layer of the EU's polity. Thus, the two cases can also be understood as a warning against analytical approaches which completely disregard the dimension of domestic politics and public discourse. They emphasize the need to regard compliance as a process which is shaped by political as well as legal means and develops through the tension between supra-national legal norms, governmental interests, and sub-national interest groups.

In this respect, the high degree of efficacy of the EU's horizontal enforcement of common policies can be attributed to at least four important interacting elements which developed over time. First, the EU incorporates the non-compliant member government into a dense network of discussions and negotiations, avoids challenging it and, thus, gives it no chance to invoke the 'sovereignty argument', since it would be the non-compliant government itself which would exclude itself from this network. Second, this dense network of discussions and negotiations not only clears the route for a common solution, but also defines all the necessary details to reach this solution effectively denying the non-compliant government any easy exit option while, at the same time, offering concessions and support. Third, this network of discussions and negotiations established over years inaugurated a specific common logic of appropriateness, a specific problem-solving rationality, which on the one hand functions as a yardstick for the earlier promises the member governments have to live up to. On the other hand, this specific rationality also shields the governments from domestic public opinion and media pressures, since it seems unreasonable to break commitments to common policies. Fourth, the EU, nevertheless, uses domestic pressure to secure compliant behaviour of the member governments. This pressure, however, is channelled by specific administrative and judicial procedures, thus strengthening the adherence to European policies without invoking national, sovereign sentiments. It is this set of non-hierarchical, non-coercive instruments which made the EU so successful in overcoming national barriers and in achieving a comparatively high degree of compliance.

References

Bleckmann, Albert (1997). *Europarecht. Das Recht der Europäischen Union und der Europäischen Gemeinschaften* (6th edn). Köln: Carl Heymanns.

Caspari, Manfred (1987). 'Die Beihilferegeln des EWG-Vertrages und ihre Anwendung', in Ernst-Joachim Mestmäcker, Hans Möller, and Hans-Peter Schwarz (eds.), *Eine Ordnungspolitik für Europa. Festschrift für Hans von der Groeben zu seinem 80. Geburtstag.* Baden-Baden: Nomos, 69-91.

Fearon, James D. (1998). 'Bargaining, Enforcement, and International Cooperation', *International Organization*, 52/2: 269-305.

Garrett, Geoffrey (1995). 'The Politics of Legal Integration in the European Union', *International Organization*, 49/1: 171-81.

Héritier, Adrienne, Mingers, Susanne, Knill, Christoph, and Becka, Martina (1994). *Die Veränderung von Staatlichkeit in Europa. Ein regulativer Wettbewerb: Deutschland, Großbritannien und Frankreich in der Europäischen Union.* Opladen: Westdeutscher Verlag.

Jacobson, Harold K. and Brown Weiss, Edith (1998). 'A Framework for Analysis', in Edith Brown Weiss and Harold K. Jacobson (eds.), *Engaging Countries. Strengthening Compliance with International Environmental Accords.* Cambridge: MIT Press, 1-18.

Joerges, Christian and Neyer, Jürgen (1997). 'Transforming Strategic Interaction into Deliberative Problem-Solving: European Comitology in the Foodstuff Sector', *Journal of European Public Policy*, 4/4: 609-25.

Löw, Norbert (1992). *Der Rechtsschutz des Konkurrenten gegenüber Subventionen aus gemeinschaftsrechtlicher Sicht.* Baden-Baden: Nomos.

Mederer, Wolfgang (1996). *Die Stellung der Unternehmen im europäischen Beihilfeverfahren* (speech held at the Studienvereinigung Kartellrecht e.V., 25 January, Brüssel).

Mendrinou, Maria (1996). 'Non-Compliance and the European Commission's Role in Integration', *Journal of European Public Policy*, 3/1: 1-22.

Neyer, Jürgen (2000). 'Risk Regulation and the Power of the People: Lessons from the BSE-Crisis', *European Integration online Papers*, 4/6.

Polley, Romina (1996). 'Die Konkurrentenklage im Europäischen Beihilfenrecht. Klagebefugnis und Rückforderung bei rechtswidrig gewährten Beihilfen', *Europäische Zeitschrift für Wirtschaftsrecht*, 7/10: 300-5.

Rahmsdorf, Detlev W. and Schäfer, Hans-Bernd (1980). 'Ökonomische Analyse des Rechts—ein Gegentrend?', in Rüdiger Voigt (ed.), *Verrechtlichung. Analysen zu Funktion und Wirkung von Parlamentarisierung, Bürokratisierung und Justizialisierung sozialer, politischer und ökonomischer Prozesse*. Königstein: Athenäum, 94-108.

Rawlinson, Frank (1993). 'The Role of Policy Frameworks, Codes and Guidelines in the Control of State Aid', in Ian Harden (ed.), *State Aid: Community Law and Policy*. Köln: Bundesanzeiger, 52-60.

Reufels, Martin (1997). *Europäische Subventionskontrolle durch Private. Partizipation der Unternehmen an der EG-Wettbewerbsaufsicht über staatliche Beihilfen*. Köln: Carl Heymanns.

Rosenstock, Manfred (1995). *Kontrolle und Harmonisierung nationaler Beihilfen durch die Kommission der Europäischen Gemeinschaften*. Frankfurt a. M.: Peter Lang.

Sinnaeve, Adinda (1999). 'State Aid Control: Objectives and Procedures', in Sanoussi Bilal and Phedon Nicolaides (eds.), *Understanding State Aid Policy in the European Community. Perspectives on Rules and Practice*. Maastricht: European Institute of Public Administration, 13-27.

Slot, Piet Jan (1993). 'Procedural Law of State Aids', in Ian Harden (ed.), *State Aid: Community Law and Policy*. Köln: Bundesanzeiger, 36-49.

—— (1999). 'EC Policy on State Aid: Are the Procedures "User-Friendly"? The Rights of Third Parties', in Sanoussi Bilal and Phedon Nicolaides (eds.), *Understanding State Aid Policy in the European Community. Perspectives on Rules and Practice*. Maastricht: European Institute of Public Administration, 81-97.

Snyder, Francis (1993). 'The Effectiveness of European Community Law. Institutions, Processes, Tools and Techniques', *Modern Law Review*, 56/1: 19-54.

Tallberg, Jonas (1999). *Making States Comply: The European Commission, The European Court of Justice, and the Enforcement of the Internal Market*. Lund: Studentlitteratur.

Victor, David G., Raustiala, Kal, and Skolnikoff, Eugene B. (1998). 'Introduction and Overview', in David G. Victor, Kal Raustiala, and Eugene B. Skolnikoff (eds.), *The Implementation and Effectiveness of International Environmental Commitments: Theory and Practice*. Cambridge: MIT Press, 1-46.

Weiler, Joseph H. H. (2000). 'Does the European Union Treaty Need a Charter of Rights?', *European Law Journal*, 6/2: 95-7.

Wessels, Wolfgang (1997). 'An Ever Closer Fusion? A Dynamic Macropolitical View on Integration Processes', *Journal of Common Market Studies*, 35/2: 267-99.

Winter, J. A. (1993). 'Supervision of State Aid: Article 93 in the Court of Justice', *Common Market Law Review*, 30/2: 311-29.

Young, Oran (ed.) (1999). *The Effectiveness of International Environmental Regimes. Causal Connections and Behavioral Mechanisms*. Cambridge: MIT Press.

Index

abattoirs 209–10
absorption 15, 159, 168, 170
accountability 18, 21, 22, 46, 83, 101
   to parliaments 86, 89
   see also 'negotiation-accountability dilemma'
acquis communautaire 54, 57
ad hoc committees 69, 70
ADAPT initiative 186
adaptability 139, 187
adaptation 12, 53–81, 161, 177
   costs of 15
   flexible 21
   smooth 20
   symbolic 15
   voluntary 14
adjustment costs of 16, 19
   EU capacities for 21
   institutional 17
   national patterns of 16
administrative differentiation 142–4
administrative procurement 30
AFSJ (area of freedom, security and justice)
   project 130
AFSSA *(Agence Française de Sécurité Sanitaire des Aliments)* 209
Agenda 2000 process 84, 92, 93, 94, 96, 98, 99
Agrarian Council 206
agreements:
   mutual 18
   'national' 165, 169
   'regional growth' 170
Allison, G. T. 158
allocation of resources 137
Ambrosius, G. 177
Amsterdam Treaty (1999) 27, 29, 41, 56, 60, 130, 175, 183, 190
Anselmann, N. 34
ARENA programme 2, 7
arenas 13, 20, 21, 46, 67
   core 86
   decision 125, 137, 140, 142
   functional differentiation of 148–50
   fundamental trends 53–4
   implementation 140
   institutional 144

Armstrong, K. A. 11 n., 195
Auel, K. 82 n.
Australia 188
Austria 73, 89, 208
authoritarian bureaucracy 26
autonomy 14, 16, 21, 30, 33–4, 65, 122, 139, 149
   connection and 140

balance of power 17
'Banana-case' 44
bargaining 115
   competitive 18, 89
   distributive 18, 87
Bauer, H. 28
Belgium 73
benchmarking 13, 18, 187, 190, 191–2
Benford, R. D. 125
Benz, A. 17, 18, 71 n., 86, 135, 148, 154 n., 158
Berger, P. 26
Berlin Summit (1999) 92
best practices 6, 14, 18, 21, 92, 182, 183, 188
   labour markets and 192
Beyme, K. von 88
Bierwagen, R. 33
binding decisions 112
Birgelen, G. 40
blame avoidance 122
Bleckmann, A. 211
Böckenförde, E.-W. 45
Bogdandy, A. von 13, 14, 26, 27, 28, 30, 33, 34 n., 43 n., 46
Bonn 209
boomerang patterns 123, 124
border control 219
Borries, von 32, 43
Börzel, T. 162
Britain 2, 3, 4, 6, 7, 46, 185
   Council presidency 145
   decision-making not predictable 87
   'goodness of fit' 5
   New Labour victory (1997) 183
   pre- and post-integration 8
   workfarist approach 186
   see also BSE
Brugère-Picoux, Jeanne 210
Brunsson, N. 160, 162

BSE (bovine spongiform encephalitis) 203, 206–11, 218, 219, 220–1
Bulmer, S. J. 11 n., 40, 42 n., 43, 44, 45, 46, 71 n., 159, 195
Bundesrat 43, 44, 91, 97, 98, 102, 211
Bundestag 43, 44, 97, 98, 99, 100
Búrca, G. de 34 n.
Burch, M. 159

candidate states 6
CAP (common agricultural policy) 63
Capelli, F. 38
capital markets 179, 188
capitalism 177
Caporaso, J. 162
Cardiff process 184, 185
Caspari, M. 212, 214
Cecchini report (1985) 182
CEN (Comité Européen de Normalisation) 36
CENELEC (Comité Européen de Normalisation Electrotechnique) 36
centralization 41, 70, 72, 202
Cerny, P. G. 179
CFP (common fisheries policy) 63
CFSP (common foreign and security policy) 63
change:
　capacity to resist 19
　constitutional 56–60
　institutional 14, 15
　material 16, 167, 170
　policy 156–7, 170–1
　social 195
　structural 186, 194
　symbolic 15, 163, 165, 168, 169, 170
　'third order' 162
checks and balances 77
CIA Security 38
citizenship 28, 125, 127
'citoyen' and 'bourgeois' 189
civil liberties 22
closeness and openness 138–9
co-decision 59, 61, 64, 96
coercive means 28, 202
coherence mechanisms 140, 141, 142, 145, 149
　effectiveness of 147–8
Cohesion Fund 96
Cohn-Bendit, D. 128 n.
collective action 127, 130, 131
collective choice 87, 89, 92
collective decisions 11
Cologne process 184, 185

comitology 24, 32, 70, 216, 218
Committee of the Regions 65
Committee on Budgets 95
Committee on Regional Policy 95
commodity markets 179
'common good' 47
communicability 117
communication 27, 29, 40, 103, 120, 125, 138
　administrative, legislatively relevant 39
　daily 148
　networks 25, 26, 28, 39
　rational 120
　transnational 77, 113, 117, 121
Communication on Openness in the Community (1993) 31
competence 21, 29–30, 60, 65, 71, 77, 141, 168
competitive advantage 19
competitiveness 180
　international 185
　regional 186
complementarity 179, 180
complexity 22, 41, 65
compliance 12, 38, 125–6, 149, 161, 201–2
　horizontal enforcement and 203–6, 215
compromises 146–7, 169
conceptual approach 26–8
connectedness 139
consensus 70, 84, 143, 178
　building 42, 45
　national or sectoral 76
　'new Keynesian' 185
consociation 20
constitutionalization 126
constructivism 7
control:
　of the controllers 215–16
　parliamentary 17
Conzelmann, T. 161
Coombes, D. 56
cooperation 19, 39, 59, 61, 64, 101, 154, 191, 219
　foreign policy 178
　JHA 21, 111–14, 115, 116, 119, 121, 122, 126
　loyal 29
　projects to improve 189
　transnational 77
coordination 12, 21, 100, 139, 191
　administrative 14
　central 69–70
　employment policy, open method of 18
　horizontal 70

INDEX   227

intergovernmental 18–19, 190
inter-ministerial 68, 71
intra-ministerial 68
legislation 37
open method of 192
positive 150
CoR (Committee of the Regions) 85, 101–2
COREPER (Comité des Représentants)
    40, 42, 43, 45, 46, 66, 68, 70, 145
COSAC (Conference of Community and
    European Affairs Committees) 72–3
cost-benefit analysis 3
Council of the European Union 28, 32,
    63–4, 67, 70, 85, 94, 124, 146, 188, 192
  balance of power 183
  BSE saga 208
  competitive bargaining 18
  decision-making processes 144
  employment crisis 182
  'grand' legislation 24
  introduction of 178
  'negotiation-accountability dilemma'
    and national parliaments 88–90
  presidency 31, 60, 96, 113 n., 129 n.,
    130, 144, 145, 185
  Regulations 33, 220
  Rules of Procedure 40
  sectoral formats 60
  social welfare reform 189
  unanimity in 58, 59, 60
  working groups 41, 42, 43, 146, 147
Council of Ministers 63, 70, 98, 145
coupling:
  loose 117, 138–42, 149
  strict 90–2
Court of First Instance 217
courts 38, 74–5
  see also Court of First Instance; ECJ
Cowles, M. G. 162
Craig, P. 27
Cram, L. 128
credit claims 129
cross-sectoral issues 87, 163
Curtin, D. 32

Dahl, R. A. 83
DCL (directory of Community legislation
    in force) 62 n.
Dean, M. 182, 185
decentralization 70, 73, 92–3
decision rules 89
  incompatible, strict coupling of 90–2
decision-making 12, 19, 21, 22, 26, 43,
    45, 65, 117, 137, 138, 156

blocked 112, 129
de-institutionalization of 18, 100–3
differentiation of 142
dilemma of 58
domestic responses to 158–63
evolution of procedures 62
inter-organizational 143
joint 13, 67, 141
national 68, 122
new regulation proposals 144
not predictable 87
regional ministers and 73
rules 60
salience of 71
sequencing 139–140, 145–8, 149
splitting-up of 20
spreading of responsibility for 77
transparency of 103
defection 58
defence 3, 4, 8
deinstitutionalization 18, 100–3
delegitimation 128
DellaCananea, G. 24
democracy 17, 18, 22, 33
  problem in EU 82, 83, 85–92
Denmark 70, 74, 178
  parliament 55, 72, 89
'departmentalization' 97
Deppe, F. 18, 19
deregulation 181, 182
derogation 17
Deutsch, K. W. 119 n.
deviant behaviour 20
DFG (Deutsche Forschungsgemeinschaft)
    2, 3
'dialectical interpretation' 138, 139,
    140
dialogue 28, 184
Diekemann, K. 32, 33, 46
differentiation 138–42
  Europeanization and 77
  functional 140, 142–50
  procedural 60
diffusion processes 115
Directives 34–5, 37, 71
'dirty' communitarizations 60
'dissidence' 139
distinctiveness 139
division of labour 190, 191, 194
division of power 72, 84 n., 100
Doméneche, R. 92
domestic response 154–74
Dreier, H. 25
Due, O. 28

Eberlein, B. 158
ECJ (European Court of Justice) 20, 28, 32, 38, 59, 74, 124
  BSE 207
  challenge of decisions 213, 217–18
  compliance cases 201, 204–5
  direct access to 212
  powers 214–15
  state aid control cases 220
economic and social partners 166, 169
ECSC (European Coal and Steel) Treaty (1952) 60
Edelman, M. 161
Eder, K. 3, 21, 22
EDF (European Development Fund) 137
educational systems 194
Eduskunta 72
EEC (European Economic Community) Treaty (1957) 57
efficiency 20, 59
embargoes 206, 208, 209, 210, 219
Employment Committee 65
employment policy 175–200
  open method of coordination 18
EMS (European Monetary System) 59, 177, 178
EMU (Economic and Monetary Union) 59, 68, 177, 181
Engels, F. 180
'enhanced cooperation clauses' 65
EP (European Parliament) 24, 32, 37 n., 39, 59, 62 n., 67, 72
  characteristic of 85
  Council and 18, 86–8, 91, 96–7, 100, 102
  national limited power 82
  national parliaments and 94–100
  plenary sessions 60
  resolution on BSE 206
  roles of 61, 64
  see also MEPs
ESC (Economic and Social Committee) 86, 102
ESRC (Economic and Social Research Council) 2, 3, 5, 6, 7
Essen 182
Esslinger, T. 82 n.
ethics 26
European Central Bank 65, 185
European Commission 20, 24, 59, 94, 95–6, 124, 136, 191, 201
  administrative differentiation 142–4

benchmarking 13, 18, 187, 190, 191–2
BSE saga 206, 208–9, 210–11, 216, 218, 220–1
coherence mechanisms 142, 149
competencies 164
compliance 202
cooperation between member states and 219
DGs 36, 60, 101, 102, 103, 130, 137, 142–3, 144, 145, 148, 149
financial support 212, 213–14, 217
fund-specific actor structures 137
German participation in 25
goal of 128
infringement proceedings 204–5, 215
Länder ministries and 169
links as a power base 29–39
mediation 97
on-the-spot checks 215–16
opinions from CoR to 102
role strengthened 193
subsidies 214, 217
White Papers 179, 182
'European Employment Pact' 184
'European Employment Strategy' 149
European governance:
  interdependent 10–23
  policy proposals 101
  state aid control law 220
  structural funds 163, 165
European law 46, 74–5, 89, 126, 202, 220
  effectiveness of 201
  unity of 19–20
European Year Against Racism (1997) 120
Europeanization 5, 15, 53, 121–6, 176, 194
  conceptualizing 54
  designer 7–8
  differentiation and 77
  intensified, demand for 179
  partial 180
  under scrutiny 65–75
  understanding of 190
  uneven 19, 180, 195
evaluation 15, 166–7
Everling, U. 29, 38, 45
evolutionary model 59
executive agencies 60
executive power 12, 14, 39, 91
  under pressure 17–18

fairness 33
Falke, J. 24, 32
federal ministries 25

federalism 28–9
feedback 65
  see also 'organized feedback loops'
Felder, M. 18, 180
Fifth Republic 97
financial sanctions 220–1
Finland 72, 73
  see also Tampere
Fischer, Andrea 209
Fischler, Franz 221
'fitness' 5
'flanking measures' 112
flexibilization 182
Florence 208, 209
Folketing 72, 89
Food and Veterinary Office 216
fordism 185
foreign relations 25
'fortress Europe' 112, 120
fragmentation 13, 21, 68, 135–53
France 16, 30, 71
  Délégation de l'Assemblée Nationale pour l'Union européenne 97, 98, 99
  embargo on British beef 206, 208, 209, 210
  Sénate 98
  socialists 183, 184
free-rider positions 58, 202, 203
freedom 129
  see also AFSJ
Freisenhahn, E. 25
'French experiment' 178
Fronia, J. 35, 38, 39 n.
Fuente, A. de la 92
functionalism 91
fusion approach 77

General Affairs Council 145
geographical units 137, 149
Germany 2–8, 16, 67, 71, 97
  Basic Law 46, 98
  Commission participation 25
  constitution 28
  Constitutional Court 17 n., 55
  Council and 39–47, 73
  decision-making not predictable 87
  embargo on British beef 206, 208, 209–10
  labour market projects 189
  national rules 216
  regional policy 93, 168, 169, 170
  structural funds 165, 166
  see also Bundesrat; Bundestag; Länder
Gil-Robles, A. 96

Giolitti, A. 143
Glatthaar, C. 32
globalization 176, 179, 195
good practice 6
'goodness of fit' 5, 159
governability 141, 142
governments 14, 25, 73, 128–9, 136, 202
  and administrations 67–71
  centralization of power 41
  changed balance inside 68
  changing attitude of 130
  conservative 184
  control of 17
  criticism at home 19
  distributive bargaining 18, 87
  divided 86–8
  monetary and fiscal discipline 178
  monopoly of 123
  participation of 70
  powerful 97
  sub-national 91
Greece 74
green papers 31
Grewe, W. G. 25

Häberle, P. 25
Hall, P. 58, 156, 162
Hallstein, W. 41 n.
harmonization 15, 32, 86, 191, 192, 194
Hartley, T. C. 32
Haverland, M. 162
Hayes-Renshaw, F. 40, 87 n.
Heclo, H. 136
hegemony 46, 176, 180, 191, 194, 196
  social-democratic 184
Heinelt, H. 20, 21, 136, 158
Héritier, A. 11 n., 25, 42 n., 101, 103, 162, 175
Hermes, G. 46
heterogeneity 22, 27, 30
hierarchies 26, 27, 34, 41, 70, 77, 116, 140, 146, 191
Hix, S. 56, 64, 86
Hoffmann-Riem, W. 26
Hogg, Douglas 221
Hooghe, L. 143
horizontal enforcement 20, 201–24
horizontal fragmentation 21, 137
Hufen, F. 24
human capital 188
human rights 127
Hyde-Price, A. G. V. 5

'ideas' 139, 140, 141
identity 130, 138
  common 125
  democratic 17
'illusory community' 180
Immergut, E. 156
incentives 92, 183, 202
individuals 196
inflation 184
information 26, 27–8, 29, 40
  Commission's gathering of 30–8
  exchange of 140
  filtering 149
  first-hand, access to 127
  parliaments deprived of 102
  policy-making 98
INGOs (international non-governmental organizations) 129
innovation 189, 193
insecurity 122
institutional spillover 15
institutional structures 17
institutionalization 70, 184
  representative democracy 85–6
integration 3, 4, 6, 8, 17, 74, 131
  academic research on 2
  complexity and ambiguity of 22
  dynamics of 56
  functional scope of 53
  intra-state consequences of 41
  legal, sub-national 12
  major steps of 135
  market 19
  multi-level governance 114–21
  national parliament reaction to 97
  new modes of 194–6
  new quality of 190
  new reality of 176–81
  policy-specific 195–6
  political 26, 119, 130
  salience of 75
  social 26, 116
  specific forms of 191
  symbolic, justice and home affairs 130–1
  vertical 116
interconnectedness 12
interdependence 10–23, 75, 179
interest groups 32, 33, 64, 86, 91
intergovernmental conferences 11, 19, 183
intergovernmentalism 21, 58, 60, 121, 127, 178
  rationalized 59
international law 33
International Political Economy 179

international relations 19
internationalization 176, 179, 180
interpenetrated polities 13, 39, 157–8
interventions 141, 143, 180, 187, 191
'intrusion'/'invasion' 139
Ipsen, H.-P. 27, 28
Ireland 69, 167, 169, 170–1, 178
  see also Northern Ireland
isolated implementation 15
isolation 168, 169, 170
Italy 67

Jachtenfuchs, M. 29
Jacobson, H. K. 203
Janning, J. 40, 43, 46
Japan 178
Jeffrey, C. 6, 40, 42 n., 43, 44, 45, 46
Jessop, B. 177, 180
JHA (justice and home affairs) 59 n., 63, 111–34
  cooperation in 21
  see also AFSJ
Joerges, C. 10 n., 24, 26, 42, 101
'joint decision trap' 135
judicial review 218–20
justice and home affairs, *see* JHA

Kapteyn, P. 26
Kaufmann, M. 27
Keohane, R. O. 12 n., 16
Keynesianism 180, 182, 185
Kirchhof, P. 28
Knill, C. 162
Kohler-Koch, B. 16, 27, 33, 40, 154 n., 190
Kohl, Helmut 46 n.
Kooiman, J. 11 n.
Kretzschmar, Hans 210
Kühn, J. 43, 45 n.

labour market policy 137, 182–9
  passim, 192
  best practices and 191
  Europeanized 194
  regulation of 193
Ladeur, K.-H. 28
Laffan, B. 69
'laid down' procedures 14
Länder 43, 55, 97, 98, 102, 168, 169, 210
Lang, J. 14, 15, 135
law:
  administrative 27
  constitutional 25
  harmonization of 32
  supra-national 13, 24

see also European law; international
      law; rule of law
learning:
  lifelong 188
  mutual 21
  network 191
  organizational 20, 21, 139
  precondition for 143
legal acts 62
legal framework 24, 30, 32–4
  common 13
legislation 31, 34, 37, 38–9, 57, 75
  Commission's right to initiate 34
  coordination of 37
  'grand' 24
  integrated 35
  national 64
  secondary 63
  technical 37
  see also DCL
legislative power 12, 13, 14
legitimacy 11, 20, 31, 125, 126, 127
  democratic 82, 92, 103
  economic 187
  'input' 101
  'natural' 27
  problems of 179
Lehmbruch, G. 82 n., 86
liberalism:
  'advanced' 182
  'embedded' 178
  neo- 196
Lijphart, Arend 84
Lisbon 185, 188
local governments 86
'logic of influence' 91
Lord, C. 87
Louis, J.-V. 28, 29
loyalty 125, 130
  federal 28–9
Luckmann, T. 22
Luhmann, N. 25, 27
Luxembourg process 149, 183, 184, 185,
      187, 188, 190, 191

Maastricht Treaty (TEU, 1992) 27, 30, 41,
      46, 56, 63, 65, 68, 183, 211
  reactions to 76
macroeconomic crisis management 169
Majone, G. 27, 28
Major, John 207
Malek, T. 144
Mancini, F. 28
March, J. G. 11, 58, 117

market forces 211, 213
market liberalization 181
marketability of individuals 196
Marks, G. 136
Marx, K. 180
Maurer, A. 13, 14, 54, 56, 65, 66, 71 n.,
      77, 189
Mayntz, R. 11 n., 140 n.
Mazey, S. 30 n.
mediation 97, 179
Meier, G. 29
Meijers, H. 32
Mentler, M. 32, 44
Mény, Y. 10 n., 26, 30–1, 33, 34
MEPs (Members of European
      Parliaments) 73, 96, 96,
      98 n., 129
Meyer, J. W. 123
Meyer, P. 40, 43, 46
microeconomic reasoning 188
migrant groups 124
Mittag, J. 13, 14
modernization 188, 194
monitoring 13, 20, 114, 116–18, 131
  critical 22
Moravcsik, A. 29 n., 41, 59, 194
Moreau Defarges, P. 29
Muller, P. 26, 30, 33, 34
multi-level governance 56, 60, 66, 71,
      73–4, 76, 77, 82–110
  coordination costs 21
  democratic deficiencies 21
  integration of 114–21
  intergovernmental negotiations to
      126–30
  policy implementation 12, 154–74
  'standard model' of 112, 121

'narrative fidelity' 117
national constitutions 28, 66
national governance 14, 15–16, 24, 39,
      126, 202
  division of labour between European
      and 190
  European politics permeates 121
  overall dominance of 111
national institutions:
  EC/EU system and 65–75
  supra-national institutions and 24–52
  see also courts; governments;
      parliaments
national interests 87, 90
  representation 46–7
Nationalrat 89

INDEX

NATO (North Atlantic Treaty Organization) 3–4
'negotiation-accountability dilemma' 17, 88–90, 98
negotiations 17, 126–30, 140, 145–8
neo-corporatist systems 16
neo-institutionalism 159
Netherlands 70, 71
Nettesheim, M. 33
networks 13, 68, 130
   communication 25, 26, 28, 39
   cross-cutting 20–1
   decision 136
   implementation 137
   information 26, 37
   interaction 28
   inter-administrative 206
   policy 20–1, 54, 136, 137
newspapers 207, 208, 210
Neyer, J. 19, 42, 101, 206
NGOs (non-governmental organizations) 32, 64, 65, 96, 127
   see also INGOs
Nice Treaty (2001) 56, 57, 178
Nicolaïdis, K. 59, 194
Niessen, J. 127
non-compliance 19, 58, 204, 214, 215, 218
'non-participation' procedure 61
non-state actors 168–70
normative force 115
norms 5, 15, 20, 21, 46, 141, 159
   constitutional 55
   legal 33, 205
   procedural 140, 149
   substantive 149
North, D. C. 159
Northern Ireland 220
Norton, P. 95
Norway 2, 7
notification requirement 34, 38
Nye, J. S. 12 n., 16

objectives 19, 22, 149, 182, 187, 191, 194
   management by 190
   policy, unclear 40
   quantitative 190
   reducing the number of 92
   shared 18
obligations 28, 29
   binding 19
   reporting 34–9
Official Journal 213
Olsen, J. P. 7, 11, 58, 117, 160, 190
openness and closeness 138–9

'opportunity structures' 66
'organized feedback loops' 21, 136, 137
Orton, J. D. 138, 139, 140, 141
overarching constitutional principle 28–9

package deals 135
paradigms 140, 141
parallel systems 160, 161, 162
parliaments 17, 18, 41, 55, 71–3, 77, 85
   accountability to 86
   Council members' pressure by 88
   deprived of information 102
   EP and 94–100, 101
   'negotiation-accountability dilemma' and 88–90, 98
   strong 97, 98
   weak 97, 99
   see also Bundestag; Eduskunta; EP; Folketing; Nationalrat; Riksdag
party competition 14, 17–18, 89
Paterson, W. E. 40, 42 n., 43, 44, 45, 46, 71 n.
Peck, J. 186
'people's voice' 117
permanent representation 45, 145
   see also COREPER
Pernice, I. 28
Peters, B. G. 11 n.
Pierre, J. 11 n.
Pitschas, R. 24, 27
policies:
   binding 131
   common 202
   competition 214
   defence 8
   education 189, 190
   foreign 8, 178
   fragmentation of 13
   'good' 136
   implementation of 67, 154–74
   ministries affected by 68–9
   national 5–6, 179
   redistributive 94, 135
   re-regulation 184
   security 8
   shared 3
   'soft' 190
   structural 20, 21, 92–103, 144, 148, 154–74, 190
   see also CAP; CFP; CFSP; employment policy; fragmentation; labour market policy; regional policy
policy communities 20, 21, 136

policy-making 11, 12, 14, 21, 65, 89, 100–3, 126
  communitarian frameworks for 53
  compartmentalization of 44
  empirical studies on 92
  exclusion from process 61
  executive negotiations in 17
  fragmented systems 135–53
  harmonization of 86
  influence in decisive stage of 97
  information on 98
  joint 93
  legal frameworks for 64
  national 91
  'standard model' of 115
  strong assembly 72
  successful instalment of structures 54–5
  uniform 76
policy mix 185
Political and Security Committee 65
'political field' 114–18
political power 41, 65, 115
political steering 12–13
politics 1, 56, 116, 129, 162, 191
  constitutional 11
  contentious 118
  'dramatic' 120
  Europeanization of 121–6
  informal 7
  institutional 90–2
  Keynesian 182
  limited scope of 182–6
  national 5–6, 54, 122, 123, 179, 183
  neoliberal 196
  regulatory 215
  Schumpeterian 182
  security 122, 128
  supply-side 182
  supra-national 123
  symbolic 118
Portuguese Council Presidency 60 n., 185
'post-Nizza process' 91
power differentials 19
PR (public relations) 118, 120, 128
prerogatives 67
Priebe, R. 32
privatization 182
problem-solving 21, 56, 184, 192, 195, 205
  common philosophies 191
  effective 204
  supra-national 53
procedural differentiation 60
procedural rules 32
procedural skills 54

productivity 180
programming 164–6, 168
Prussia 41 n.
public-private divide 12, 14, 19
public spheres 22, 117 n., 119–21, 122, 126, 130

QMV (qualified majority voting) 59 n., 60, 64
Quermonne, J.-L. 26, 30, 33, 34

racism 120, 128 n.
Radaelli, C. 162
rapports d'information 99
ratchet effect 56
rational choice 11
Raustiala, K. 203
reality 26, 27, 176–81
  one-sided perception of 34
redistribution 28, 94, 135, 185
referendums 178
Reflexionsgruppe 40
reforms 14, 16–17, 46, 70
  regional policy 92–4
  social welfare 189
  structural funds 20, 92, 97, 99, 135–8, 142, 147, 182, 193
  treaty 58, 61, 65, 86
regional policy 20, 95, 143, 168
  implementation networks 137
  reform 92–4
regionalization 73, 170
regulations 13, 16, 27, 33, 149, 201–2, 206
  intergovernmental 22
  labour market 193
  market-oriented 179
  product-related 37
  structural funds 146, 155–66, 194
  technical 34–5, 36
Rein, M. 144
resistance 21
responsiveness 21, 139
  ideological 120
  institutional 118, 119
restrictions on trade 35
retrievability 117
Rhodes, R. A. W. 1, 10 n.
Richardson, J. 30 n.
rights 33, 113
Riksdag 72
Risse, T. 162
Röhl, H. C. 40
Rosenstock, M. 211, 214
Rowlands, S. 127

rule-making procedures 33
rule of law 131
rules 140, 141
ruling majority 41

Sach, 42
scapegoating 122
Scharpf, F. W. 20, 27, 29, 42, 64, 83, 87
Schengen Treaty (1999) 120 n., 126
Scheuing, D. 24
Schlink, B. 29
Schmidt, M. G. 83
Schmidt, V. A. 16, 162
Schmidt-Aßmann, E. 27, 29
Schmitter, P. C. 11 n.
Schön, D. 144
Schreckenberger, W. 39
Schumpeterianism 180, 182, 189
Scientific Veterinary Committee 207
SEA (Single European Act, 1992) 56, 214
secondary law 24
secrecy 118, 120, 122, 126
Secretariat 70
'securitization' 112
security 3, 4, 7, 21, 123
 national 129
 see also AFSJ
self-interests 58
Selmer, P. 44
sensitivity 16, 20–2
sequentialization 139, 140
side-payments 135
single market 31, 34, 35, 38, 178, 179, 214
Skolnikoff, E. B. 203
Slot, P. J. 38
Snow, D. A. 125
Snyder, F. 201, 205
sociability 189
social cohesion 185
social contagion 13
social embeddedness 181
social justice 189
social protection 183
social security 189
socialization 147, 189
sovereignty 129
 credible commitments to delegate 59
 loss of 88
Spain 69–70, 73, 96, 185
'spatio-temporal fix' 177
special committees 99
sponsorship 144
SSC (Scientific Steering Committee) 209, 210

standards 36
 technical 13, 34, 37, 39
standing committees 71
Standing Veterinary Committee 206
standstill clause 35
state aid cases 220
state-centred polities 16
state-watching activities 122
statehood 25
 characterized 28
Statz, A. 177
Steinberg, R. 41
strategies 19, 76, 116
 bargaining 87, 89
 employment 192
 negotiation 69
 non-hierarchical, non-coercive 20
 problem-solving 21, 192
 socialization 189
Streeck, W. 196
structural funds 14, 21, 144, 146, 148, 154–74
 loosely coupled 149
 redistribution of 94
 reform 20, 92, 97, 99, 135–8, 142, 147, 193
 regulation 146, 155–66, 194
sub-national state actors 167–8, 169
subsidiarity 192–3
subsidies 14, 136, 165, 217
 control of 211–14
supra-national institutions 215
 national institutions and 24–52
supra-national procedures 59
Sweden 72, 165–6, 167, 169–70
symbolic mobilization 125
synergy 6

Tampere Council Presidency 113 n., 129 n., 130
target setting 18
task forces 143–4
Taylor, R. C. R. 156
Teague, P. 192
TEC (Treaty of the European Community) 11, 19, 29, 30, 32, 36, 45, 46, 85, 212
technical issues 148
technical standards 13, 34, 37, 39
'technoculture' 34
territory 28, 194
TEU, *see* Maastricht
third parties 213, 215, 216–18
'third way' 189, 196

Thuringia 210
Tidow, S. 18
Tocqueville, A. de 25
transaction costs 20, 58
transnational resonance 22, 114–21, 123, 124–5, 126, 130–1
transnationalization 180
transparency 21, 22, 103, 118, 124
'travelling actors' 54
treaty matters:
  building 56
  provisions 60–5
  reforms 58, 61, 65
  revision 59
  violation procedure 218–20
Trenz, H.-J. 3, 21, 22
TREVI group 59
'troika' 87 n.
Turin European Council Meeting (1996) 206
'two-level game' 88

unanimity 58, 59, 60
United States 178, 186, 188

VerLoren van Themaat, P. 41
vertical fragmentation 21, 137
Vesting, T. 41
vetoes 90, 91, 100
  ex ante 89
Victor, D. G. 203
vulnerability 16–22

Wallace, H. 40, 56, 87 n.
websites 31 n., 206 n.
Weick, K. E. 138, 139, 140, 141
Weiler, J. H. 10 n., 27, 205
Weiss, E. B. 203
welfare 180, 186, 187, 189
Wessels, W. 13, 14, 29, 32, 54, 68
Westlake, M. 60
White papers 31
  European Governance (2001) 10 n., 179
  Growth, Competitiveness, and Employment (1993) 182
Wiesenthal, H. 139
Wildavsky, A. 136
Winter, G. 24, 32
Winter, J. A. 206
Wolf, D. 19
workfare 180, 186, 187, 188, 189
working groups 41, 42, 43, 66, 102, 146, 147
World Health Organization 207
WTO (World Trade Organization) 33
Wuermeling, J. 40
Wulf-Mathies, Monika 193

Youngs, R. 178
Yugoslavia (former) 4

Ziltener, P. 178
Zuleeg, M. 28